The Rag Trade

THE RAG TRADE

The People
Who Made Our Clothes

Pam Inder

AMBERLEY

Front cover: 'How to get this year's sleeves into last year's jacket!'

Back cover: 'Should you like to sit down, my dear?' 'Yes, but my dressmaker says I mustn't!'

First published 2017

Amberley Publishing
The Hill, Stroud
Gloucestershire, GL5 4EP

www.amberley-books.com

British Library Cataloguing in Publication Data.
A catalogue record for this book is available from the British Library.

ISBN 978 1 4456 5729 5 (print)
ISBN 978 1 4456 5730 1 (ebook)

Typeset in 11pt on 15.5pt Sabon.
Map illustration by Thomas Bohm, User Design, Illustration and Typesetting.
Typesetting and Origination by Amberley Publishing.
Printed in the UK.

Contents

Acknowledgements and Prefatory Notes

I would like to thank the following people and institutions for their help and support:

Allhallows Museum, Honiton; Ruth Blair; the British Library; Cheltenham Local History Library; Helen Clark; Donna Coulson; Cumbria Record Office (Barrow-in-Furness); Christine and Michael Endacott; Gloucestershire Record Office; Hampshire Record Office; Denise Harman; Valerie Hawkins; Herefordshire Record Office; the Jewish East End Celebration Society; the Jewish Museum, London; Norman Lambert; Lambley Local History Society; Lancashire Record Office; Leicester Arts and Museum Service; Leicester University Library Special Collections; Leicestershire Record Office; Leintwardine Local History Society; the National Library of Scotland; Nottinghamshire Record Office; Plymouth and West Devon Record Office; the Victoria & Albert Museum.

Illustrations

The author and publisher would like to thank all the people and organisations who have supplied us with images for this publication. Every attempt has been made to seek permission for copyright material used in this book. However, if we have inadvertently used copyright material without permission/acknowledgement we apologise and we will make the necessary correction at the first opportunity.

Nineteenth-century money

There are numerous references to prices and wages throughout the book and these are all in 'old' currency – pounds (£), shillings (s.) and pence (d.). There were twelve pence in a shilling and twenty shillings in a pound. There were also halfpennies and quarter-pennies (farthings) and guineas (21 shillings). It is impossible to convert nineteenth-century prices into modern ones with any degree of accuracy – the balance between the costs of housing, food and clothing, for example, varies so much over time. However, the figures below are based on conversion tables provided by the National Archives, and give some idea of the changing value of £1's worth of twenty-first-century money at various points in the nineteenth century.

1800	£33	1850	£58
1810	£34	1860	£43
1820	£41	1870	£46
1830	£49	1880	£48
1840	£44	1890	£60
		1900	£57

Introduction

I always enjoyed working in the City Archives in York. Tucked away in a corner of the Art Gallery[1] and run almost entirely by volunteers, it was a friendly, quirky little place. Mid-morning and mid-afternoon, the entire office came to a standstill as staff, volunteers and readers all crowded into the tiny common room for tea, coffee and homemade cakes. For twenty minutes or so we all chatted about our projects and exchanged tips and stories – then it was back to work, refreshed and, hopefully, reinvigorated. One afternoon I described the letters I had recently found in Barrow-in-Furness. They were from a middle-aged widow to her dressmaker, and it was clear the poor lady was drinking heavily – week after week she had her dressmaker in Ulverston send her bottles of whisky – 'and the Doctor says it must be old' – packed into corset boxes and carefully wrapped in garments being sent 'on approval', so as to disguise her growing addiction from the prying eyes of the local carrier! It was a very human story and the consensus in the tearoom that afternoon was that I should turn it into a novel.

That piece of research is long finished and became part of my PhD thesis. Since then I have co-authored several books and written various papers, some of them about workers in the clothing trades; however, until now Mrs Fenton's dressmaker and her corset boxes of whisky have remained under wraps. No doubt her story would make a novel, but I have decided to tell it straight, along with the stories of a number of other clothing workers, as one of a series of single-chapter biographies. Truth may not really be stranger than fiction – but it is sometimes more powerful.

The broad sweep of history is made up of the lives and experiences of countless millions of individuals – this book tries to rescue a handful of them from obscurity. Only one of my subjects, George Odger, the shoemaker trades unionist, has any sort of national profile. A little is known about one or two of the others in their home districts, but most of them have never before been written about, and that is one of my objectives – to remind readers just how much fascinating material is out there, waiting to be discovered. At this point it may be helpful to explain that each of the biographies can be treated as a separate entity, rather like a short story, rather than as part of a sequence making up a definitive history of the clothing industry.

However, though they could never provide a complete picture, the individual histories do tell us a good deal about the trades my subjects practised, as well as about the lives of working people in the nineteenth century. A few of the documents I have found – such as Elizabeth Taylor's letter to her sister-in-law in 1850 – are actually of considerable historical importance. Elizabeth's letter was not written with any agenda – it was simply an explanation to her brother's wife as to why she was changing her job – but it demonstrates just how hard even quite senior dressmakers were expected to work. Similarly, I believe the tragic story of Adolph and Ella Kushner's baby daughter is as powerful an evocation of what could happen when a family became destitute as any number of pages of statistics.

I have tried to show people's lives in the round rather than recounting a series of anecdotes. People are more than the jobs they do or the odd episodes that happen to them. Most of my subjects worked long, hard hours for meagre wages – but they also had homes and families, interests and skills. They gardened and went fishing, visited friends and enjoyed walks in the countryside, made music, played cricket, went to the theatre and celebrated national events with feasts and fireworks, parades and parties.

For most of my working life I was a museum curator, working with collections of costume, and I am therefore very familiar with the sorts of items my subjects made. I have handled, identified, catalogued and displayed such things, and have even, on occasion, made replicas of them. I have studied tailoring, learnt to make Honiton lace, watched knitting frames in operation and made many a garment on my grandmother's nineteenth-century German sewing machine. I am therefore well-placed to understand and appreciate the skills that many of my subjects used in their day-to-day lives and this, I believe, lends an extra dimension to my study.

Since the 1950s, a plethora of glossily illustrated books on the history of dress have been published; they deal in exhaustive detail with the costume of men, women and children, of the rich, the poor, tradesmen, country folk – even of royalty. There are books of photographs and fashion plates, and others that tell us about hats and shoes, bags and purses, umbrellas and parasols, underwear and stockings. There are trade histories and histories of individual firms. What is lacking is information about the *people* who actually made clothes.

The reason is obvious; given the enormous numbers of people employed in the nineteenth-century clothing trades, very few paper records survive. There are numerous odd bills and apprenticeship indentures. There are records of clothing workers who came to the attention of the authorities – people who resorted to petty crime to make ends meet, desperate individuals trying to prove their right to poor relief, women seeking bastardy orders and employers who went bankrupt – but sets of records full enough to allow us to reconstruct lives and careers are few and far between. The law obliged businesses to keep records, but there were no auditors to satisfy, no VAT inspectors, no HMRC to which to report, and such records as were kept were often extremely sketchy.

However, sources do exist – a cache of letters here, a daybook there, odd diaries, memoirs, reports and newspaper articles. They are scattered across the country and there are not a great many of them, but it is resources such as these that I have used in this book to illuminate the lives of a handful of workers in the nineteenth-century clothing trades. The eleven workers whose lives I describe in the following chapters must stand proxy for the hundreds of thousands of nameless, faceless artisans who ensured that their fellow countrymen and women were decently attired and shod. The individuals featured are not necessarily typical, but nor are they atypical; aspects of their lives reflect experiences shared by many others in the same lines of work – be it difficult clients, problems getting bills paid, trouble with the law or the effects of grinding poverty. Some were successful, others were not, and, as we shall see, the dividing line between the two was a narrow one and often depended on luck as much as on judgement.

Pamela M. Inder
September 2016

The Nineteenth-Century Rag Trade

'Poverty must, above all things, avoid the appearance of poverty,' Sylvia warned her readers in *How to Dress Well on a Shilling a Day*, a book published in 1876. Of course, ladies who had a shilling a day – or £18 5s a year – to spend on clothes were certainly not poor by nineteenth-century standards. Many women – governesses, ladies' maids, dressmakers and the wives of small tradesmen, for example – were expected to dress respectably on a fraction of that sum and were equally anxious to 'avoid the appearance of poverty'.

In the class-conscious nineteenth century, clothes were very important. Outfits had to fit and flatter, and to demonstrate to the world the social position of the wearer – or at least the position to which they aspired – without being unnecessarily gaudy or showy. At the same time they had to conform to the latest fashion as illustrated in a host of magazines and fashion plates, while giving the impression that the wearer was not so shallow as to be overly interested in what they wore. It was a careful balancing act. Dressmakers, tailors and shopkeepers had to guide and advise their customers, tactfully steering them away from making inappropriate choices and helping to disguise their bodily imperfections by careful styling and judicious padding.

Throughout the century, fashions – particularly in women's wear – changed markedly from decade to decade but, at any given time, there was remarkably little deviation from the style that was deemed to be *à la mode*. If a lady in 1820 or 1850 or 1880 or any other decade had written about 'my new black silk day dress', her contemporaries would have had a very clear idea of what that dress would have looked like. Dresses were very different in the 1820s, 1850s and 1880s but, in any one of those decades, all day dresses – black silk or otherwise - would have been very similar; any variation would have come in the trimming and detailing. Only the very poor, the very rich or the very famous dared ignore the dictates of fashion. To do so was social suicide. This meant that, in the course of their working lives, garment makers, especially dressmakers and tailors, would continually have had to be learning new ways of cutting out and making up. (See image section for examples.)

Of course, at the bottom end of the social spectrum there were always individuals for whom new clothes were an unattainable luxury. They were dependant on second-hand clothes dealers when they had a few pence to spare and on charitable donations when they did not. They accepted whatever clothes they could find, however incongruous, and wore them until they fell to pieces. For example, in 1861, the journalist Henry Mayhew described an old man in a cheap lodging-house:

His clothes were black and shiny at every fold with grease, and his coarse shirt was so brown with long wearing, that it was only with close inspection you could see that it had once been a checked one; on his feet he had a pair of lady's side-laced boots, the toes of which had been cut off so that he might get them on...

But even this individual was luckier than the nine-year-old 'mud lark', or Thames scavenger, dressed in rags, who told Mayhew he 'remembered once to have had a pair of shoes, but it was a long time since'.[1] At any given time, such people only had the clothes they stood up in; they seldom had needles and thread with which to repair their garments, or soap with which to wash them. If the worst came to the worst, they would (after 1834) have had to enter the workhouse, where they would have been decently clothed but in garments that were coarse and humiliatingly recognisable. Estimates vary, but throughout the nineteenth century between 10 and 25 per cent of the working population would fall into destitution for at least part of their lives.[2]

For everyone else, however, new clothes and shoes were nearly always bespoke. Not until the 1870s and 80s were ready-to-wear garments generally available, and even then the shops that sold them often employed seamstresses who would turn up hems or let out seams so that the garments fitted their wearers as fashion decreed they should. This meant that, proportionately, there were far more people earning their livings as garment makers in nineteenth-century Britain than there are today. Even small villages would boast one or two tailors, shoemakers and dressmakers (usually listed as 'milliners' – in the nineteenth century the term did not necessarily mean someone who only made hats). For the first half of the century, those clothes and shoes were all made entirely by hand. The only exceptions to this rule were stockings and other knitted items. Knitting frames were developed in the sixteenth century and, by the nineteenth century, most knitted garments sold were machine made – though even machine-made knitwear had to be assembled by hand by 'seamers'.

Garment making was therefore slow, laborious work – but, nevertheless, nineteenth-century customers were led to expect unbelievably speedy service. To quote just one example, on 28 December 1840 Barbara Hill, a travelling dressmaker, arrived at the Manor House in Little Longstone in Derbyshire to make a dress for fourteen-year-old Emma Jane Longsdon to wear on New Year's Day. Barbara must have sat up all night to complete it, for the following day it was ready for Emma to wear.[3] Working extraordinarily long hours when there was an order to be completed was accepted practice in the nineteenth-century clothing industry, and dressmakers like Elizabeth Chaffard actually advertised speedy service (see Chapter 2).

There is a reasonable amount of evidence[4] in the form of diaries and account books to suggest that even the comparatively well-to-do had fewer clothes than do their twenty-first-century counterparts. This was partly because many fabrics were of a higher quality than we see today, meaning garments lasted longer and could be altered and remade as fashion changed; it was also partly because clothes were comparatively costly throughout the nineteenth century. A new pair of men's boots, for example, cost more than most labourers earned in a week, while a silk dress such as a tradesman's wife might wear to church cost the equivalent of a month's wages for a village schoolmistress.

We are today accustomed to the idea that labour is expensive, even when materials are relatively cheap. In the nineteenth century, the reverse was the case. A tailor or dressmaker's profit was often the same as the price of just one yard of the fabric they were making up for their customer. Fabrics came in narrower widths than they do today, so the yardage required for garments was greater than we might expect. Suitings, tweeds and heavy woollens were the widest (hence the term 'broadcloth') and could come in 38-, 54- and occasionally 60-inch widths; alpaca, cashmere and some fine woollens could be 40 inches wide; serge was sometimes as wide as 32 inches. No other fabrics came in anything wider than 30 inches, and silks, 'fancy materials like brochés, pekins, [and] crepe de chines ... [were] all very narrow, less than 27 inches.'[5]

Prices for goods other than foodstuffs remained remarkably stable throughout the nineteenth century – a reel of cotton cost 1*d* in 1800 and it still cost 1*d* in 1899, for example. The following prices are culled from a variety of personal account books and day books kept by people in different parts of the country at different dates, but they give a good indication of the price-per-yard of fabrics in everyday use throughout the century.[6]

Woollen cloth for a labourer's coat (i.e., the cheapest available) – 2*s* 6*d*
Fine woollen cloth, various weights and colours – 9*s* to 24*s*
Tweed – 5*s* 6*d* to 9*s*
Plain or figured silk – 2*s* to 10*s* 9*d*
Taffeta – 6*s* 6*d*

Satin – 8s 6d to 10s 6d

Velveteen – 2s 8d

Calico – 3d to 1s 2d

Lawn – 6d

Printed cotton – 1s 6d to 2s 9d

Muslin – 4½d to 6d

Flannel – 1s 2d to 2s 3d

Barnsley shirting – 6d to 9d

Holland (linen) – 1s 6d to 2s 9d

Norwich crepe – 10½ d

Velvet ribbon – 2½d to 7d

Satin ribbon – 1s 10d

Wages in the clothing trades varied enormously depending on the experience of the worker, the size of the firm and the type of clientele for whom they catered. We shall look at the incomes of individuals chapter by chapter but it may be useful to make some general points. Throughout the century a pound a week was reckoned to be the wage on which a working man could comfortably support a modest family – but, in 1880, Charles Booth estimated that some 178,000 East Enders fell below that poverty line.[7] In fact, some professional men did not earn a great deal more – schoolmasters' annual salaries, for example, ranged from £50 to £100.[8] Women, of course, earned less and there were fewer opportunities open to them – the average female weekly wage in 1888 was found to be 12s 8d[9] and, by that measure, wages in the garment making trades do not look too bad. The wage for a skilled dressmaker – a 'first hand' or workroom supervisor – in an elite establishment could be up to £120 a year, though in a less prestigious firm she would have been lucky to make £70. Assistants' wages ranged from £30 to £70 for live-in workers (who would work longer hours but did not have to pay for their keep) and between 8s and 12s a week for workers who lived out. Wages in the tailoring and shoemaking trades were only slightly higher, even though the workers were usually male. All the clothing trades relied very heavily on the work of apprentices, who were usually unpaid and may in fact have had to pay a 'premium' up front – anything between £3 and £50 – for the privilege of receiving a training.[10]

Regardless of how good a service they provided, the people who made our forbears' clothes had to contend with a problem that is still with us today; customers who were unwilling to pay the market price for their garments. Today firms outsource production to countries where labour is cheap, plentiful and compliant. In the nineteenth century, employers paid their workforce as little as they could get away with, and had them work unreasonably long hours. Even so, wealthy customers were often tardy in paying their bills, sometimes with disastrous consequences for the firms they patronised. To quote just one example: in Leith in 1816, society milliner Magdalene Dunbar went bankrupt with a staggering £2,549 2s 6¾d worth of bad debts from her rich and titled clients.[11]

For the first half of the period covered in this book, the clothing trades changed very little. There were some attempts to improve the lot of dressmakers after the *Children's Employment Commission Report* of 1843 was published, with its litany of complaints about long hours, poor management and low wages.[12] A benevolent association was set up in London, and artists and novelists drew on the report to paint pictures and write stories to raise awareness of the problem – but, when the Commission reported again in 1864[13], it was found that little had changed.

The tailors and shoemakers – in the big cities at least – were more militant and organised than their sister dressmakers. Both tailoring and shoemaking had been guild occupations since the Middle Ages, so there was a long history of mutual support. They organised strikes and campaigned vigorously for better wages and conditions, but there were usually too many men desperate to fill the strikers' places for agitation to have much effect.

However, by the 1870s, England was changing. The death rate fell and the population grew. More and more people lived in towns and an increasing number of them belonged – or aspired to belong – to the middle classes. And the rag trade began to change too. Most importantly, from the employees' point of view, the Workshop Acts (when they were enforced) limited the number of hours workers in any workshop with more than five staff could be expected to work. It also became easier to get a proper training. For years, there had been criticism that many employers did not teach their apprentices properly; they simply used them as dogsbodies to do boring jobs, such as making buttonholes and sewing on brush-braid[14], but failed to show them how to assemble garments or fit customers. In an overcrowded market employers feared that a fully trained, able apprentice might eventually set up a business in competition to their own.

One important factor in improving this situation was the rise of the department store – by 1870 most towns of any size had at least one. Most department stores had started out as drapers and, even in their expanded form, most concentrated on the sale of clothing, shoes, millinery, fabrics, household textiles and furnishings. The establishment of workrooms for tailoring, dressmaking, millinery, upholstery and so on was thus a logical extension of the department stores' services. The rates the stores offered were usually competitive – the workrooms were subsidised by the profits made in other departments, and fabrics and sundries were acquired at cost, which was a considerable saving. From the workers' point of view, conditions tended to be better there than with private firms. Their working hours were usually in line with those of the stores' other employees; the purpose-built workrooms were relatively comfortable and well-lit; the stores did not fear competition from their employees and so provided a better and more complete training than apprentices in small firms received. Furthermore, department stores did not charge premiums for training; many provided boarding houses for their work people and took a paternalistic interest in their welfare.[15]

The improvements in training may have started in the department store workrooms but, by the end of the century, most towns also had technical schools that offered classes in sewing, dressmaking, tailoring and pattern cutting. Numerous books were published, often

Grantham Journal, 16 November 1878.

Yorkshire Post, 20 May 1875.

Advertisement for lay figures from *The Drapers' Record*, 1895.

by the teachers of these classes[16], purporting to instruct readers in the art of making clothes. Gradually this type of training began to replace – or at least to augment – the often unsatisfactory apprentice system.

Little by little the trades also became more mechanised. Sewing machines began to come into use in the 1850s, though to begin with they were awkward to use and the trickier parts of a garment – setting in sleeves or stitching flimsy fabrics, for example – would still be done by hand.[17] Within a little over a decade, however, the majority of clothes and shoes were stitched by machine and sewing machines were in use in most dressmaking, tailoring and shoemaking workshops by 1870. Commercially produced paper patterns came into general use in the 1870s, though many experienced tailors and dressmakers still preferred to make their own. A whole industry developed supplying dressmakers' and tailors' dummies, 'kilting machines' that would do permanent pleating, buttons, woven name-bands and a whole host of other more or less useful goods and services. Trade magazines came into being: *The Drapers' and Milliners' Gazette of Fashion, The Milliner's, Dressmaker's and Warehouseman's Gazette* in 1870, and *The Tailor and Cutter* in the 1860s, for example.

The growth of the railway network allowed salesmen from wholesale firms in the big cities to travel the country, bringing catalogues and brochures and offering to supply fabrics, partly made shoe-uppers, caps, bonnets and a host of ready-made goods that could be delivered by rail to remote stations at surprisingly moderate prices.[18]

This, then, was the background against which our subjects lived and worked.

PART 1

DRESSMAKERS

'A Willing Horse': Elizabeth Chaffard (1821–1867), Edinburgh

My dear Louisa,

If I have not answered your kind letter before it has been more for want of time than inclination for really my mind has been so much occupied lately what with one thing and another – of some you know, I mean leaving here. Miss Goulding is just returned from London she has engaged a French Dressmaker I could not put up with her temper any longer its an old saying and a fine one with them 'work a willing horse to death' in my part I told her from ½ past 7 till 11 and sometimes 12 was quite hours enough for any old work horse and Madame Schoelcher who lived with us a year was always asking me to join her so I made up my mind to try this winter to see if it will answer, if not I can always take another situation in the spring. She is very clever and I have not the slightest doubt we should do very well if can only get up the first year – the worst is the furniture to buy for we must have a decent showroom. I wish I had a friend to lend me twenty pounds – would not mind paying good interest. In a year – but that's the 'rub'. The ladies are all so fond of me in Edinbro – there are few good dressmakers there and you see it being three years I am so well known. I expect to go in about a month. What will they say when they find I am in Edinbro for tho I have never told them they think I am going into business in Brighton, they were very much put out when they found I would not stay again but I could not swallow the last tiff she and I had without cause. She thought it would all blow over again but when she found I was determined she said I should not have to take another situation she would rather give me £35 per annum and then she offered 40 the next day but I had gone to[o] far with Madam to retreat or they would have persuad'd me to stop another year. [Had] she known it she would have had a person working under me all the summer. You see they cannot get anyone to do the stays and dresses and we make nearly as many stays as dresses – that will make it all the better for me in Edinbro each one for themselves and both for us all I ask is she would now [leave me alone] I feel very unsettled – however we must trust in Providence. I would not care if I had a little more money first going off but really know its working hard for nothing as I am compelled to dress pretty then washing and books [from which to make dress patterns] cost me a great deal. Madam is trying for a house. Mrs M— is going to London tomorrow. I am glad to hear the children are getting on so well …

Your very affectionate sister,
Elizabeth Taylor[1]

The letter is undated but it must have been written sometime towards the end of 1850. 'My dear Louisa' was Elizabeth's sister-in-law, the wife of her elder brother, George Taylor. He was a hairdresser and the couple lived in Elizabeth's home town of Brighton; they had three small children – Fanny, who was Elizabeth's particular favourite, George and William. At the end of 1850 Louisa was heavily pregnant with her fourth and last child.

Even in the early nineteenth century, the conditions in dressmaking establishments and the long hours worked by dressmakers were causing concern but, despite the publicity that accompanied the reports published in 1843 and 1864, most ladies seem to have persuaded themselves that their own dressmaker was a charming woman who paid her staff properly and would never overwork them.

This enabled them to ignore how quickly she produced dresses and how little she charged. Elizabeth's letter is important because it was not written with any agenda; she was simply stating the facts of her working life.

Elizabeth was born in 1821, in Brighton, the daughter of mariner Adam Taylor and his wife Elizabeth, née Short. In 1841 the family were living on East Street. As well as her elder brother George, Elizabeth had two younger sisters, Anna (or Ann) and Mary Ann. Elizabeth was twenty at the time of the census in 1841, but she is not recorded as being in employment – perhaps she was between jobs, as it is likely that by that date she had completed an apprenticeship. Girls could begin their training as young as nine or ten, though most were in their teens. Formal apprenticeships were becoming less common by the middle years of the nineteenth century, and girls often trained with a neighbour or family friend; sometimes they were paid pocket money but more often they worked out their training unpaid. In some cases their parents would have paid a substantial premium – anything between £3 and £50 – to get them started. Apprenticeships varied in length – in a few places the traditional seven-year apprenticeships were still in force, but most girls served between two and five years. Ambitious girls like Elizabeth often then worked another unpaid period with a different firm as an 'improver'. Thereafter she would have taken a post – or probably a series of posts – as a 'second hand' or assistant before graduating to the position of 'first hand' or workroom supervisor.[2]

To be well known in Edinburgh, Elizabeth would have had to have been a senior dressmaker, even though it seems she was paid less than the £35 that Miss Goulding offered her. Ladies met the person who took their orders and supervised their fittings, but they seldom knew the backroom staff who did most of the actual making-up. She was twenty-nine when she wrote the letter to Louisa; she would therefore have had fourteen or fifteen years' experience in the trade and would already have seen women's fashion go through a series of changes. When she was a young apprentice, women wore short-waisted dresses with enormous sleeves, puffed out over swansdown pads or little cages. Necklines were wide and often quite low, and day dresses were worn with big collars or 'pelerines', sometimes of fabric to match the dress and sometimes of lace or embroidered muslin. The 1840s saw sleeves become more and more fitted, while waists became longer and skirts got fuller and fuller, worn over layers of starched petticoats. Within a few years those petticoats would be replaced by the crinoline cage, and skirts would reach unprecedented dimensions (see plates 1 and 2).

Elizabeth seems to have been quite enterprising. We do not know where Miss Goulding had her establishment but Elizabeth seems already to have worked for firms in Brighton, London and Edinburgh, and she was quite prepared to move again. Early in 1851 she and Madame Schoelcher did indeed set up in business together in Edinburgh at 99, Princes Street – the first advertisements for the new firm appeared in the Edinburgh press in February. At census time (30–31 March) in 1851, Elizabeth's sister, Mary Ann Taylor, was working for the firm and is listed as 'assistant dressmaker'. Mary was then twenty, ten years younger than Elizabeth, but presumably she too had served out an apprenticeship and had a period working as an improver. This advertisement appeared on 3 July.

The firm's advertisements continue to appear throughout the summer but, for some reason, Schoelcher and Taylor did not prosper.

---

99 PRINCE'S STREET, EDINBURGH

--

MESDAMES SCHOELCHER & TAYLOR
MILLINERS, DRESS and CORSET MAKERS,
Respectfully beg to announce that their Stock of
BONNETS, CAPS, CLOAKS, CORSETS, RIBBONS, FLOWERS, &c for the Summer Season, is replete with every article in the most correct taste; and at Prices exceedingly moderate.

Ladies *en passant* can have any article of dress made in the first Parisian Style, on the very Shortest Notice.

On 9 October an advertisement appeared advising customers that Mme Schoelcher had recently returned from Paris with news of the latest fashions – but tucked away in a column of the *Edinburgh Evening Courant* of the same date was another advert offering the sale of £500 worth of 'general stock' to drapers and mercers – from 99 Princes Street. Two more advertisements for the firm appear that October, but the sale of stock does not seem to have raised enough money to keep them afloat. No advertisements appear for Mesdames Schoelcher and Taylor after October, and it seems that the business closed down.

Elizabeth and Mary moved back to England and found work as paid employees – something of a come-down after a heady seven months of working for themselves – but it was not long before their fortunes changed for the better. On 17 September 1856 the two sisters had a double wedding at the church of All-Hallows-by-the-Tower, in the City of London. Elizabeth married Leonard Ferdinand Chaffard – always known as Ferdinand – and Mary married John Carmichael. The Chaffard marriage was recorded in the *North British Advertiser* for 20 September 1856. Several members of the Taylor family came to London for the ceremony – the witnesses were the women's brother, George Taylor; their brother-in-law, William Phillips, husband of their sister Anna; and George's daughter, Fanny. Fanny was a governess – an educated young woman with a clear, neat signature. No doubt Anna Phillips and Louisa, George's wife, and some of their other children were there as well.

Ferdinand Chaffard was French and described himself as a 'hatter' but by that it seems he really meant traveller for a hat-making firm back home in Limoges. He probably met Elizabeth through her work. Many dressmakers also made hats, and he may well have visited her employers with his samples and brochures of hat shapes that could be ordered from France and trimmed to their customers' requirements. Of John Carmichael we know much less. On his marriage certificate he is listed as 'government clerk', the son of Duncan Carmichael, a corn merchant. It is likely that this was Duncan Carmichael, the miller in Crieff in Perthshire, but we cannot be sure. It seems that John died in 1862.

Ferdinand and Elizabeth went to Edinburgh soon after the wedding and Ferdinand set up in business as a 'French hatter' at 70 George Street – the first advertisements for the firm appeared on 5 February 1857. For a time Elizabeth seems to have been a lady of leisure and, on 2 June 1861, she gave birth to a daughter they christened Marguerite Elizabeth Marie but who was always known as 'wee Lizzie'. The birth was announced two days later in the *Caledonian Mercury,* which gives some indication of the family's social standing.

Before and during the early years of the marriage, Ferdinand made several long trips to France, visiting family and looking after his business. He wrote to Elizabeth every few days. The early letters are in French – had Elizabeth learnt French at school? It seems unlikely. Perhaps she had picked up a smattering of the language from colleagues – her former partner, Madame Schoelcher, was a Frenchwoman from Strasbourg. However, it seems she did understand the language, for there are a series of letters, in very flowery French, written to her by a business friend of Ferdinand's and it is obvious that she also wrote to him – though of course she may have written in English. Later, presumably as Ferdinand's grasp of the language improved, he began to write in English, though his grammar and spelling remained idiosyncratic, and when he could not remember the English word he used the French one – 'the trees have no *feuilles* [leaves] yet' being a typical example. Numerous nineteenth-century letters between husbands and wives survive, and many of these now sound very stilted – addressed to 'My dear wife', or even 'My Dear Mr Smith'. Ferdinand dispensed with any such formality. Elizabeth was '*Ma bonne* Lizzie', '*Ma chère*/my darling Loo Loo' or '*Ma chère Ange*', and his letters end by sending her '*mille baisons* [a thousand kisses]' or 'a million kisses to my Loo Loo'.

However, what is most remarkable about the fifty-plus letters of Ferdinand's that survive is just how little they say. We learn that it took three days for a letter from Edinburgh to reach him in Limoges and that Elizabeth was keeping him updated by sending him copies of the Edinburgh newspapers. He detailed his travels, visiting cousins who were 'great grand brandy merchants', his sister-in-law and her new husband and an old uncle out in the country. It rather sounds as if Ferdinand and Elizabeth might have been planning to move to France – 'about the cottage there is nothing fine enough for us but they can build it', he wrote in one letter. He described the weather – cold and wet or unseasonably snowy or too hot – and listed his every cough and sniffle. He was still only in his mid-thirties but he comes over as a complete hypochondriac. He visits doctors, but tells Elizabeth that it would take too long to explain all they had said to him. Later he describes how he is getting up late, breakfasting on chops and beefsteak and feeling stronger, and assures her that he is not drinking too much – *'peut etre une bouteille ½ en tout par jour'* [perhaps half-a-bottle a day]. He also made solicitous enquiries about Elizabeth's health, which is not so surprising as she must have been pregnant for at least some of the time he was away. There also seem to have been some problems with creditors, which he airily dismisses: 'Those that call on you for money tell them that I will be back soon and I settle with them they think I am a Scotch man to run away in bank rupt'! and in a subsequent letter he tells her sternly not to 'pay anybody for me in my absence.'

Ferdinand was a sentimental man. He sends his 'compliments' to the family dogs, Monsieur Bosco and Monsieur Tasso. Monsieur Bosco was obviously his favourite and he sends messages promising him long walks, telling him he was not to go out in the snowy weather because his 'new suit' was not warm enough, and talking about him having sessions 'in the tobb'. Unlike most dogs, it would seem Monsieur Bosco enjoyed being bathed! After one visit Ferdinand arrived back in Edinburgh shortly after Elizabeth had left for a holiday in Brighton. He writes to her there, telling her that he put her nightcap on the pillow beside him at night and 'Mr Bosco was so please when I comm back that he jump on the bead and keep all the room for him self and I had bad sleep. <u>Tasso</u> hes very quiet.'

None of Ferdinand's letters mention wee Lizzie, so perhaps he stopped travelling after she was born or perhaps those later letters were lost.

Wee Lizzie was to be an only child – Elizabeth was forty when she was born – and soon after her birth Elizabeth joined forces with Ferdinand as 'Chaffard et Cie, milliners and dressmakers', trading from 2 Castle Street, just off Princes Street (see plate 3). Soon afterwards, Mary Carmichael joined them. For four or five years the firm prospered, building up a loyal clientele among the well-to-do and titled of Edinburgh, and across much of Scotland. We do not know how many staff they employed, but there were probably at least a dozen, spread between the millinery and dressmaking departments. Ferdinand integrated into the Edinburgh business community and joined the local Freemasons' Lodge. Wee Lizzie grew up playing in the shop and workroom and became a favourite with her mother's customers. She was petted and indulged. At a time when few children celebrated birthdays, Mary wrote to her brother George to tell him that Lizzie had had a rocking horse for her birthday 'and she is hardly off it'. Lizzie was probably three. George had sent her a book and a 'sachet' of some sort, and Mary thanked him and described how the little girl enjoyed drawing: 'she is always busy with her pencil.' Mary's own baby girl had died in infancy and she seems to have treated little Lizzie almost as a surrogate daughter.

Brighton is a long way from Edinburgh and it seems wee Lizzie never met her Taylor grandparents. They both died in 1865 and, in a letter later that year to 'Dear Parfy', an aunt, Elizabeth says how sad she is that her mother and father had 'never seen my Lizzie'. Parfy had obviously written to her about her inheritance as Elizabeth tells her she would like her 'Mother's keeper' but had no need of her father's watch as 'I have no boys'. A keeper was a decorative ring, supposedly worn to prevent other more valuable rings from slipping off the wearer's finger. Elizabeth also tells her aunt that Lizzie often asked about her Brighton cousins – presumably she had never met them either. Her Uncle George and Aunt Louisa had four children, all much older than Lizzie, and her Uncle William and Aunt Anna Phillips had three little boys and a baby girl, Louise. John, the middle boy, was almost the same age as Lizzie; William was a few years older; and the youngest, little Ferdinand, had even been named after Lizzie's father. To an only child, these unknown faraway relatives must have seemed fascinating.

She would get to meet them soon enough. By the mid-1860s, Elizabeth's health was failing. Sometime in late 1865, she, Ferdinand and four-year-old Lizzie left Edinburgh for a holiday in Brighton in the hope that the sea air, warmer climate and familiar surroundings might do her good. After a time Ferdinand returned to Edinburgh, leaving Elizabeth and their little daughter in Brighton. He wrote to her frequently, with more news of the firm – 'the showroom look very well Jane has been very busy today. She write to you tomorrow … The start date is next Thursday but don't hurry yourself.' Inevitably there was more news of the dog: 'I am goan to put Bosco in the tobb on Sunday'. At this stage Ferdinand clearly expected Elizabeth to recover and re-join him in Edinburgh; meanwhile Mary Carmichael ran the dressmaking side of the business and sent regular accounts of it to Elizabeth.

Then, on 28 February 1866, with Elizabeth and Lizzie still in Brighton, tragedy struck. Ferdinand died at home in Edinburgh of '*ascites* and *anasarca*' (fluid retention and massive swelling) resulting from cirrhosis of the liver. Elizabeth had obviously been right to worry about his drinking. We do not know whether she travelled to Edinburgh for the funeral – Victorian women did not always attend funerals even of their nearest and dearest, for fear of giving way to emotion in a manner that contemporary society found embarrassing – but she certainly decided that she was not going to return there to live. She found lodgings in Brighton and then rented a place of her own, 22 Cobden Place in Prestonville. There was a long correspondence with poor Mary in Edinburgh about winding up her affairs. Ferdinand had had property in Edinburgh and Mary had to deal with his rather inefficient solicitor: 'I wrote him a sharp note and have heard no more.' She also had to deal with despatching her sister's belongings to Brighton.

Elizabeth had originally planned to rent somewhere unfurnished but, as her health declined, she decided that would be 'too great an undertaking' and chose a furnished property, though presumably it was quite sparsely furnished given the number of items she had sent from Edinburgh. The removal was entrusted to the firm of Darlington & Hopper on Frederick Street and there were numerous payments to them – including 1s 6d for a 'bed chair', which was probably some sort of contraption for an invalid. It rather sounds as if the firm were also renovating some of her furniture – one load was delayed 'until the paint [was] sufficiently hard to pack'. Elizabeth obviously became irritated by the delays and wrote to Mary about a Brighton firm that shipped goods by sea and would have been a good deal quicker; however, she does not seem to have transferred her business to them. Various items were left behind in Edinburgh. In one letter Mary writes that she is making an inventory of those of Elizabeth's possessions 'for which I am responsible' and, in a later one, she assures her that her furs are safe and that her patterns are still in the ottoman. Commercially produced paper patterns were not generally available until the 1870s; a dressmaker's patterns, drafted from pictures and diagrams in magazines, were her stock-in-trade. Even if she did not anticipate working again, Elizabeth wanted to be sure they had not been lost. In September 1866 the bank seems to have closed Elizabeth's business account and Mary sent her a cheque for the balance: £48 13s 7d.

This was quite a considerable sum and it would seem that the Chaffards had lived comfortably. Among the surviving papers are bills for purchases Elizabeth had made from high-class Parisian firms – 210 francs worth of jewellery from the Maison de Confiance, 54 Boulevard de Sebastopol, for example, and underwear from Zoe Brisac et Soeurs, a Parisian lingerie business. It also seems she had shares in the Brighton Baths Company – one letter in the collection gives Elizabeth's brother, George, power to act on her behalf in dealings with them.

Chaffards were an up-market establishment and Mary wrote of visits to London and Paris – Elizabeth had probably made similar visits during her time as head of the firm. These trips do not seem to have been all work and no play. A letter survives from another 'Lizzie' to her mother describing a visit to London with her Aunt Mary, and it begins 'Champagne Charlie is my name' and goes on to detail outings to theatres and exhibitions. 'Elizabeth' was a Taylor family name – this 'Lizzie' is not Elizabeth Chaffard (Lizzie Loo Loo) or 'Wee Lizzie', who was still a small child, but George Taylor's youngest daughter, Susan Elizabeth. George's eldest girl, Fanny, became a governess; one of his sons became a clerk; and the other joined him in the hairdressing business. His youngest child, Susan Elizabeth – or 'Lizzie' – became a dressmaker like her aunts. She would have been about fifteen when the letter was written and it may be that she had gone to Edinburgh for a holiday; however, it is equally possible that she was serving an apprenticeship there at her aunts' firm.

Between 1865 and 1867 Mary sent Elizabeth almost weekly bulletins about the state of the business and they give us a unique insight into the life and attitudes of a reasonably prosperous dressmaker in the mid-nineteenth century. When Mary was away, their 'first hand', Miss Margaret Taylor (no relation), wrote to Elizabeth in her stead and, among other news, thanked Elizabeth for the information she had sent about the latest trends. Living in the fashionable resort of Brighton, Elizabeth would have known about new fashions sooner than her sister and former colleagues in Edinburgh. One letter sent while Mary Ann was away in Paris gives a particularly clear picture of the firm's activities and of Elizabeth's relationship with her staff.

Dear Mme Chaffard,

... I make a cheque for £10-5s which Lady Ross sent here last night. Thank you for your description of the fashions. We are making two dresses for a Mrs Baird staying at the 'Alma Hotel' a black figured silk out of the showroom, the trimming I have copied from your letter and a fine black repp which we got from Gray and Macfarlane, both made 'Princess' shape. We are still continuing busy. Mrs Dobell and her sister have sent a material for two dresses, when out fitting them on they made kind enquiries after your health and Mrs Dobell desired me to give you kind compliments. A Box from Paris has arrived today which they are unpacking but I have not seen the contents as yet. We are still getting on nicely but I shall be very glad to see Mrs Carmichael home again. There is no word of Miss Stark going to be married but indeed I could not spare her for any such thing ...

    With kindest love to Lizzie and a kiss and kindest regards to yourself,
    Margaret Taylor

Miss Taylor was head of the dressmaking department and poor Miss Stark, who could not be spared to go to her own wedding, was her second in command. Miss Stark was a talented worker. On one occasion, when Miss Taylor was away and Miss Stark was in charge of the workroom, Mary wrote to Elizabeth describing her work as 'first class'. Miss Taylor's letter is written in a beautiful, neat hand. No doubt she was anxious to impress her employer, but dressmakers in high-class establishments were often well-educated young women.

    Chaffards often attracted big, prestigious orders. 'I have been very busy', wrote Mary proudly in one letter:

Yesterday had a visit from Mrs Lawson for mourning – one of the Oliphants of Coullie [in Aberdeenshire] is going to be married and I had to arrange for her as they are to be in tomorrow in prospect of the trousseau of which I think there will be at least five silks all in stock as I looked them over yesterday ...

But though no doubt the order was a lucrative one, it was also a lot of work. 'I am fairly worn out tonight,' Mary admitted a few days later:

... have had such a heavy day with the Oliphants. I was from twelve till four without ceasing speaking and advising and arranging as all was proposed to them first and then the intended had to go over all again ... I think at present there will be about twenty-one dresses without jackets, crinolines, bonnets, etc. and all have to be done by first week in October without other orders and Miss Taylor away for her holiday. I don't think you will see me till the first week in October – I decided them for fourteen today <u>all stock</u> but two with which you will be pleased. I did not feel very strong after they left – but am better tonight.

The dresses would have been fairly similar to the one shown in plates 4 and 4a–d. The huge crinolines of the 1850s continued to be popular – crinolines are cumbersome but they flatter most figures. In the early 1860s the shape changed slightly, to be fuller at the back than the front, and this trend increased as the decade progressed. Dresses were often made with a separate bodice and skirt, with the bodice shaped to accentuate the fullness at the back of the skirt. Some dresses even had a separate 'tablier', which was like a short gathered apron worn at the back rather than at the front. Sometimes Mary went into considerable detail about what she was making:

I enclose patterns of the principle dresses the one white and gold with butterflies in all diamond shaped in front with a butterfly in each corner and each side a plaiting of tarlatan going the entire way round the skirt with a row of gold cord in the heading puffs on other part go from top to bottom of the skirt ... I've tried a sketch of it.

It is to be hoped the sketch was clearer than the description! Unfortunately very few of the letters are dated, so we cannot be sure who it was who was going to be arrayed in white and gold with butterflies.

Mary described the sort of business they were doing:

We are keeping busy – <u>not driving</u>... Just had a visit from Miss Walker in getting a Bonnet, sold a grey silk yesterday and Mrs William

Steward brought a dress to be made and Mrs Abercrombie sent three dresses from that new house in Glasgow.

'That new house' was probably a department store. Department stores sold ready-made dresses – very much a novelty in the 1860s – but they nearly always had to be altered to fit.

Have been busy making mourning for David Stewart's wife who has lost a sister and Jane Maclain writes in today saying her dress pleased her so much and wanting a muslin badly – I think I told you that blessed Mrs Hamilton – Mrs Nollingeye's sister – the one who played the <u>harp</u> – brought a dress to be made ...

Got such a pretty grey straw hat so light the bateau shape sold three already trimmed velvet same shade and veil same colour ...

One of the Miss Hawkins is going to be married – they've been staying in London since they got those white glacé dresses. Mrs Hawkins came in – she gave me a compliment when she said she had been to four places before me – Simpsons, Hackwoods, Camerons, Youngs – for a tulle bonnet – but she could not fix so I fixed her ...

Mary could obviously be quite firm with indecisive customers. Chaffards offered a good service and she knew it. She criticised the shoddy practices of other millinery firms – 'three parts of them buy a frame and cover it' – and was quite proud when Mrs Hay Gordon called to get Chaffards to remake a bonnet she had bought in London '<u>because nobody liked her in it</u>.'

Clients obviously had a close relationship with the sisters. One former client – a Miss C. Vinck – even sent a present for wee Lizzie, and told Elizabeth she was planning a trip to Brighton and would like to visit. She went on, 'I see Mrs Carmichael regularly in Edinboro and I am very pleased that the business continues good, she certainly sends out some of the handsomest dresses I see anywhere and deserves success.'

Another customer, Fanny Sansome, sent cards for wee Lizzie's album and, even while complaining about being overcharged, Susan Hill sent kisses to 'your little daughter'. Dressmakers knew their clients well and were aware of all their health issues: Mary writes of Mrs Sansome coming in with blue, pinched lips, having just recovered from a bout of dysentery, and of a pregnant client with 'another bad breast'. Relationships between senior dressmakers and their customers were surprisingly intimate.

Mary also often grumbled about customers who were inconsiderate:

> Had a visit on Saturday afternoon from Miss Bateman had a cup of tea – just in the midst – walked in Lady Borthwick – wanted a Bonnet this was half past six and wanted me to unlock and turn out everything. I told her I knew there was nothing really she would like but could shew her some Tuesday ...

> Mrs D Mackenzie Clark Marman, Elizabeth Maclaine that was, has removed to this address Tighnabruaich near Greenock. I have two dresses for her I think I told you in a former letter and [she] has the coolness to say 'Pay Carriage of Box' ...

Tighnabruaich was on the other side of the country, up the Firth of Clyde on the western side of the Kyles of Bute, which was probably a two day journey in the 1860s; 'carriage of the box' would have been pretty expensive.

'The Kempes have just come in and paid their bill – with a deduction of course ...' Miss Kempe had owed £38 19s and Major Kempe £1 4s.

Customers who expected instant service were another problem. Mrs Logan Home's mourning was 'only ordered at two and all has to be finished for tomorrow as she goes to Ireland at three.'

The letters also contained local gossip. Elizabeth's former partner, Mme Schoelcher, had set up in business again in Edinburgh in 1856 at 103 Princes Street. The dissolution of the partnership back in 1851 had left a bitter taste and the sisters seem to have had little to do with their near neighbour and former friend, so there is an unmistakeable hint of schadenfreude in Mary's letter: 'Did you see in the paper I sent the E. Schoelcher and Co bankruptcy?'

And there were the inevitable grumbles about staff. 'Miss Muir is giving notice to go to Rimingtons. I suppose Miss Nicoll has persuaded her as they were great friends.' But a week or two later she wrote, 'Miss Muir has not been long in repenting – would be glad to come back.' Like most employers, Mary resented staff demands for more pay: 'Wages are higher as you know by Miss Stark who has of where at first she had half the sum and workers are not to be had ...' was her somewhat incoherent complaint about one of her best workers.

The mid-1860s saw a series of strikes both in Paris and in London. The biggest of these was the tailors' strike for more pay and shorter hours, which lasted from April to October and did a great deal of damage to the trade while failing to achieve its objectives. 'Strikes are the order of the day,' *The Caledonian Mercury* told its readers:

> The working tailors are gradually gaining their point; and some twenty or more of the larger houses have been forced into submission. Two or three delegates from the London Trades Union have come over to encourage the members of the association here, and to bring them substantial aid in money. The hairdressers promise to go out on strike next and I suppose we shall find them supported by your trades unions after the same fashion.[3]

The hairdressers' action was short-lived but Mary Carmichael was deeply unsympathetic. 'What a case with the Hairdressers – our lot will be next I shouldn't wonder,' she grumbled. And in another letter she wrote sarcastically, 'I should never be surprised at our lot wanting their hours shortened it seems such a pity to work till 9'. She and Elizabeth had trained at a time when employees were expected to work to midnight or later when an order required it; the Factory Acts had restricted the hours factory owners could demand of their employees, and moves were afoot to extend this legislation to smaller businesses. Mary thought it totally unnecessary.

The relationship between the sisters was not without its difficulties, however. It sounds as though Elizabeth had been careless in keeping records. 'I said Mrs Hunter of Craigerook was already entered in the book – you have entered it over again,' Mary told her, soon after Elizabeth left Edinburgh. On another occasion she forwarded a letter from Miss Younger of Kirkhill, Gosbridge, who had received a bill from Elizabeth but '... will thank Mme Chaffard to let her know what were the articles furnished [for 1gn] as it is so long since that she does not even remember the lady they were for ...'. Later there were problems with Susan Hill of 137 High Street. Susan had paid the firm thirteen guineas in settlement of her bill, but was outraged to receive a letter from Elizabeth telling her she had only paid £5 and £8 13s was still outstanding. Mary assured Miss Hill it was a mistake and apologised profusely – but her irritation with her sister for putting her in such an embarrassing position is almost palpable.

Several times she asks Elizabeth to send the pass books for their bank account – presumably they had been packed and taken to Brighton by mistake. On another occasion she asked Elizabeth about items for which she had been responsible – 'Please will you let me know the cost of stock marked,' and again – 'think you misunderstood me in regards to Mrs Antrobus. I intended today not to charge the firm with more than I had received for your own account.' Mary herself seems to have been a meticulous record keeper. Soon after Ferdinand's death, Messrs Horne, Horne & Lyell, a firm of solicitors, was called in to sort out his business affairs and wrote to Elizabeth describing Mary in glowing terms. Its representative was impressed by

the excellent style in which the Day Book has been brought forward, and the ready proffer of Mrs Carmichael to give every explanation and assistance in her power, he does not anticipate the difficulty and labour which he expected.

We can watch Mary becoming progressively more resentful of her sister, who was still drawing an income from the business but doing nothing to earn it. 'How do you think I could keep house on £28?

I hold my own accounts and I have had the £80 same as you except the £5 due,' Mary grumbled. Things got increasingly heated when Elizabeth misread the books. 'I cannot believe I have worked a year for nothing. Did you not check all payments on the large books with the others?' Mary wrote and, later, when Elizabeth accused her of cheating and keeping money for herself she became really angry: 'as to honesty I should scarcely have sent you twice over if I had any intention of being otherwise.' A few weeks later she was still justifying herself – 'I think you are rather hard on me for I know there are not many could have done as I have' – and it rather looks as if at that point Elizabeth paid Mary £500 to carry on. She needed the business to provide her with an income and, if she could not run it herself, she was dependent on Mary to do it for her.

For her part, Mary thought Elizabeth was extravagant. On at least one occasion Elizabeth tried to explain why she was taking such large sums from the business: 'You think the money goes fast, remember, we are a family of four adults and two children. Mrs Broad [a servant] has 7s a week ... then the provision is [provisions are] such a price here ...' It is not clear who the 'four adults and two children' were – perhaps at the time this letter was written she and Lizzie were staying with George and Louisa.

But Mary was not to be placated:

I have tried hard to do my best and have a happy mind that my part has been kept – as far as my strength allowed. Since I was ill before Christmas I have not been nearly as strong. You well know the credit that was always required ... There is not to my belief a penny in bad debts.

Getting bills paid was not always easy – wealthy ladies were notorious for paying their bills late. A letter from a Miss Shaw illustrates this. She sent £3 'on account' and wrote that if they 'will kindly wait a little for the balance Miss Shaw will feel deeply grateful. Miss Shaw also desires to thank Mme Chaffard for her kindness in waiting so long as it is ...' Colonel Mason's wife wrote from Gosport in a similar vein, wishing Chaffards' staff a happy New Year and hoping 'to send part of my debt very shortly.' Part of the problem was that even well-to-do ladies had an allowance from their husbands or fathers to pay for their clothes, and this money was usually doled out at quarterly intervals. These women had seldom learnt to budget and were used to having what they wanted when they wanted it – and the tradespeople with whom they dealt suffered accordingly. Mary may eventually have secured all the payments due to her, but in one letter she lists the sums owed to the firm; they totalled a whopping £373 16s 7d and were due from seventeen customers, including Mrs Abercrombie, who owed £47 2s 10d, and 'Lallesay' – probably the inhabitants of a house of that name – who owed £157 19s 10d.

She was often very busy:

I am overwhelmed with work. I have ten dresses to turn out this week and cannot see my way clear one little bit so do not expect to hear from me before Monday. I could not sleep last night with the worry ...

It must also have been galling that the firm was still in Elizabeth's name. One letter from Miss Fenwick of Bywell Hall, Stockfield-on-Tyne, praised the firm's work highly:

Miss Fenwick writes to Mme Chaffard to say she got her dress yesterday and is so much pleased with it, she considers it perfectly lovely and quite what she wanted it fits very well indeed and is altogether perfect – Miss Fenwick now wishes Mme Chaffard to make her sister, Mrs Barnard a dress like the <u>white</u> dress in the modes, made of the same material as the one she made Miss Fenwick only in white and trimmed with black velvet and buttons the same as in the modes the length of the skirt must be just the same as Miss Fenwick's, the waist cut square, and if Mme Chaffard will begin the skirt as soon as possible Miss Fenwick will send the size of the waist in a day or two. Mrs Barnett would like the dress to cost about £4-4s ...

However, the dressmaker responsible for this perfect garment – and who would also supply Mrs Barnett – was actually Mary Ann Carmichael.

But there were lighter moments. Shortly before setting out to spend the Christmas of 1867 in Brighton, Mary wrote to wee Lizzie, offering to bring her a hat with a bird on it and telling her a story about 'the little boy who would sell her his wee sister for a horse and cart and some sweeties' – he must have been the child of one of her customers. For her part, it seems wee Lizzie sent her aunt lots of pressed flowers in her mother's letters.

In one letter Mary asked for little Lizzie's measurements, as they were making her a dress and 'Miss Taylor has no pattern of Lizzie so if you send her size as soon as you can'. In another she wrote,

> I think you scarcely understand me in regard to the material for Lizzie's jacket – the pattern I sent is so uncommon it was only a little slip I could cut from the one in stock it cannot be bought by the yard or I would not have proposed marking down the one here – would you object to her having a sealskin hat with white gossamer veil and white wing – the newest thing out and so pretty.

Mary still took a maternal interest in her little niece and was anxious she should look her best.

The proprietors of Chaffard et Cie were all comparatively young. Ferdinand was just forty-four when he died in 1866 and Elizabeth was the same age. Mary was ten years younger. But neither of the sisters was strong. Dressmakers worked long hours, and dressmaking is sedentary work, requiring concentration and attention to detail. Clients could be difficult and demanding. Profit margins were always narrow and success involved meticulous book-keeping and calculation. As proprietors of the business, the sisters may not have sat sewing late into the night, but they still worked long hours and the profession had taken its toll on them both. Elizabeth wrote of rheumatism in her arms and shoulders, gum-boils and a swollen face, of being 'languid' and hoping 'nature air' would restore her to health.

Mary admitted to being unwell, over-tired and forgetful, and told her sister that 'Dr Malcolm' said she was suffering from 'debility' and recommended rest and bathing in tepid sea water.

Sometime in November 1867 Mary set off for her long-awaited holiday in Brighton, leaving Chaffard et Cie in the capable hands of Miss Taylor. No doubt little Lizzie was excited at the prospect of seeing her aunt again. She was just four when the family left Edinburgh two years previously and so she probably barely remembered what her Auntie Mary looked like. Nevertheless, there had been regular letters and presents; there was the promise of smart new clothes and the 'hat with a bird' to look forward to; there would be gifts and cards from her mother's customers in Edinburgh; and if Lizzie had any memories at all of her aunt they would have been of a woman much younger than her mother, one who petted and played with her.

Elizabeth's health had been poor for months and, by the time Mary arrived in Brighton, she was seriously ill, bedridden, coughing and struggling to breathe, and little Lizzie was spending much of her time with her uncles and aunts as her mother could no longer care for her. The family seem to have taken it in turns to sit with Elizabeth, and it was her brother-in-law, William who was there on 3 December when she died of 'inflammation of the lungs'. It was a terrible start to Mary's holiday but worse was to come. Mary herself was weak and exhausted when she left Edinburgh; the long journey must have been trying and no doubt on arrival she had had to do her share of nursing. Within days of Elizabeth's death Mary was running a high temperature and complaining of stomach pains. She had 'gastric fever' – a form of typhoid. She was too ill to be moved and died at Elizabeth's house, 22 Cobden Place, on 16 December – and again it was William Phillips who was at the deathbed. Mary was thirty-seven. Little Lizzie was just six; her father had died the previous year; and, in the space of two weeks, she had lost her mother and the aunt who had been like a second mother to her. It must have been a terrifying time for a small child.

Ferdinand Chaffard and Mary Carmichael both died intestate, so the business passed into the hands of their solicitors, Messrs Horne,

Horne & Lyell. Elizabeth left around £3,000, which went to her brother George to pay her debts and support little Lizzie. No doubt the solicitors kept Chaffards' staff on for a few weeks to finish any outstanding orders but, on 26 February, the *Edinburgh Evening Courant* advertised the customer list and 'goodwill' of the firm for sale. They also advertised a series of clearing sales of stock. On 27 May there was an announcement to the effect that the business had been transferred to the Miss Reids at 5 South Hanover Street, and this was followed by a statement from the Miss Reids themselves saying that 'every effort would be made to give satisfaction'. There were more clearance sales, including a sale of household goods and showroom fittings, which show that Chaffards had been a very luxuriously appointed establishment; the walls had been lined with seven 'large and elegant Mantlepiece and Pier Mirrors' and the room was lit with flickering gas lights adorned with lustres. There were rosewood cabinets, chairs upholstered in Utrecht velvet and a damask-covered couch for customers to recline on if the whole business of choosing a dress became too much for them. Curiously, there was also an 'Elizabethan Bed', though it is not clear whether this was for decoration or use.

But, although the Misses Reid had no doubt paid highly for access to Chaffards' customer lists and records, 'goodwill' was a less purchasable commodity. Chaffards' reputation had relied on the quality of the goods they produced and the relationships the staff forged with customers – and these were things the Misses Reid could not buy. Miss Murray, who had been head of the millinery department, moved to Inverness to run the millinery department at Cumming & Campbell's in Church Street, and the firm's advertisements stressed her former connection with Chaffard et Cie. The firm's reputation was obviously known right across Scotland. Margaret Taylor, Mary's invaluable 'first hand', went into business with a relative as 'the Misses Taylor' at 4 Hope Street, off Charlotte Square 'at the request of some of Mme Chaffard's most esteemed customers'. The firm's advertisements appeared in the *Edinburgh Evening Courant* throughout 1868. They remained in business until 1870/1, when Miss Taylor moved to a slightly less prestigious address, 75 Broughton Street, for a couple of years before closing down altogether. Perhaps she did not have enough capital to tide her over when the 'esteemed customers' were tardy in paying their bills.

Wee Lizzie was brought up in Brighton by her Uncle George and Aunt Louisa; she became a music teacher and, in 1888, she married a Belgian, Frank Dusterwald, who worked as a clerk to a wine merchant. They had two sons but Lizzie was widowed young in 1894. She died in 1940. How much did she remember of her mother, of her cossetted early childhood in Edinburgh and of riding her rocking horse in the palatial mirrored showroom at 2 Castle Street?

It seems likely that the letters on which this chapter is based were kept to remind her. Most of them are addressed to Elizabeth Chaffard and would have been in her possession when she died. However, a few letters from and about her must have been added by family members, as was a photograph taken by a Brighton photographer in the early 1860s (see plate 1). It is not identified but is almost certainly of Elizabeth. Sadly, Lizzie's grandchildren seem not to have been particularly interested in the history of their great-grandparents and their business. The collection of letters was put up for auction in 1963 and was bought by the National Library of Scotland.

'One Good Example': Rebecca Thomas (*c.* 1830–1902), Cheltenham

The year was 1870 and Edward Brydges was out of his depth. Edward was an attorney and solicitor and, sometime in 1861/2, when he was still in his early thirties, he had been appointed clerk to the Cheltenham Borough Council. Part of his role was to implement new legislation when it affected the Council.

The 1867 Workshop Regulation Act came into force on 1 January 1868, but it seems Edward made no attempt to publicise the fact. For a year. This is strange because, when the Improvement Committee or the Turnpike Trustees met, or the Council did anything else of general interest, he normally published a notice about their deliberations in the local press. It seems likely that the decision to keep quiet about the new Act was not Edward's alone.

The Workshop Act was designed to limit the working hours of people employed in small workshops and to bring them in line with the provisions of the Factory Acts of the previous decade. It applied to workshops with more than five employees and prohibited the employment of children under the age of eight, limited children's hours to six a day and reduced the working hours of 'women and young persons' to no more than twelve hours in any given period of twenty-four. Sunday working was prohibited and so was working after 2 p.m. on a Saturday. There were a great many other provisions about the education of children in part-time employment and the work children under eleven were to be banned from doing – notably metal grinding and 'fustian cutting' – and there was a long list of exemptions and special cases.

Implementing the Act in full would have had serious financial implications for small businesses, however, and many of the town councillors were businessmen; there was a lot of vested interest at stake, which is probably why Edward kept quiet. However, in June 1869, he finally decided, or was persuaded, that the proprietors of workshops in Cheltenham really did need to be made aware that new legislation had been passed, and he penned a long letter to the *Cheltenham Examiner,* setting out the provisions of the new Act in detail.[1] In January 1870 he seems to have been advised to do more and there was a flurry of correspondence. First he wrote to Mr Earnshaw, the local factory inspector, asking about posters, where should he get them and how many? Mr Earnshaw advised him to contact the town clerks of Gloucester and Marlborough for advice, which he duly did. At the end of January, he heard from Robert Missiman in Marlborough, who gave him the address of the government printing agent, sent him a brochure about implementing the Act and told him Marlborough had had 300 posters printed. Edward followed this advice and, in due course, received a set of large posters from the printers in London:

BOROUGH OF CHELTENHAM

Notice is hereby given that since the first day of January 1868 the following provisions have been and are now in force under the

WORKSHOP REGULATION ACT 1867 ...

A list of the provisions of the Act followed, with all its sub-clauses, exemptions and exceptions. The posters cannot have been easy to read because there was so much detailed information on them, but orders were given that they were to be displayed prominently around the town. Edward Brydges had done his duty, albeit belatedly.

Then, a few weeks later, he received an anonymous letter, addressed to him as 'Publick Officer':

> If you have anything to do with inspecting the workrooms in Cheltenham you will be doing a great kindness on the part of the dressmakers by inspecting Miss Thomas, 13 Promenade after 5 of a Saturday evening, there the young people are kept in an underground place till 8 or ½ past or loose [sic] their place when every other business is closed ...

It is not clear whether it was the appearance of the posters that prompted the letter, but the timing does suggest that it might have been. Details of the Council and its employees were published monthly in the *Cheltenham Chronicle,* so the writer would have had little difficulty in tracking him down. The letter placed Edward Brydges in an extremely awkward position. Then, as now, a complaint had to be investigated – but he decided he would have to get his facts absolutely straight first. A prosecution, he probably reasoned, would be very bad publicity for the town ...

Miss Rebecca Thomas and her mother had arrived in Cheltenham from Clifton in or around 1860 and had set up a very respectable business on The Promenade, one of Cheltenham's main shopping streets (see plate 8). They employed up to ten young women and catered for a superior class of customer. There had never been any hint of scandal associated with the business and Edward had no wish to make waves. He would have known, of course, that dressmakers always worked long hours – but probably considered it light work, not particularly demanding or tiring. After all, even ladies sewed.

However, Edward did as the law required, though he, the anonymous letter writer and the dressmakers themselves seem to have misunderstood the Act – it was actually illegal to employ people after *two* in the afternoon on a Saturday, not five. Edward despatched Mr Morgan, Inspector of Nuisances, to 13 The Promenade on the evening of Saturday 14 May and, sure enough, nine young women were still at work. When Mr Morgan questioned them, it became clear that they regularly worked on Saturday evenings. He reported back to Edward.

Edward Brydges was now in a quandary. He wrote to the local factory inspector, Hugh Granger Earnshaw, asking for his advice – given his experience in implementing the Factory Acts, what course of action did he recommend? Were there not exceptions for people working in retail and was not a dressmaker a retailer of dresses? On 19 May he had his reply. In Mr Earnshaw's view the case was clear-cut; the exception made for small shopkeepers would not apply to Miss Thomas as she employed more than five people and, anyway, Mr Earnshaw thought the argument that she was a retailer was a very questionable one. She had nine employees, so she was guilty on nine counts – and besides, there were other issues; he had obviously made enquiries. She was accused of overworking her employees generally, not just on Saturdays, and of not allowing them the hour-and-a-half to which they were entitled for meals and of hurrying them to finish eating before they were ready so they could get back to work. Furthermore, one young woman, Julia Fisher, was a special case, as she said she had often been expected to work after 9 p.m. He finished by saying that the case was a strong one and that 'One good example is worth a thousand precepts. I would exhaust the case and prosecute it rigorously.' Hugh Earnshaw was a hard-headed Lancastrian.

Edward prevaricated; this was the first offence of its kind in Cheltenham, could they not be lenient? Miss Thomas was a highly respected businesswoman – perhaps a warning would suffice? Mr Earnshaw strongly disagreed and took it upon himself to interview some of the girls concerned, and then, on 21 May, he wrote to Edward again: 'I listened to the clear, modest and (I well believe) true statements of a set of girls whose listless manners and wearied looks bespoke the long hours of jading toil ...' Once again, Mr Earnshaw urged him to prosecute – but still Edward dithered. On 27 May Mr Earnshaw sent him two closely written pages stressing that it was the Council's bounden *duty* to enforce the Act as stringently as possible; and then the following day he sent another letter, probably intended to stiffen the young man's resolve by offering his active support: 'If you think I can serve your case against Thomas on any point – as a witness or by my appearance ...'

Things were getting worse. In despair, Edward wrote to Whitehall. Surely the new Act did not apply to dressmaking businesses? We do not have his letter but he received an acknowledgement of it on 3 June and then a reply, dated 11 June 1870, arrived from S. J. O. Liddell, making it clear that there was absolutely no exemption to the Saturday working rules for milliners and dressmakers.

Meanwhile, Rebecca Thomas had got wind of what was going on. The inspector's visit had alerted her to the fact that there was a problem, but it is clear that someone else was giving her inside information. A letter from Rebecca had arrived on Edward Brydges' desk on 30 May pleading ignorance of the law she was accused of breaking. Another, undated, letter arrived from a Mr Henry Page, saying that Rebecca was in fact the injured party, that she had no idea who could possibly have accused her and stressing that she really was unaware she had broken the law. We do not know for sure who Henry Page was, but he was probably the furniture dealer on the High Street, a fellow tradesman. Rebecca Thomas may have been ignorant of the law but she was certainly not ignorant of the other accusations being levelled against her, for Henry Page answered them on her behalf. She denied ever having hurried the girls over their meals; on the contrary, their tea was provided free by the firm because some girls lived too far away to be able to go home and back in the half-hour she allowed them each afternoon. This tea was a generous bonus; it was not 'part of their hire.' Of course, this was irrelevant – the fact that the tea was free did not mean that the girls were allowed to enjoy it at leisure. She admitted some girls had worked late the evenings before her 'show' – but claimed they had asked to be allowed to stay on to help get things ready, and that she had not obliged them to do so.

Dressmakers all had 'shows' or 'fashion days' at the start of each season, where they displayed new fabrics, fashion plates and accessories, and entertained their customers. The shows often took place after the proprietor had visited Paris or London and had returned with samples and pictures. Rebecca's advertisements tell us that, in the 1860s at least, she made annual trips to Paris.

The case finally came to court on 14 June. Edward Brydges prosecuted, Mr Jessop defended and Mr Earnshaw was there to oversee proceedings on behalf of the Crown. Three young women gave evidence – Julia Jeens, Agnes Forty and Mary Ann Pardington – the other girls seem to have valued their jobs too much to stand up against their employer in court. In addition, the prosecution were obviously trying to do their best by Rebecca Thomas. The *Cheltenham Chronicle* reported the case that evening and explained:

> There were in all ten cases [this suggests that perhaps one dressmaker was absent on the Saturday of Mr Morgan's visit – he only interviewed nine], but this being the first prosecution under the act, and on account of the expense to which it would put the defendant, they thought it would be straining the law a little too tight to issue ten summonses.

So what do we know about Rebecca Thomas and her firm? She was born in Bristol in about 1830, the third child of grocer Edward Thomas and his wife Rebecca. She had an elder brother and sister and a younger sister, Elizabeth, who also became a dressmaker. In 1841 Rebecca and Elizabeth were at a boarding school run by a Miss Mary Burfoot, where they would have learnt needlework, and they both seem to have served their apprenticeships in Clifton or Bristol. Their parents seem to have separated – by 1851, they were both running grocer's shops but living at separate addresses. Sometime around 1860 Rebecca and her mother moved to Cheltenham and set up in business at 13 The Promenade, leaving the rest of the family behind in Bristol, and by 1861 the older Rebecca is listed in the census as a 'W' – widow.

Rebecca's career up to this point would have followed a similar trajectory to Elizabeth Chaffard's – apprenticeship, time as an 'improver', then second hand, then first hand. After a few years she, like Elizabeth Chaffard, would have been in a position to set up on her own.

The Promenade was a fashionable address. It would have cost quite a lot of money to lease or rent the premises and more money again to set up the workrooms and showrooms such an establishment required. It seems likely that this came from the sale of one or both of the family grocery businesses in Clifton. The numbering on The Promenade has changed over time but, when George Rowe published his *Illustrated Cheltenham Guide* (1845 and 1850), number thirteen was Shipton's Library and print shop. It is almost certain this is the building Rebecca took for her business and it does not appear to have a basement – though it is just possible that there was one that could be approached from the rear of the building.[2] When Rebecca's accusers spoke of 'an underground room' therefore, they probably meant a cellar rather than a basement with windows.

Rebecca was just thirty in 1860 but presumably she was highly skilled – her business would not have survived otherwise – and as early as 1861 the firm was employing seven girls, so they did not start

13 The Promenade. Rebecca Thomas took over this shop in or around 1860. When George Rowe sketched the shop it belonged to a print seller, Mr Shipton. From Rowe's *Guide to Cheltenham*, 1845. (Courtesy of Cheltenham Local and Family History Library)

small and then expand. It may be that old Mrs Thomas, Rebecca's mother, had some dressmaking experience before her marriage – certainly the 1861 census lists her as head of the firm and the girls' employer – though the press advertisements always describe the proprietor as 'Miss Thomas'.

In 1863 Rebecca was interviewed by the *Children's Employment Commission*:

> I have only three residents, two apprentices and one paid hand; our day workers vary from six to nine or ten, in the season we very rarely work longer than from 8am to 10pm: it is very seldom that we work till 12. I have one machine, we do not use it for more than an hour or two in the day, but even that saves one or two extra hands. Our workroom, unfortunately, is on [sic] the basement and rather low pitched; although it is large, and we never have very many in it, and only three gas jets, it is often very hot. There certainly are inconveniences attached to having day workers, but others are not to be had. I do not think, speaking of the business generally, that so many respectably connected girls are apprenticed to it as there used to be 15 years ago; many now are taken without premium by persons in a small way of business; they live at their own homes and give their work for nothing for some time after they have learned enough to be useful.[3]

The commissioners were interested in the conditions in which young people and children lived and worked, which was why Rebecca's testimony concentrated on apprentices and training. Long hours were something the Commission had highlighted in their report in 1843. Rebecca would have known this and, like most employers, she was keen to play down the length of time her staff worked; however, it is evident that the hours her workers complained about in 1870 had been pretty much the norm seven years earlier – and would certainly have been considered perfectly acceptable when Rebecca herself trained. This does not justify her breaking the law but probably explains why she did not see it as particularly wrong.

Rebecca's preference for live-in staff as opposed to day workers is also understandable – no doubt even in 1863 it was easier to bully live-in workers.

The comment on the lack of 'respectable connections' of girls going into the trade is interesting – it looks as though Rebecca saw herself as socially superior to many of her staff and thought the dressmaking trade was becoming less rigorous. This may also be why she appointed Julia Jeens as her 'first hand' – Julia was certainly well-connected; her brother was a solicitor. Samuel Jeens, Julia's father, was the baker in Glastonbury, a prosperous tradesman. Julia was sent away to boarding school at Culmstock in Devon and was there until she was sixteen; this was a family who valued education and wanted their children to have genteel jobs. By contrast, young Julia Alderslade, Rebecca's sixteen-year-old apprentice, came from much lower down the social ladder. Her father was a 'bill poster' – a precarious occupation in more ways than one.

Sewing machines were relatively new in 1863 and their use had been criticised by some writers, who thought the rhythm of the machine affected women's internal organs – hence, no doubt, Rebecca's insistence that her machine was not much used. Not everyone agreed. Mrs Gilling, a dressmaker at Promenade Villas, a stone's throw from Rebecca's establishment, told the commissioners she had three machines and that she

should like every dressmaker to use them, they save much labour and also enable you to pay at a higher rate those whom you employ, whether machinist or finisher. Much more work can be put in too, we should never put 100 yards of trimming in a summer dress if it were all to be done by hand.[4]

By 1870 machines were increasingly widely used and it is quite probable that Rebecca Thomas was using them more too.

We have some clues about the wages she was paying in 1870 and it is unlikely that they had changed much since the firm was set up. Mary Ann Pardington was being paid 7s a week as a nineteen-year-old out-worker, and this was probably fairly typical of the wages the other girls received. They were much of an age and 7s to 8s was the standard wage for an assistant dressmaker countrywide. Sixteen-year-old Julia Alderslade was an apprentice or an 'improver' and would not have been paid at all. However, Agnes Forty's £40 a year was a substantial wage. She was not the head dressmaker – that was Julia Jeens – but she was probably Julia's second in command. Julia herself would have received considerably more – probably somewhere around £70–100. She was still comparatively young but she had come all the way from Warrington to take the post, so she must have thought it was worth her while.

The dresses Miss Thomas's workroom made in 1870 would have looked very similar to those Chaffard et Cie were making shortly before Elizabeth Chaffard and Mary Carmichael died – full-skirted dresses worn over a 'crinolette' with all the fullness at the back. Two-piece dresses with long bodices were in vogue and – as Mrs Gilling said – the ubiquitous sewing machines now enabled garments to be lavishly trimmed in a fraction of the time it would have taken to apply decoration by hand. Over the next decade the fashionable shape would change: skirts would become less full and flatter at the front until, by the 1880s, the crinolette was replaced by the bustle (see plates 6 and 18). Rebecca's business records do not survive but, from the location of her business, we can deduce that she was working for a fashionable clientele and, from the size of her staff, she must have been doing a brisk trade.

In court Julia Jeens gave evidence first. She had worked for Miss Thomas for just six weeks from 7 April as head dressmaker and was due to be paid quarterly. There were ten other dressmakers, two of whom were under eighteen, and she, Miss Forty and Miss Pitt lived in; the others all lived at home.

They all started work at 8 a.m. The live-in staff were allowed a quarter-of-an-hour for breakfast – never more – sometime between 8 and 9 a.m. The 'outdoor' workers ate before they left home. They had half-an-hour for dinner at 1 p.m., never an hour, though the outdoor workers went home between 1 and 2 p.m., and they all had a quarter-of-an-hour for tea. The outdoor workers had theirs in the work-room, while she and the other live-in staff ate in the parlour. They had been especially busy before Miss Thomas's show days, which had been 13 and 14 April. Julia had worked until a quarter-to-midnight on the eleventh and till a quarter-past on the twelfth. On 30 April (a Wednesday) she, Miss Forty and Miss Pitt worked till twenty-five to eleven and on the following day (Thursday) they worked till after nine. She had never known any of them leave work before eight on Saturdays.

Miss Thomas had sacked her on 23 May and had not allowed her to work her month's notice. She also threatened her saying 'she would blame me and she knew what I was.' Rebecca Thomas obviously suspected Julia Jeens of being the whistle-blower who had alerted Edward Brydges to the fact that the law was being broken. It seems an entirely reasonable – if unproven – assumption.

Agnes Forty spoke next. She had been with Miss Thomas for three years and six weeks, was paid £40 a year and also lived in. Her hours of work were supposed to be from 8 a.m. to 8 p.m., but she generally worked to 9.30 or 10 p.m. and she confirmed Julia's version of the time they were allowed for meals, although she said they only 'had about ten minutes for breakfast' and were 'expected to start work immediately we finished.' The live-in workers were supposed to have supper after they finished work, so it was often 10 p.m. or later before they got their last meal of the day. She admitted that occasionally in summer when they were not busy they might stop work at 5.30 or 6 p.m. on Saturdays – but said it did not happen often. She went on,

The indoor Assistants always had to work after the outdoor ones when anything had to be done – I have been very ill through overwork and have been obliged to leave in consequence – Miss Thomas told me she did not believe I was ill it was only my temper – I gave Notice to leave on 26th April before the Inspector came. After he came she raved at me and told me I had behaved in a most brutish and disgraceful manner ...

Agnes confirmed Julia Jeens's version of the hours they had worked before the show and on 30 April, adding that that evening she had asked Miss Thomas if they could have supper before they finished work 'as I was almost dying for want of it', which is why she could clearly remember the exact date and the time they finished, but neither she nor Julia explained why they had had to work so late that particular day. Agnes also added a telling detail: Miss Thomas used to draw the blinds at 5 p.m. on Saturdays to make it look as if the business was closed. 'I have remonstrated with her and I have tried to get her to close at five on Saturdays. She has always said, "The work must be done."'

But there was another part of Agnes's story that did not come out in court. A month's wages seem only to have been paid for a full month's work – despite the fact that a monthly wage could easily be divided into weekly parts. Agnes had given notice on 26 April and so should have worked to the end of May to complete her notice. In court Agnes claimed she left on 14 May because she was ill, but in the account she gave to Mr Morgan she said Miss Thomas had thrown her out. Agnes had therefore not received her last lot of wages, so her brother wrote to Miss Thomas on her behalf requesting that they be paid. Rebecca had replied in a very high-handed fashion:

> Miss Thomas is anxious to close her transaction with Miss Forty therefore she is willing to forgo the fortnight's salary and only on this account does she do so, as Miss Forty is perfectly aware the law is entirely on Miss Thomas's side. Had Miss Forty given proper notice her brother would have been aware of it and not have so readily decided the month's salary should be paid in lieu of Miss Forty's service which he did …

Rebecca must have been well aware that the law was not on her side but she wanted to blame and intimidate her former employee.

Mary Ann Pardington was the last of the girls to take the stand. She lived with her sister at 21 Manchester Walk and was supposed to work from 8 a.m. to 8 p.m. for 7s a week. She did get an hour for lunch because she went home for it, but said they 'were obliged to keep the time punctually.' She confirmed that tea was served in the work-room but said they didn't always get a quarter-of-an-hour in which to have it. She, too, often worked after 8 p.m. – she had worked till 10.30 p.m. on 12 April, and till 9.30 p.m. on 23 April and 7 May. These answers seemed rather too pat to the prosecution and she was asked how she could be so sure. She replied that there was a clock in the workroom. She too had had a run-in with Miss Thomas after Mr Morgan's inspection: 'I gave Miss Thomas a week's Notice on 14th May, the night Mr Morgan came – Miss Thomas told me I had exaggerated.'

The inspector, John Henry Morgan, was the last to give evidence. He had visited Miss Thomas's on 14 May at about 7.20 p.m. with a Justice's Order and found nine young women at work in a basement room. Two of them were under eighteen. They all said they worked 8 a.m. to 8 p.m. six days a week and had an hour-and-a-quarter for meals – of the ones who were not in court only Julia Fisher had admitted that she sometimes worked till after nine. He listed the women, giving names, ages and addresses:

Agnes Forty, aged 20. Lived in
Annie Watson, aged 18. 25, Grosvenor Street
Julia Alderslade, aged 16. 32, Ambrose Street
Mary Jane Pitt, aged 18. Lived in
Mary Ann Pardington, aged 19. 21, Manchester Walk
Julia Fisher, aged 19. Golden Valley
Julia Jeens (or Jeans), aged 25. Lived in
Sarah Osman, aged 17. Victoria Street
Luisa Cowley, aged 21. 12, Mitre Street

Then he added the most damning piece of evidence of all: 'Miss Forty and Pardington has been discharged since my Inspection for the Candour of there replies' [sic]. What is striking is how young most of the girls were – small wonder that they were too afraid to speak out against their employer, especially when they saw how she bullied the girls who did.

The court found against Rebecca Thomas – the fact that she had sacked two of her accusers told heavily against her – and she was fined £1 plus costs for each of the three indictments. It was a derisory sum, one she could well afford, and though the case was reported in the papers there is nothing to suggest that it in any way affected her business.

Within the year most of the nine young women on Mr Morgan's list had left Rebecca Thomas's employ. In 1871 Agnes Forty was working as a draper's assistant and living just a short distance from her old employer in a boarding house for her store's employees in Promenade Villas. Annie Weston had moved to Great Malvern and was getting experience in a millinery establishment. Mary Jane Pitt, who as a teenager had come from Newport as a live-in apprentice to Miss Thomas, was still dressmaking, but at Awre, on the edge of the Forest of Dean. Julia Fisher had gone back home to Golden Valley and was living with her widowed mother and brother next door to the Golden Pheasant, the pub that her father once ran. She and her brother, Solomon, both described themselves as 'assistants' and seem to have been working for the new landlord. Luisa Cowley and little Sarah Osman are untraceable in the census, and Julia Alderslade and Mary Ann Pardington were both still living with their families in Cheltenham. Mary Ann had been sacked, so she must have been working for someone else; Julia may or may not have still worked for Miss Thomas.

And what of Julia Jeens who, in all probability, set the whole case in motion? When she left Cheltenham she went to stay with her brother and his family back in Warrington. Did the fact that he was an attorney have any bearing on Julia instigating the case against Miss Thomas? Was Julia a troublemaker or an honourable young woman who took her role as head dressmaker to mean she should fight for her colleagues' rights? She was engaged to be married – did she make the case because she knew she would soon be leaving? We have no way of knowing. We do know that Julia Jeens never worked as a dressmaker again; in the summer of 1871 she married George Edwin Chatwin, a 'provision dealer' with a shop on Bury New Road in Manchester, and, within the decade, they had a son and four daughters. By 1891 the business had prospered and they had moved it to Blackpool, where Julia ran a seaside boarding house alongside her husband's shop.

There is no question that Rebecca Thomas was breaking the law quite flagrantly – even though Mr Jessop, acting on her behalf, urged that it was not 'an extreme case'. One wonders what his definition of 'extreme' would have been. It does sound as if she was something of a tyrant – but there again, so was Elizabeth Chaffard's employer, Miss Goulding, and so, probably, was Mary Carmichael. Rebecca was unlucky in finding a member of staff confident enough to take her to task and charismatic enough to rally her staff against her. Henry Page's letter suggests that she was being made a scapegoat and in a way she was, as Hugh Earnshaw was determined to make an example of her, and it may be that, for a while at least, other dressmakers in Cheltenham and elsewhere broke the new law and overworked their staff just as callously as Rebecca did. The profit margin in dressmaking was always dismally low and an ambitious dressmaker, who was anxious to make a respectable profit, keep her customers happy by producing elegant dresses in a matter of hours and unwilling to turn clients away, had to work her staff to the bone. The Workshop Regulation Act was designed to prevent such abuse and, as time went by, it gradually became more effective in doing so.

In April 1887 Rebecca Thomas was still advertising her services (see advertisement overleaf), but she ceased trading in 1888[5] and retired to Somerset. She is listed in the 1891 and 1901 censuses as being of 'independent means', which means that she had saved enough from her business to provide her with a pension – obviously her ruthlessness had paid off.

In her late sixties Rebecca developed Parkinson's disease – for someone whose career had depended on meticulous needlework, the loss of motor function must have been especially hard to bear. For the last month of her life she was paralysed and eventually her heart gave out. She died on 22 July 1902, aged seventy-three. She ended her days at Falcon Lodge, a sort of retirement home, run by former coastguard Charles Anderson and his wife Sarah. No friends or family came to nurse her and it was Charles who was with her when she died. In her will Rebecca left the little money she still had – £74 17s 1d – to the Andersons; this was probably part of the agreement she made with them when she moved in. It was a sad and lonely end, but it is probably as well she did not survive much longer. The £74 would not have enabled her to pay her way for more than a year or two; when it was gone her only option would have been the workhouse.

MISS THOMAS, 13, PROMENADE

COURT MILLINER

WEDDING and MOURNING Orders, DRESSES and COSTUMES complete,
executed by
competent hands in the Newest French Styles

'Dear Mrs Pattinson': Elizabeth Pattinson (1862–1935), Ulverston, Cumbria

'To Sam and Elizabeth!'
'To the happy couple!'
'Their good health!'

No doubt the regulars in the bar of the Hare & Hounds were happy to toast the marriage of the landlord's son. John Pattinson was the publican and Samuel Smith Pattinson, his eldest boy, married Elizabeth Sarah Simpson at St Mary's, Ulverston, in October 1884. They spent their honeymoon on the Isle of Man.

In an isolated small town like Ulverston, everyone knew everyone else's business and they would all have known the Pattinsons. John's younger son, Isaac, was probably the cause of a good deal of bar room gossip. He had emigrated to America, joined the US army and played in a military band, and his letters home detailed his regiment's exploits in exotic-sounding places such as Fort Clark in Texas and Detroit in Michigan – inconceivably remote to most of his father's customers. They were hard men – farmers and ironworkers who seldom travelled as far afield as Lancaster, a mere twenty-six miles away by rail.

Samuel, the newly-wed, was much less adventurous than his brother. 'He's got a good head on his shoulders, though,' the men probably told each other. Samuel worked as a clerk at the station. No doubt his father had put in a good word for him with the company; John Pattinson had worked as a railway guard before he took over the pub. Nineteenth-century employers were usually happy to take on the relatives of trusted staff, as they believed it bred loyalty and a sense of community. In the nineteenth century, railway workers were comparatively well paid; they got perks, such as cheap travel, and it was a job with prospects in what was then a thriving, modern industry; best of all, it was regular work. In most jobs, men could be laid off or put on short time when the weather was bad or when trade was slack but the Pattinsons were luckier than most – they would be able to rely on a fixed wage coming in each week. Samuel also had a second source of income. He acted as rent collector for old Mr Fenton. David Henry Fenton was a retired bank manager with interests in a gunpowder-manufacturing business and a series of rented houses – he had nine in Ulverston alone. He and his wife, Mary Anne, lived in a succession of houses in Kendal, in Levens, Low House at Cleabarrow (see plate 9) and, latterly, at Arnside on Morecambe Bay. They were childless and Mary Anne was restless and discontented. Whether Samuel met Mr Fenton through his job at the station, or through the pub, or the bank, or in some other way, we do not know, but from the tone of their surviving correspondence theirs was something more than just a business arrangement and it continued throughout the Fentons' various moves.

Samuel had married a neighbour's daughter – Elizabeth's family lived just a stone's throw from the Hare & Hounds, round the corner in Upper Brook Street at No. 10 where her father, Moses Simpson, and one of her brothers worked as wood-turners. She had been born a few miles away but the family had moved to Ulverston when she was just a little girl – the young couple had probably known each other since childhood. She and Sam seem to have saved quite a substantial sum of money with which to start their married life and their first home was 8 Upper Brook Street, next door to her parents.

In 1982, the then owner, Mr Lawson, discovered a large bundle of late-nineteenth-century bills and correspondence in his attic and donated them to the Cumbria Record Office.[1] They form the starting point for this chapter and give an insight into the lives and financial affairs of three very different women – Elizabeth Pattinson, her niece Maggie Simpson, and their client-from-hell Mary Anne Fenton.

Elizabeth had trained as a milliner – as we have seen, in the 1880s 'milliner' was synonymous with dressmaker; it did not necessarily mean someone who only made hats. Millinery and dressmaking were respectable jobs – poorly paid like all women's work, but the sort of employment that was suitable for a well-brought-up young girl like Elizabeth Simpson. She had begun her training in 1877 when she was fifteen, but a letter from her cousin, Jane Simpson, had expressed surprise. 'I hope you like it. It will be a nice pastime for you,' she wrote, which would suggest that Elizabeth's family did not really need her to earn her own living. They do seem to have been fairly prosperous; the houses in Upper Brook Street are solid, stone-built, three-storey properties. However, Elizabeth must have enjoyed millinery for, over the winter of 1884/5, she set up in business on her own account.

The bundles of papers tell us a good deal about how she did so. It is not always possible to tell which bills were for the couple's home and which relate to Elizabeth's new shop – payments for plumbing and gas services could be for either, though clearly the ones for sign-writing and insuring plate-glass windows (for 4s a year with the PG Insurance Society) were for the business. Unusually, Elizabeth chose not to work from home, even though their house was quite large enough to allow a room to be used as a shop. Instead she rented a tiny, two-storey place on the corner of King Street and Upper Brook Street, a few yards down the hill from her home and in a prime position in the shopping centre – it was built into the angle of an 'L' shaped shop that faced on to the main road (see plate 7). In Elizabeth's day it was a separate building with space for a little shop on the ground floor and a workroom-cum-storeroom upstairs, though today it forms an annex to the larger shop next door.

Sam and Elizabeth were childless but they adopted a niece, Maggie Simpson, the daughter of Elizabeth's brother James. Such informal adoptions were quite common in the nineteenth century, although it is hard to see why James and Margaret Simpson gave up their baby daughter. She was their first child, born in 1883 a matter of months after their wedding, and she seems to have moved in with the Pattinsons when she was quite little and while both her parents were still alive. Perhaps – because of illness or injury – Elizabeth and Sam knew they would never be able to have a family of their own, and the arrangement with James and Margaret Simpson was an early example of a sort of surrogacy. We cannot know for certain.

Whatever the reasons for her adoption, Maggie Simpson had as privileged a childhood as a working-class family in 1880s Ulverston could provide. She had music lessons from Margaret Speight, a local piano and violin teacher who wrote that she considered Maggie 'a regular little genius and [felt] quite proud of having such a pupil'. Maggie was then ten years old. She was taken to children's operettas performed at the Drill Hall by the local Congregational Band of Hope; a programme for their 1893 production of *The Fairy Grotto* survives. They went on holidays – in 1890 the family travelled to Edinburgh by way of Kendal, Carlisle, Jedburgh and Galashiels. And when she left school – if not before – Maggie's aunt taught her to sew and to trim hats. In due course she was to inherit the business on the corner of King Street.

Ulverston in 1881 had a population of 10,001 but it also served a wide rural community. In 1882, two years before Elizabeth opened her shop, there were eighteen drapers' shops in the town, sixteen firms offering millinery and dressmaking, and eighteen offering tailoring. No doubt most of these 'firms' consisted, as Elizabeth's would, of one person, perhaps with an apprentice to run errands, pick up pins, thread needles and do boring jobs like hems and buttonholes. Nevertheless, it would seem that Elizabeth had chosen to enter a crowded market and it is hard to see how she – or anyone else – could have made a profit.

Her horizons did not extend far beyond Ulverston and at first she relied heavily on local tradespeople. Her sewing machine came from J. B. Kay, the Ulverston sewing machine agent, though she could probably have got it cheaper in Lancaster or Barrow. A local sign-writer, Edward Dickinson, wrote her 'frieze and door' and charged her 6s 9d for it. Later, in 1892, he varnished a display screen for her and re-glazed and renovated a show case, charging 6s and 2s 3d respectively. She placed her first stationery orders with Weeks & Fletcher, an Ulverston printer and stationer, who supplied her with a thousand millinery bags (for caps and bonnets), a hundred bill heads for 15s 3d and five hundred 'flower bags' (paper bags with a floral pattern on them) for 4s. The numbers are telling; she clearly did not expect to sell a great deal. Fairly soon, however, she discovered that the Midland Printing Works in Birmingham offered much more competitive rates.

She even bought odd hats – which presumably she trimmed for her customers – from J. H. Barrow, 'tailor, draper and gentleman's mercer' in Ulverston Market Place and from W. D. Higgins, another Ulverston draper. To oblige customers who could not be bothered to trail round the shops themselves, she would buy fabrics and sundries from most of the drapers in the town – including items from Joseph Postlethwaite, 'woollen and linen draper, silk mercer, hosier, haberdasher and hatter' and M. A. Hughes, 'hatter, hosier and outfitter', both of whose shops were just a few doors away from her own. They sold to her at a tiny discount, which became her profit when she passed the goods on to her customers. But soon the bulk of her supplies came from out of town. No doubt as her business became established she was targeted by sales reps arriving by train from Manchester, London, Nottingham and Ripon. We have no way of knowing whether Elizabeth ever visited their warehouses herself or whether she relied entirely on catalogues and samples, but most of her goods seem to have been ordered by post and sent by rail. Odd little notes survive from her suppliers:

March 18th, 1891 ... Sorry we cannot do the mob cap and Jack Tar cap ...
November 9th, 1895 ... Sorry we are sold out of the brown hat have sent the nearest ...

April 23rd 1895 ... Sorry this is the nearest we have in all white,
can have at any time made exactly to pattern, say ¼ doz of any
kind ...

But Elizabeth did not buy in ¼ dozens – she bought in ones or maybe
twos. On one occasion she ordered a single widow's cap, price 1s 1½d,
carriage (by rail to Ulverston station) 3d – all the way from Manchester!
No doubt the recently widowed customer who bought it was grateful –
but probably much less surprised than we might be that a big city firm
was prepared to supply a tiny provincial milliner with a single item.

Detailed records survive for Elizabeth's expenditure during the
period October 1886 to December 1887 – by which date she had been
in business for almost three years. Batho, Taylor & Ogden, 'suppliers
of millinery goods', and Peel Watson & Co., 'manufacturers of baby
linen, underwear, sun bonnets, aprons, etc.', both of Church Street,
Manchester, were her main suppliers and with them she spent totals
of £141 8s 1½d and £107 11s 6½d respectively. S. J. Watts & Co.
of Manchester, 'suppliers of ready-made clothing, laces, trimmings,
aprons, etc.', received just £9 12s 6d worth of her business over the
fourteen-month period, and Rayner & Lee, 'wholesale dealers in
straw bonnets, ribbons, flowers, feathers, millinery, etc.', of North
Bridge, Ripon, got even less. This level of expenditure did not
change – though the firms with which she traded did – between 1887
and 1902 when she handed her business over to Maggie.

Much of Elizabeth's trade was in ready-made goods. Some of the
stock books survive – in 1891, for example, her stock of ribbons,
feathers, laces, trimmings and sundries was valued at £248 12s 6d.
By 1900 that had risen to £349 4s 8d. She made a few garments; it
is hard to know how many customers she had, but garment-making
seems to have been a comparatively small part of her business. Not
for Elizabeth were the fifteen-hour days and overnight working
that so many dressmakers reported to the Children's Employment
Commissioners in the 1860s. No doubt Maggie helped as soon as
she was old enough and, unlike many dressmakers' apprentices, she
probably got a thorough training.

We do, however, know a good deal about Elizabeth's relationship with one of her clients. Sometime in the late 1880s Mary Anne Fenton, wife of the man for whom Samuel Pattinson acted as rent collector, decided that it would be a kindness if she patronised Sam's wife's business. It was also convenient. When Samuel arrived each week with the Ulverston rents – probably using his concessionary pass as a railway worker to travel by train to their nearest station – he could bring goods for her to see or garments for her to try on. Mary Anne was a nervous woman, who believed herself to be an invalid, and this way she avoided making uncomfortable journeys. Mrs Fenton wrote regular letters to Elizabeth, in which her garrulous voice comes over quite clearly, and she was obviously a lady who knew what she wanted, even if she often had difficulty explaining herself.

Low House, Windermere
March 28th 1891
Dear Mrs Pattinson,
Will you please send me a white sailor hat for our little maid – a plain white or cream band – if it requires trimming a crimson silk one – she's nearly 14. I like quite a bright hat for her. Have you any pinafores likely for her – I got a nice one from you sometime ago – Holland and braid. I want one that is neat and will wear well and be useful – if you would send 3. Also a smart little apron for my Cousin – she is a very little body and generally wears a black dress – so I want a nice apron for her. She is very dark haired so I think you will manage to send something that will suit her. Have you any kind that would suit me? Perhaps you would send one or two. I want some terra cotta ribbon to tie an antimacassar with about a yard please ...

Low House, Windermere
Saturday
Dear Mrs Pattinson,
My bonnet arrived safely and is very pretty but rather small. I think if I had strings of a rather wide lace it might be better and

will put them a little forwarder so as to make the side of the face a little more – and please make me a bow to fix on for it – and tie the lace – it soon looks shabby. If you have not any wider lace please send me ½ yard same as the strings – and the bow as well. Please send same time a pair of grey thread gloves for our maid – quite cheap ones – to wear with a grey beige frock and please send me two little dress bows – pale yellow – perhaps with a bow the lace would be wide enough – but will leave it to you – we will be glad to see any of you on Friday if you will let us know we will meet you. Our kind regards to all. We had such a pleasant day in Ulverston ...

[No address or date]
Dear Mrs Pattinson,
Kindly send me postal order for £1-1-0 that I can send away and not made payable to myself. I am getting a warm garment for a present to my husband on his birthday and don't want him to know about it – please post it at night as when we get them in the afternoon Mr F generally gets them himself ...

Mrs Pattinson was soon running all sorts of other errands for her in the town.

[no address or date]
Dear Mrs Pattinson
... Will you kindly send some little useful article suitable for a 3 month old baby boy to the following address ...

It was a present for the child of an old servant – and Elizabeth was not on any account to spend more than 2*s*!

[no address or date]
Dear Mrs Pattinson,
... My husband was very pleased with his presents and the hat does beautifully for him ... My hat fits very comfortably but after the soft

silk that would bend any way it feels rather stiff – I like it very much but am returning it to have some more trimming on – some loops from the crimson round to the other side 2 fill it up and I think if they were made of the plain velvet they would look well – just – little fancy bows on loops and I would like a bow at the back where the gauze is tied on 2 fill it up a bit – Mr F thinks it a beautiful hat but I think it a little juvenile – but the members will make it all right – the velvet both plain and ribbed is very pretty. Some thought a bit of feather trimming would look nice – but leave it to you – I don't like great spreading bows – the crimson one is very nice – the canvas is very nice but I still prefer thick Turkey red cotton whether in skein or on ball and few skeins of dark blue thread they go well try them – will return one or two of the things and perhaps your husband will bring my hat and a few more aprons 2 look at – perhaps coloured or Holland – what a trouble I give you …

One imagines a stylish hat gradually being turned into something resembling a hanging basket – how Mrs Pattinson and Maggie must have sighed! Letters arrived at the shop every few weeks and Mrs Pattinson probably came to dread them.

… the dress is rather white but I can soon remedy that – but the cape is too short – it just cuts me off in the worst place for me and shows all the worst part of me – fortunately it just fits a friend …

I like 2 falls and quilting on other people but not on myself – it makes me too round and plain …

I think I had better have a net hat it would be more serviceable – I have seen you with a shape I like – good brim and a little raised at one side. Don't put any standing up stiff bows – I don't like them – but I would like a little white to relieve the black, and rather full net – not to be stiff – but you know what suits me pretty well now. I like the back of my head protected well the sun makes it ache. Please let me have it soon …

Can you send me a pr of silk gloves. I like pure silk with double
[woven] tops – they wear so much longer ...

Mrs Graham has been over lately so I have all sorts of things to
tell you – please bring a little cheap brown trim for Jenny's hat ...
Do you have any scraps for Jenny's patchwork?

The broach is very pretty and will last a lifetime – my cape is
very nice and fits well is just one thing I would have liked a little
different ... astrakhan down the points as wide as the collar ...

The cloak came all right – it is very nice – and a good size but
I think a collar would improve it. I mean a little upper cape like the
one on [my] cloth dyed cape –

... my dress would be better with a good bow at the back ... would
ribbon or crepe be best – I think perhaps ribbon would be the most
durable ... make what you think best –

Alterations to garments that did not meet with a customer's approval
had to be made at the dressmaker's own expense – Mrs Pattinson
would not be paid extra for remaking the cloak or adding the
astrakhan trimming or making the bow for the back of the dress.
And it would seem that Mary Anne Fenton was unwilling to pay full
price for anything:

Could you tell me what a black hat would cost with a little
trimming – as inexpensive as possible. If you wish I can write again
but I cannot afford anything expensive ...

David Fenton died early in 1896 and, as was the custom, his widow
had to go into deep mourning. For a year and a day she would be
expected to wear heavy black, trimmed with crepe, and a widow's
cap. At various points throughout the year the crepe trimmings
would be shortened until, at the end of the year, she could do without

them altogether. She would then have to wear plain black – no white collars or cuffs – for another year. After that she could wear coloured dresses again but it was deemed heartless and disrespectful to be too anxious to discard your mourning. Many widows never wore colours again. Not surprisingly, the letters from 1896/7 are much concerned with Mrs Fenton's mourning clothes. She was parsimonious and resented every penny she spent; she was also plump and had difficulty finding styles that suited her; and she felt the heat and found heavy mourning fabrics uncomfortable. Mrs Pattinson had her work cut out to find garments that would satisfy Mary Anne Fenton.

20th Feb 1896
… I am glad my dress has come back the price of Crepe Cloth is hard but Aunt Mary is going back to Southport soon and has a bundle of crepe she is going to give me – will send it to you – please put quite a thin lining into it as it is a heavy dress and the back of the neck was low and has been altered and it was tight across the chest – otherwise a very comfortable dress …

Crepe was a difficult fabric. It was hard to clean, prone to develop rusty spots where the dye leached out and over time it flattened or went limp and shiny. Mary Anne hated everything about her mourning – this was a lady who liked crimson bonnets and wore dresses with yellow ribbons. At the very least she wanted to wear pretty embroidered crepe rather than plain – though both she and Mrs Pattinson must have known that it was totally inappropriate for widow's mourning.

My dresses are getting very dirty and I can't yet wear the alpaca it is too bright my cousin sent me the patterns from Liverpool but there might be some as cheap in Ulverston … I have a nice black silk skirt but it might be better lined … I get so overheated and then take cold easily. I thought a little cape without any lining just to reach below the waist would be nice – would you give me your advice please. I can't afford anything expensive I have had a great deal of wear out of the crape clothes and if I live it will do well for winter ... I do so dislike being fitted on it need not be made quite the same just a change somehow and a little crape – there is a kind of embroidered crape would be nice for cuffs and about the saddle ... I need 2 get nice readymade dresses for under 30/-. I am giving you a deal of trouble but will be much obliged to you. When you send my bonnet would you send a bottle of whisky from Mackereths 3/2 proof Scotch – Dr Mason said I had to have some ... I think this pattern would be nice over some thin lining ... if you can get the material in Ulverston as cheap or cheaper it is all right ...

More about this dress I am afraid it will be heavy but please line it with the thinnest possible lining for in winter I can wear an extra petticoat. I saw some of the crepe embroidered with dull not bright silk and it is very pretty and would look nice for cuffs or anywhere else you might think for I would like this dress to be nice as its to last for a long time – it would take about 2¼ [yards] for a cape ... I saw a cape the other day with the embroidered crepe down the points and on the shoulders and it looked very well. I would like the cape lined with black like enclosed or something like it ... I do not want this cape now – it would be too hot – but before it is made we can have a talk about it some day when you come over for I would like it a good shape – the crepe cloth I have always catches up a bit at the back – please don't put any stiffening in the back of my dress or hook and eye in front ... you will think I am faddy. I have never been able to get over top the lily wood but perhaps we can get over before they are done I will be very glad to see you ... What sort of sleeve did you think of making?

Mary Anne was depressed, lonely, and struggling to keep her husband's businesses going – her income depended upon them. Samuel seems to have taken more and more responsibility for her properties and, in return, she seems to have become increasingly friendly with the Pattinsons. She often urges them to visit and signs her later letters to them 'with kind love'. She also seems to have taken to the bottle – and she relied on her good friend Elizabeth to keep her supplied with whisky.

I think I had better get you to send me tomorrow a bottle of whiskey – the Dr says it must be old ... if you would pack it in a corset box it would be all right, I think ...

Please send 2 bottles of whisky and some wine for a lady here ... please get them to make it into a safe parcel and put a plain label on – not theirs – if they put glass with care they charge more – so I think if given to the guard it would come all right ...

I want you kindly to send a bottle of whisky by [Mrs Harrison] – same as before – made into a parcel – and 2 borders for my bonnet please ...

Could you run me up a quite plain apron or send me a yard of material and 6 yards of navy blue ribbon for Jenny Storey's white hat you sent me in summer and 1 BS whiskey please 3/- ...

Could you send me another bottle of whiskey in a little box like last time and perhaps it would do with cloak so that Mrs P need only have one parcel and a little 6d needle book ...

Was Elizabeth shocked or sympathetic? We have no way of knowing. Certainly she continued to supply her pernickety customer with aprons and whisky and bonnets and wine until Mary Anne's death in 1898.

It is tempting to feel sorry for Elizabeth Pattinson as she struggled to keep her little shop going, wrestling with suppliers who could not provide the goods she ordered, clients who expected her to make and remake their hats and dresses as cheaply and speedily as possible, who relied on her to source goods that met their pettiest requirements, supply patchwork pieces for their maids and – in Mary Anne's case – to conceal their growing alcoholism from the prying eyes of neighbours and carriers. But we need not pity her, for – and this is the really surprising thing – Elizabeth Pattinson was making a comfortable profit from her small business.

For several years in the 1890s she kept a monthly account of her income and outgoings. 1897 was a typical year.

Month	Income	Expenditure	Profit/loss
January	£12-8s-2 ½d	£18-11s-6d	-£6-3s-3 ½d
February	£18-2s-11 ½d	£7-14s-2d	+£10-8s-9 ½d
March	£22-16s-5 ½d	£13-14s-6d	+£9-1s-11 ½d
April	£21-16s-2d	£19-13s-11d	+£3-2s-3d
May	£30-18s-11 ½d	£17-15s-4d	+£13-3s-7 ½d
June	£36-17s-4d	£21-1s-6d	+£15-15s-10d
July	£24-13s-3d	£22-4s-11 ½d	+£2-8s-3 ½d
August	£25-11s-1 ½d	£14-0s-11d	+£11-10s-2 ½d
September	£21-0s-1d	£5-9s-3d	+£15-10s-10d
October	£15-4s-5d	£20-11s-8d	-£5-7s-3d
November	£25-12s-3d	£11-18s-2d	+£13-14s-1d
December	£19-7s-7 ½d	£5-1s-0d	+£14-16s-7 ½d

Total profit   £98-2s-0d

Elizabeth was averaging nearly £2 a week profit at a time when £1 a week was reckoned to be the minimum on which a working man could expect to provide for a wife and family – though, of course, many managed on much less. The Pattinson family could have lived quite respectably even without Samuel's wages. However, there is no proper breakdown of this income and expenditure – Elizabeth's figures were scribbled in pencil on the back of old calendars.

In many ways Elizabeth Pattinson seems to have been a shrewd businesswoman, succeeding when many small dressmakers-cum-haberdashers failed or went bankrupt. She seems to have been fortunate in having enough capital to start her business without a loan – whether this was money she and Samuel had saved or a gift from one or other of their families, we do not know. Her shop was in a prime location. She managed to maintain a balance between profit from sales of ready-made goods and items she made or customised – consequently she had time to make all the alterations fussy customers like Mary Anne Fenton required without losing too much money. Had her order book been full, other customers would have suffered and spending that extra time would have cost her dear.

She resisted the temptation to expand. Many firms overreached themselves and took on staff who cost more in wages over the course of a year than the firm earned. Even a semi-trained 'second hand' who could sew but was unable to fit customers or cut patterns would cost about 8s a week, while the average profit a small-town dressmaker made per dress was around 5s. One woman, working unacceptably long hours, could probably make three dresses a week – though, of course, in reality the simpler parts of each job would have been done by apprentices or part-trained 'improvers'. It took a good business head to work out the most profitable ratio of staff to orders, and keeping it small and simple was often the best policy. Studies show[2] that many of the most profitable businesses were in the hands of a group of 'principals' (owner/workers) – usually pairs and trios of sisters or friends. A single 'principal' did less well – while she was with clients, no work was being done, or her unsupervised apprentice (if she had one) slacked and made mistakes. As the proprietor's niece and heir to the business, even as an apprentice Maggie Simpson had more incentive than most to work hard and concentrate on what she was doing, so Elizabeth had no need to employ expensive staff. However, her figures do include occasional payments to 'Ida'. Maybe she was someone who helped out at busy times – again, a more sensible solution to the problem of a temporary glut of orders than taking on full-time employees. Elizabeth was also fortunate in that most of her customers seem to have paid cash – even Mary Anne Fenton was assiduous about paying her bills. Samuel's concessionary rail passes and connection with the railway made it possible for goods to be delivered to country clients at cut-price rates, which was no small consideration. Crucially, if Elizabeth had a bad month – and January and October were notoriously bad months – there was always Samuel's income to tide the family over. No doubt Elizabeth and Maggie worked hard. Shops in the 1880s and 1890s opened for long hours and clients were demanding. But from her relationship with Mary Anne Fenton we can also deduce that Elizabeth Pattinson was exceptionally obliging, and discreet – qualities much prized by nineteenth-century customers. Maybe that was the key to her success.

She reaped her reward. In 1902, aged just forty, Elizabeth Pattinson retired and handed her business over to Maggie. Maybe she still helped out at busy times – but her name no longer appears in the trade directories. At the same time the family moved away from Upper Brook Street to a new house in Hoad Terrace, on the northern edge of the town. Samuel continued to work, but Elizabeth was now a lady of leisure.

Maggie married in the summer of 1907 and moved away from Ulverston, and the little shop on King Street was sold. Samuel and Elizabeth lived on at Hoad Terrace into the 1930s.

PART 2

TAILORS

'Three Hours at Home from the Effects of Drinking': Samuel Attwood (1792–1870), Basingstoke

Samuel Attwood liked a drink. His diary[1] is peppered with references to time off work to recover from evenings of over-indulgence; in July 1821, for example, he wrote, 'one day to get over Mr May's licence dinner'. Licence dinners seem to have been held in all the local pubs to celebrate the renewal of the innkeeper's licence and to thank the regulars for their continuing patronage. There were a great many pubs in Basingstoke – twenty-seven at the time the 1831 directory of the town was compiled – and Samuel frequented most of them, though his favourites seem to have been the Black Boy on Church Street (kept by his relative, John Attwood), the Feathers, the Goat, the Golden Lion and the Ship. And, when he was not celebrating licence renewals, he was drinking and feasting with the other groups to which he belonged – the cricket club, the band, the Freemasons, the coroner's jury, the smoking club at the Black Boy – even the church choir and the Parish Council.

Fortunately Samuel's employer was his father, Abraham Attwood. Abraham was a tailor, and he and his wife Dina had four sons and a daughter: Samuel, Mary, George, Bill and Roger. Abraham apprenticed all his boys to the tailoring trade. Samuel was the eldest, some four years older than George, the next brother in line, but it seems to have been George who went into the family business first. They would both have served apprenticeships, perhaps with their father, perhaps with one of their father's friends. As in dressmaking, traditional seven-year apprenticeships were becoming less common in the early nineteenth century – three- and five-year terms were more common.

The boys were clearly quite well-educated, and they were fortunate in having a good school in Basingstoke – St Mary's Boys' School, which was founded in the sixteenth century. They would have stayed at school until they were at least fourteen or fifteen; a five-year apprenticeship, beginning when they left school, would have meant that by the age of twenty they would each have been fully qualified. That seems to have been the age at which George joined his father, but Samuel had to wait several more years, during which presumably he worked for someone else.

Perhaps Abraham was worried about Samuel's rackety ways. Certainly Samuel was nearly twenty-five, newly married and the father of a baby daughter, before Abraham took him into the firm as a journeyman in March 1816. It very much looks as if the diary, which began that month, was written at his father's insistence to keep track of how much time Samuel spent at work, what he did and how much he earned. 'You are a family man now,' Abraham may have said, 'you need to know what you have to spend so you can look after Grace and the baby properly. The drinking has to stop, my boy. Babies and hangovers don't mix.' The drinking did not stop for some years and there were no more babies – but Samuel caught the diary-writing habit and carried on keeping a journal until a few weeks before his death.

His early entries describe the state of trade in general terms week by week – 'Not in want of work', 'Plenty of work but not busy', 'A little brisk' or 'Rather at leisure' – and his weekly income for the first few years was somewhere between fifteen shillings and a pound. This was a perfectly respectable wage but it was certainly not generous. Samuel does not tell us how much Attwood's charged their customers, but the account book of fellow Basingstoke tailor

Robert Mansbridge, kept between 1811 and 1820, gives us some clues.[2] Mansbridge usually charged seven to nine shillings for making a coat, 3s 6d to 4s 0d for making a waistcoat and 3s 0d to 7s 0d for making a pair of breeches. Making a suit of clothes was around 16s 0d and a pair of flannel drawers was 4s 0d, plus the price of the flannel, which cost 2s 3d a yard. The firm also did various repairs, for which they usually charged between 6d and 2s 6d.

Throughout the nineteenth century fabric was expensive; buff kerseymere (a woollen fabric) and 'baragon' (a cheaper wool) cost ten and four shillings a yard respectively, for example, and they were the fabrics that Mansbridge's used most for coats, waistcoats and breeches. Calico for lining cost sixpence a yard. When they were short of orders Mansbridge's made garments for stock, which were then sold ready-made: a pair of patent cord breeches cost £1 to £1 2s 6d; a 'Buff Cassimere Waistcoat' cost 16s 6d in October 1817; a pair of velveteen breeches also came in at 16s 6d; and a cloth great-coat was two guineas. These garments from stock were cheaper than those made to order, as the following bills illustrate:

March 1816, Breeches for John Cooper

Making	3s-6d	
1 ⅜ cord at 12s a yd	16s-6d	
Callicoe	2s-0d	
Pockets and faceings [sic]	1s-0d	
Buttons and trimmings	2s-6d	Total: £1-5s-6d

October 1816, Coat for Mr Watson

Making a coat	9s-0d
4 yds Duffle	£1-4s-6d
1 ½ yds brown Irish	2s-0d
(linen for lining)	
1 yd fustian for pocket	1s-6d
10 buttons	1s-3d

Velveteen for collar	1s-9d	
Trimmings	2s-0d	Total: £2-2s-0d

March 1820 Coat for Mr George Kearsley

Making a coat	8s-6d	
2 ½ yds superfine green cloth @ 24s	£2-11s-0d (less 1s discount)	
Sleeve lining and pockets	2s-6d	
10 coat and 4 breast gilt buttons	2s-6d	
Padding and trimming	2s-6d	Total £3-7s-0d

Attwood's were working for a similar clientele and it seems likely their charges were much the same. This means that, to earn his week's wages, Samuel needed to make the equivalent of two coats, or four pairs of breeches or drawers, or four waistcoats. He seldom tells us what he made but, from time to time, he does record making items for himself. He does not seem to have been the quickest of workers; in November 1825, for example, he spent two whole days making a waistcoat that a speedier worker could have completed in under a day. However, as he could take time off work to make items for himself, he may have been dragging his feet deliberately. He seems to have been something of a dandy – after all, if a tailor did not dress fashionably, who would patronise his business? He writes of making himself a matching blue coat and waistcoat, a claret coat and an olive riding coat, a pair of lavender kerseymere trousers and a striped waistcoat. However, money was tight and later on the garments were often altered or 'turned' – that is, remade inside out so that the side of the fabric that had been protected by the lining was on the outside and the worn or stained outside was hidden. Turning the blue coat that he had made in 1821 took twenty hours in the spring of 1826, for example, and after three years of wear the olive coat was smartened up with a new collar.

Tailoring was not really to Samuel's taste. He was a gregarious young man, keen on sport, and he did not enjoy sitting in the traditional tailor's posture, cross-legged on a bench, sewing for hours on end with only his father or brother for company. However, for a good few years he did his best. He records buying equipment: 'June 6 1819 Bought of George [his brother who had just been to London] a pair of scissors 5 shillings and an inch measure.' A few months later he bought a more expensive pair of shears for a pound.

Inch measures were a comparatively new invention in 1819 and many tailors still preferred the old-fashioned method of using strips of paper, cut to the length of the various measures to be taken, labelled, and then pinned together and stored as a bunch. George Walker in *The Tailor's Masterpiece* gave instructions for using a tape measure that are almost insulting in their simplicity.

> In the first place, lay the cloth smooth with the double edge towards you (that is, if it be a double breadth) at the same time observe that the wool grain of the cloth runs towards the left hand, then look for the measure for the length taken to the bend of the knee, which is 39 [inches], therefore find 39 on the tape inch measure, and place it at the bottom of the cloth, and extend the measure up to the edge of the cloth from bottom to top, as at B ...

In the early nineteenth century men's coats and breeches were very close fitting; breeches were skin tight, and a really fashionable coat was so tight across the back that the wearer had difficulty using his arms (see plate 10). Careful measuring was, therefore, of paramount importance in creating a fashionable garment and George Walker devoted a good deal of his book to it. *The Tailor's Masterpiece* ran to numerous editions in the 1830s. It was based on a series of lectures that Walker had given at the London Mechanic's Institution, and he was confident that he had indeed written a masterpiece.

> It is a common remark that a handsome Coat makes the gentleman, and though this cannot be justly admitted to its full extent, it is well known, that a handsome dress, especially a well-made Coat, such a one as will be produced by adopting the

principles laid down in this work, will give a person the external appearance of a gentleman.

He included numerous diagrams showing where measurements should be taken, and each of the 'points' for these measurements was labelled with a letter between A and Q. These letters are used throughout the text rather than descriptions such as 'the distance from shoulder to elbow' or 'the length of the centre back', so the text reads rather like an exercise in code and the reader is constantly having to refer back to the diagrams.

> In the first place, consider the line from L to L (figure 2, plate the second) to be the edge of the cloth, the dots across the end the tops of them at about an inch below as at L make a short line as to B, and from there mark the length of the sleeve, which is in the measure 6, 20½ and 34 ...

George Walker was particularly keen on actual measurements, and he included instructions for measuring people with unusual figures.

> Measuring for a person who is bellied in the extreme, it is necessary to take the length or height of the principal [sic] projection of the belly ... continuing the measure under the protuberance to the length required ...

This may seem rather obvious to us, but traditionally tailors had cut coats to a series of measurements based on ratios relating to the customer's 'breast' (chest) measurement. This in fact seems to have been how Attwood's worked.

Samuel dutifully made several pages of notes in his diary about the best way to make certain garments:

> To form the fork of a pair of breeches take ¼ of the width across the thigh with ½ an inch added for riding breeches or ¼ of an inch for walking breeches ...

In marking a coat out observe the following rules 1st make the waist according to fashion or order and length allow ¼ of breast measure with ½ inch added across the back at the hind arm and 2¼ Inch added at top of back the same at the bottom of Waist (or always ⅛ of Breast Measure) allow ½ of Breast Measure from the top of Back to bottom of back save except in stout men then according to measure ...

No doubt these rather garbled notes meant something to him.

Manwaring's *The Tailor's New Guide being an Universal and Complete System of the Art of Cutting* was published in 1836 and gave yet another set of ratios, but he did include a very useful guide for making stock items, with a table describing just how much yardage would be required for different sizes and items from cloth of 30, 29, 28, and 27 inches in width 'in the double' – in other words, 60, 58, 56 and 54 inch wide fabrics. He also included a series of small printed fold-out patterns for the tailor to scale up. If these instruction manuals teach us anything, however, it is that learning tailoring from books must have been well-nigh impossible.

In 1816, when Samuel's diary begins, men wore tight knee-breeches, buckled at the knee and worn over stockings, but by the early 1820s long trousers had come into vogue. To begin with, these, too, were very tight fitting but gradually they became looser and easier to wear. Some older men, however, continued to wear breeches as late as the 1840s.

Samuel would have seen fashion change in other ways too. When he was a young apprentice, men still wore fancy embroidered silk waistcoats, at least for dressy occasions. Lengths of silk could be bought ready-embroidered with decorative waistcoat fronts; the tailor would cut these out and add a lining and backing with a strap and buckle to make them fit customers of any shape or size. By the 1820s men's dress was becoming more sober, and elaborate embroidery on waistcoats gave place to striped or patterned fabric. The cut of men's coats changed, too, particularly in terms of the shape of the lapels, the set of the sleeves and the shape of the tails at the back (see plates 10 to 13).

Attwood's customers seem mostly to have been small tradesmen, shopkeepers and farmers from nearby villages, though we do not have the firm's customer lists to enable us to trace them all. They would have wished to dress respectably and to show that they were aware of the latest fashions, even if they wanted those fashions adapted for practical use.

From time to time Samuel's father sent him to work with a colleague – perhaps to gain experience.

1819

March 7. This week at Mr Lambert's at Overton to work my wages 12 shillings per week and my board and lodging …

April 11. 3 days at Mr Lamberts and the rest of the week to work for Father …

He also spent time working with a Mr Garret. Brother George was also sent off to gain experience with other tailors – in Alresford, in Honiton and for several months with a Mr Fagg in Hounslow.

Just occasionally Samuel tells us what he was making. 'May 2, 1819. Mrs Tolfree died last Wednesday evening (kept her bed for five days) very busy making mourning'. In June 1823 he was uncharacteristically overworked. 'June 1. Very busy, obliged to put work out. Obliged to work on Sunday morning.' This was for another mourning order and these, of course, were usually required at short notice. In May 1824, for example, he was again 'Very busy with mourning for Mr Leah and Mr Barber of Dunmer who died on the 4th' and in November 1829 he spent a day helping George 'finish James Smith's mourning'. He seldom records other types of order – 'August 26th 1826. ¾ of a day to make waistcoat for Ubsdell' is a rare example. He does, however, record when, in spring, he is again able to work without artificial light. Working by candlelight with dark-coloured thread on dark fabrics is trying to the eyes, and it is clear that Samuel hated the winter months for that reason. 'Not working by candle' entries usually appear at the beginning of March and one can sense his relief.

We do not know how closely Samuel worked with his father and George in the early days of the partnership, nor do we know whether they employed other staff, but certainly after a few years he seems to have been working alone. George had set up in business on his own account in 'Oat Street', now called Wote Street, and though the family business was in Abraham's name the diaries suggest that he was semi-retired. When the diary begins, Samuel's younger brother Bill was apprenticed to a tailor in St Ives in Huntingdonshire. In March 1821 Samuel recorded 'Bill out of his time', meaning he had completed his apprenticeship. Bill was then twenty and it seems he stayed on in St Ives for a time, probably working as a journeyman for his former master; however, like Samuel, Bill disliked tailoring and he and his wife eventually went off to run a lodging-house in Shoreditch. Roger, the youngest brother, also trained in St Ives and by 1851 he had his own shop there.

After the first couple of years, Samuel's diaries record increasing numbers of extra-curricular activities:

1819
January 15. One day altering my best coat and hunting. One hour at home with the Christmas party.

Christmas parties seem to have been a family tradition. The whole family gathered together, sons came home for the duration, and evenings were spent eating, drinking, playing games and catching up on the news.

In summer, sport – particularly cricket – absorbed as much of Samuel's time as he dared spare:

1819
August 1. John Hurdle, 4 hours to finish the mourning, obliged to leave at 3 to go and see the cricket match.

The choice of words is interesting – it is doubtful whether he was actually 'obliged' to attend the match! In subsequent summers he played for the team against various opponents – Odiham were their particular rivals – and, when he got too old to play, he umpired. Cricket was a life-long passion but he was interested in other sports too:

September 19, 1819. Half a day nutting. Went to the Races ...
September 17, 1820. Washing week. 1¼ Days to go to the Races and being at leisure ...

Samuel eagerly awaited the annual race days, as most of the shops in town closed and he could take time off. He attended other, unofficial sporting events. 'April 7, 1820. One hour to see the fight on the common' and a few months later he noted a local record: a man had run twice round the local race track in nineteen minutes. He was even more impressed by the new national record for running a mile, also set in 1819, of 6 minutes, 2 seconds. Samuel fancied himself as a runner and on 29 September that year he challenged 'Mr Watson the painter' to a race on the Common and won, though he does not record the length of the race or their respective times.

He continued to attend licence dinners and other celebrations. Tailors worked long hours; when an order had to be completed, they expected to work late into the evening or even all through the night. Consequently, Samuel's evening activities cut into the time he was available to work and are recorded accordingly:

September 5, 1819. Half a day to the Licence Dinner ...
July, 1821. Dance at Farmer Quinn's. Half a day to recover.
October, 1821. Two days in London, half a day to get over it.

Even a visit to his mother-in-law was an opportunity to take time off and drink too much: 'January 6, 1822. One hour to spend at Mrs Taplin's. ½ a day to get over it ...' And, as time went by, his earlier resolution to spend more time on his work began to falter. He attended anniversary dinners to commemorate the Battle of Waterloo, dances, Freemasonry meetings and club dinners. Samuel was at the celebrations when the Prince Regent was proclaimed

King (6 February 1820) and he also took a day off for the old king's funeral; he viewed the 'Illuminations to honour Queen Charlotte' in November 1820 and attended the Coronation celebrations in July 1821. He went to the 'maying' festival each year in Basingstoke and sometimes to similar events in nearby towns and villages. He also did his best to attend any local spectacle that was going, however gruesome. In April 1820 he saw two boys 'wip'd', one at Overton 'for robbing Mr Purkis' and the other in the Market Place 'for robbing Mr Loader', and that December he watched a man being flogged for threatening to rob two women. He recorded – and therefore probably went to see – regiments that passed through the town: the 33rd on 9 October 1819 and the 12th Regiment of Foot on 4 March 1821, for example. He played cribbage and 'corks' (a form of skittles) and went on boat trips down the canal. The only remotely cultural activity he ever mentioned was attendance at a lecture on geology, then a new and controversial subject as it apparently contradicted the biblical description of the Creation, with his father in December 1820.

From time to time he travelled to London, usually with one of his brothers, occasionally with his wife, to spend a few days. In May 1821 his youngest brother, Roger, accompanied him for the first time. Roger was eighteen and it seems Samuel took him on a drinking spree: 'Three days in London, one day to get better.' Ostensibly this was work, to see the new fashions and fabrics and to check in with the tailors' guild, though inevitably in Samuel's case it was an excuse to get drunk with a different group of people. 'October 7, 1821. Two days in London and half a day to get over it'.

Samuel also played a part in local civic affairs – perhaps, as the eldest Attwood son, he was following in his father's footsteps. He was a member of the Coroner's 'Jury' and attended inquests.

April, 1819. 2 hours to attend the Jury on the body of Sam Stag.
October 4, 1820. 4 hours to attend on the jury of John Pillar alias Jackey Pollard he being found dead in the Feathers Inn stable by intoxication.

April 4, 1826. 4 hours in the Coroner's Court about Mr Blackstone who died – a visitation from God.

He attended vestry meetings to vote for parish officials and in October 1830 he was himself sworn in as a parish constable, being one of 200 new constables who were hurriedly appointed to deal with unrest among farm labourers:

… a great number of riotous persons assembled in a disorderly manner breaking all machines, demanding money, committing robberys [sic] etc.

This was the period of the 'Swing' riots, named after a mythical leader, Captain Swing, when agricultural labourers, fearing for their jobs, attacked and damaged the newly invented steam-powered threshing machines and demanded higher wages. The riots were largely unsuccessful but for a period they caused a good deal of concern to respectable people; the French Revolution was still a comparatively recent memory and middle England feared a similar revolution among the increasingly disaffected labouring poor.

Samuel's wife, Grace, and daughter, Mary Ann, scarcely feature in the diary at all. On a couple of occasions he has a day or two off work because Grace is ill and, once or twice, he writes that she is with her mother or staying with relatives – for example, 'Grace, Mrs Taplin and the Child went to Breach' (10 September 1820). However, on 21 May 1820, he recorded with what sounds like fatherly pride and affection 'The first week that my little girl attended school regularly at Miss Cox's'; later, in September 1822, he shares his concern that six-year-old Mary Ann was very ill with scarlet fever.

However, the fact that he does not write about Grace and Mary Ann does not mean that Samuel was an uncaring husband and father. Very early in the diary we find him attending sales to buy furniture for his new home. 'March 21, 1816 Two hours at Mr Penny's sale, bought a bureau £2-17s.' 'May 16. Miss Willis's sale. Bought mahogany cubbard [sic], a carpet, etc.' He made bed furnishings, whitewashed the house inside and out several times, and in May 1824 he had someone in to paper the living room. He kept pigs, built a sty for them and took time off work to slaughter them and prepare the meat. 'November, 1820. One and a half days at home to kill three pigs.' He collected and chopped wood, brewed vast quantities of beer, made elderberry and ginger wine and distilled hogsheads full of a lethal-sounding beverage he called 'red moonshine'. In 1827 he caught a lark, which the family kept in a cage as a pet. The poor little bird survived for twelve years in captivity. Home and domesticity obviously mattered to Samuel or he would not have recorded such things.

He also kept in touch with all his siblings and carefully recorded the births of his numerous nephews and nieces. He wrote regularly, if infrequently, to Bill in London and Roger in St Ives 'and sent all the news' – which in Samuel's case probably consisted of long lists of people who had died. He was fascinated by death.

As time goes by Samuel begins to complain of rheumatism in his arms and shoulders and weak eyes – typical clothing workers' complaints – and finally, in May 1832, soon after completing his sixteenth year working as a journeyman tailor, he began 'having some thought of leaving Father.' It did not take him long to decide. He spent much of the month clearing out the shop and painting it, and on the twentieth, 'I began to work at home regular having left the old shop altogether.'

He may have continued to do a little tailoring from home – in 1841 he still described himself as a 'tailor' to the census enumerator – but Samuel had embarked on a new career. For at least five years before he made his decision he had been earning less and less; he continued to keep a record of his earnings week by week until he left his father's employ. His average weekly income dropped from eighteen shillings to eleven shillings to seven shillings until, in 1831, there were weeks when he made less than five shillings. Clearly the family could not live on so little. There are clues as to what he was doing, however. In March 1829 he bought 'potatoes for sale'. In August he records 'Days marking off my goods, my own employ etc.' and he writes of frequent attendance at 'the markets'. It looks very much as if he had become a market trader, buying and selling, wheeling and dealing. This new venture may not have been wholly successful at first, however, for in the 1831 Basingstoke directory Grace Attwood appears as a 'toy dealer.' Mary Ann was fifteen that year – maybe she helped her mother. We do not know how long Grace's business lasted, but there is no mention of it in 1841, so perhaps by then Samuel was once again earning enough to support his family. Sadly, as soon as he ceased working for his father, Samuel stopped recording what he earned so we cannot be sure how successful his new venture was in financial terms.

In 1839 Mary Ann got married. Her husband was Thomas Flower, a beer seller, and the wedding took place in London; Samuel and Grace went up to town for three days to attend the celebrations. For a time the young couple lived in Basingstoke but by 1861 they were back in London with Thomas having upgraded his occupation from 'beer seller' to 'porter merchant' for the census enumerator's benefit! The couple provided Samuel and Grace with four grandsons and a granddaughter. However, by 1860 Thomas Flower had got himself into financial difficulties. He had borrowed £300 from an acquaintance called John Morgan Deere and a further £583 from Samuel, and he was unable to repay either of them. A complicated legal document[3] survives by which Samuel took on the entire debt and stood as guarantor for the couple, using as security a £1000 3 per cent consolidated Bank Annuity that Mary Taplin, Mary Ann's grandmother, had left to her daughter and granddaughter, and which was 'then standing in the name of William Garrett of Blounce Farm, Southernborough, Hants', who was Samuel's old friend and mentor. The crisis was averted and Samuel had secured his son-in-law's business and his grandchildren's future.

Diary-keeping is actually a curious activity; the way different diarists condense a day's happenings into a couple of sentences tells us a great deal about them as individuals. In Samuel's case, what it tells us is that he had an obsession with death. This may have been sparked by his membership of the Coroner's Jury, or perhaps by his

work as a tailor. Tailors were at their busiest when working on a
mourning order and it may well be that it was in their interests to
keep an eye out for local deaths; Attwood's may even have distributed
discreet leaflets to bereaved families – some tailors did. Throughout
his diary Samuel recorded local deaths but, in 1832, freed from
the constraint of recording his income and hours of work for his
father's inspection, Samuel could give free rein to his fascination with
mortality. Day after day he records the deaths of Basingstoke folk,
often with details of how they died – 'after a few days in bed', 'with
great pain and suffering', 'a man badly scalded at the brewery', 'on
the spot, hit by the Magnet Coach', 'drowned', 'George Tubb of Ale
Farm shot himself', 'the noted Probert hanged for horse stealing' –
the list goes on and on. There is the occasional record of a birth or a
marriage but, were one to rely on Samuel's diary, one would get the
impression that the population of Basingstoke declined dramatically
in the course of his lifetime. In fact, it doubled. He also records the
nicknames of the deceased – 'Mr Andrews alias Lord Cork', 'James
Kent alias Fortune Kent', 'John Knight alias Old Budget Night',
'Mrs Inwood alias Old Jogger', 'William Ackerman alias Billy Bunny'
and so on – and indulges in a little scandal mongering. 'July 25, 1826.
Jenny Hillier and Joe Gillian discovered on the 2nd July committing
an unnatural act.'

Of slightly more general interest are his comments on events in
Basingstoke. It was a small town and even quite minor happenings
broke the monotony of daily life. Samuel writes of local curiosities
like the enormous, record-breaking ox killed by the local butcher
in 1819 and the ten gold coins found in the wall of an old house
when builders were at work there in March 1820; he tells us
about the measles epidemic of 1820, the erection of a new 'May
pool', and describes novel and exciting spectacles like the hot air
balloon that passed over the town in April 1827 and the steam
coach that chugged through Basingstoke for the first time in July
1830. He records the opening of the 'new George Inn', the laying
of the foundation brick of the new Market House in June 1832
and the planting of trees in the churchyard – all interesting stuff

for Hampshire historians – but none of it took precedence over his fascination with death and disease.

He obviously kept the entries in a series of notebooks of various sizes and these have now been bound together as one volume, but what is really curious about the diary is the way the handwriting changes. The pages are not ruled and the early entries are packed close together, separated by inked lines. Sometimes the handwriting becomes so small as to be barely legible, particularly when he is clearly trying to finish an entry without turning over the page. On other pages the entries are widely spaced, and on some the handwriting is enormous, with letters up to an inch high and with only two or three entries to the page. These differences do not reflect the content of the entries and it is hard to decide whether they relate to changes in mood or perhaps, more prosaically, to Samuel having trouble with his eyes.

The final entry, in a rather shaky hand, comes on 10 January 1870:

Fred Flower [presumably a relative of his son-in-law] enlisted in the Royal Artillery. [something illegible] E Biddle the painter died at 35, two children died this week. Thomas May the brewer died suddenly at Odiham aged 40. Very bad weather.

Samuel himself died five weeks later on 18 February 1870, aged seventy-seven. He had made a will two years previously, leaving everything he owned to Grace, then to Mary Ann 'for her sole and separate use'. It was Mary Ann who proved the will: Grace was already ill and housebound and she outlived Samuel by just six weeks. His estate was valued at 'under £1000'.[4]

Would he have been more financially successful had he remained a tailor? Possibly. Of the two other Attwood brothers who stayed in the trade all their lives, George died intestate, but Roger left £1,646 13s 8d, to be divided among his nine children.[5] Given that his expenses in raising such a large brood must have been considerably more than Samuel's, this was a very considerable sum of money indeed.

'A Pair of Drawers for the Excise Officer': John Evens (1807–1885), Holbeton, near Plymouth

Young John Evens took the axe and swung it at the beam – once, twice, three times. It was seasoned oak, hard as iron. He wiped his brow and tried again. He was still feeling groggy from the voyage; he and the others had set sail from 'Wadum' (Wadham Sands, a few miles east of Plymouth) the previous day, 19 August 1832, and the Channel had been stormy and rough, tossing the little *Jane Ann* about like a cork. John was not a good sailor and he'd been horribly seasick all the way. Eventually the axe dislodged a splinter of wood. His companions cheered. John had 'made his mark,' and he was one of them now, a fully fledged smuggler.[1]

He sat down with relief. The bizarre initiation ritual was over and now he could enjoy the fish and fried eggs the inn served them, the first food he'd eaten in two days; he recorded that it tasted as good as any meal he had ever had. This was John's first visit to the French Arms in Roscoff, the inn 'it is usual for Smugglers to stop at', as he later described it.

The following day, feeling much better, he went to see two spirit merchants, 'M Malleby and M Delisle', with whom he was hoping to come to an agreement. 'I assured [them] it was the intention of myself and partner to deal honourably', he wrote later, with no apparent sense of irony. It may be that John had inherited the contact with the merchants from his father, Michael. Smuggling was often a family affair and the fact that the trip took place just a few weeks before Michael Evens died may be significant – perhaps he knew he was dying and wanted to make the introductions for his son before it was too late. Roscoff had grown into a substantial port, largely because of English smugglers, and Monsieur Malleby and Monsieur Delisle would have understood exactly what young Mr Evens required of them. Legally imported wine and spirits were delivered in large casks, which were winched off the ships at legitimate ports with proper docks. Smuggled goods were landed at night in coves and creeks, and the goods were carried away by teams of men on foot or in carts. The tubs – or bales of other goods – had to be light enough for a man to carry single-handed, probably for several miles, and so 'ankas', which were barrels holding three-and-a-half gallons, were usually used to smuggle spirits. Tea, sugar, coffee and tobacco had to be carefully wrapped in oilskin in the hope that they would survive a dunking, and the outsides of the barrels had to be fully waterproofed.

Business completed in the town, John Evens went sight-seeing, travelling some distance inland and finding that, away from the port, few people spoke English and he could not make himself understood. He was shocked to see men and women without shoes and stockings, and was scathing about the clattering wooden sabots worn by others. He comments on women doing their washing in the streams and notes that the French threshers used a flail that was different from the ones used on Devon farms. He thought the church in Roscoff was a fine one and well-kept, though he felt obliged to remark that the worshippers were all Roman Catholics; but what shocked and horrified him most of all was the discovery that the graveyard was so small that bodies were removed from the graves to make way for others before they were fully decomposed, and in that state they were placed in a 'special building' open to view – 'a disgusting spectacle'. He then went back to the inn and enjoyed an evening carousing with a group of Norwegian sailors and got very drunk.

It was a short visit, though they do seem to have brought back a cargo of wine and spirits when they were eventually able to set sail. The weather was still rough and the crew had to make three attempts before the *Jane Ann* could leave port. This meant they arrived off the Devon coast in broad daylight and had to lay out of sight of shore until nightfall, when at last they sailed into Wadham Bay and unloaded their cargo of contraband. At last, 'to no small satisfaction of myself and crew about twelve on Friday night we were clear of everything seizable in the boat and proceeded without delay to Plymouth', John wrote. It had been an exciting experience – so exciting that he wrote a careful account of it when he got home – but it seems to have put him off seafaring for life, though he was happy to sponsor and profit from others' efforts. John was not just a smuggler; he was a 'venturer', someone who took orders, organised the voyages, paid the sailors and distributed the 'things', as he called them, that they landed. It was – for a few years at least – extremely profitable.

John Evens was an energetic and enterprising young man. He had trained as a tailor and, by the age of twenty-five, he had a flourishing business in his home parish of Holbeton. He was well-educated, wrote a clear sloping copper-plate hand, and from the *Account of a Voyage to France* and diary[2] he left behind it seems that he actively enjoyed writing; he also had a good head for figures and received occasional informal payments from the churchwarden for helping with the parish accounts. We do not know where he went to school but, as there was no school in Holbeton when John was a boy, it seems likely that he went to Plymouth Grammar School, probably boarding in the town during the week. Certainly in later life he had numerous contacts there. Nor do we know where or with whom he served his apprenticeship. That may also have been in Plymouth, though there were several tailors in Holbeton itself – Richard and William Avery, Richard Martin, Thomas Stone and Richard Penwill – any one of whom might have taken him on as a favour to his father or because they thought he showed promise.

Holbeton is just nine miles east of Plymouth, but even today it feels like a different world (see plate 14). It is a picturesque little place with steep, narrow, twisting streets, stone houses, thatched cottages and pretty gardens, but it is hidden in a deep valley and approached by a network of sunken lanes barely the width of a car. In the village itself there is hardly any level space. Sadly, John Evens's cottage and his orchards have disappeared to make way for the village hall and its car park, and a row of houses now stands on what would have been the bottom boundary of his land, but the memory of his home survives in the name of the house opposite: Orchard Cottage. The fifteenth-century spire of the parish church, perched on a mound alongside Vicarage Hill, would have been visible from his house, and the exterior would still be familiar to him, though the interior has been extensively remodelled. It is approached by a flight of stone steps partway up Vicarage Hill, which must always have been something of a challenge for those worshippers who were aged or infirm. The school, which John would have seen established and which his children attended, lies just below the churchyard, at the top of those same stone steps.

Most of Holbeton's inhabitants were farmers, farm labourers or small tradesmen – a butcher, a baker, a grocer and several blacksmiths, tailors, shoemakers and carpenters. There were two pubs, the George and the Union, and several 'sellers of beer'. The parish encompassed a series of hamlets – Membland, Luson, Ford, Creacombe, Battisborough and Mothecombe – and a number of outlying farms. The River Erme, a little way to the east of the main village, was navigable by vessels of up to 70 tons as far as Mothecombe and there was a coastguard station there (see page 110 for map).

The soil of the South Hams is rich and red and fertile; everything grows prolifically, including the wild flowers, which, in early summer, are glorious. There are swathes of pale yellow primroses, studded here and there with tiny purple violets, great drifts of smoky-blue bluebells, wild garlic with its spiky white flowers and broad, pungent-smelling leaves, pinky-red campion and ragged robin, tiny pink cranesbill with its feathery, russet-tinged leaves, delicate white stitchwort and creamy Queen Anne's lace. The surrounding countryside seems almost designed for clandestine activities. Travellers in the lanes would be almost invisible to watchers in the fields above, even in broad daylight, while the twists and turns mean that, even on the lane itself, people and vehicles are soon out of sight. It was in the steep banks, some of them 10 or 12 feet high, that border these lanes that sympathetic farmers allowed John and his companions to dig 'private places' or hidey-holes where they could stash barrels and bundles or even hide themselves. This is what John Evens means when he writes of putting things 'in the hedge'. The greatest danger for the men transporting contraband was meeting the coastguard round a hidden corner in one of these deeply sunken lanes; then there would be no escape, for the banks are all but vertical and are topped with thick, prickly hedges (see plate 17). However, the smugglers outnumbered the coastguard many times over and had an elaborate system of lookouts and signals that – usually – protected them.

John was an only child and his father, Michael, died in 1832, leaving his son the family smallholding with its two orchards of cider apples, three fields ('Watergate', 'Veal's Portlehead', 'part of Frogmore') and a strip of woodland, with a total rateable value of 4s 9d.[3] Not only was John then responsible for the care of his widowed mother, Ann, he was already a married man with two small children of his own. In addition to his tailoring and farm work, and his occasional jobs for the parish council, he was then appointed parish constable – essentially the local police officer. It was an unpaid, and not particularly arduous role; he only seems to have been called upon once or twice a year, to deal with minor thefts, recalcitrant servants and the occasional unexplained death. Nevertheless, it gave him status in the community.

We can only presume that John's tailoring and farming were a cover for his illegal activities, for they must have made far less money, but nonetheless he took them seriously. He lists more than eighty clients for his tailoring work, and he made them coats and suits, trousers and flannel drawers, waistcoats and smocks; he also seems to have specialised in making clothes for their young sons. It is interesting to note that he made 'smockfrocks' – most writers on costume subscribe to the idea that these were made at home by working men's wives and lovingly embroidered with symbols that depicted their trades. John Evens's smocks were probably much more utilitarian, made of coarse cotton or linen, and with the plainest of embroidery to hold the smocked areas in place (see plate 15). For coats, breeches and waistcoats, he used mostly fustian and 'cassimere' (kerseymere), both relatively cheap woollen cloths, while 'everlasting breeches' and 'kneecaps' were his best-selling items – sturdy work wear for farmers and labourers, fishermen and sailors. Kneecaps, according to George Walker's *The Tailor's Masterpiece*[4], were

> cut from the fork to the foot, as the legs of a pair of Trousers, or rather Overalls with buttons down the side, and in size not tight, but tolerably close to the legs, especially at the bottom, where they must fit as precisely as a Gaiter ... These are the best things that can possibly be contrived either for COACH TRAVELLING or for RIDING ON HORSEBACK.

No doubt they were equally useful for keeping warm when unloading cargoes of contraband in the dead of night.

John also made bed-furnishings, tarpaulin covers for carts, sacking bags – anything, in fact, that his customers asked for. We do not know what he charged but prices seem to have been fairly similar across the country.[5] John Evens's customers were mostly local labourers, seamen, tradesman and farmers, but he also did work for the schoolmaster; the relieving officer; Captain Bignell, who was one of the churchwardens; and, bizarrely, on at least one occasion in January 1838, he made 'a Pair of Drawers for the Excise Officer'. The officer is unnamed and we cannot be sure whether or not he knew or cared what John Evens and his companions got up to on dark nights on the nearby cliffs and beaches.

John kept a diary between 1836 and 1840, and in it he lists a good many tailoring orders. He seems to have been a quicker worker than Samuel Attwood. For example:

1836

February 10. Mended covering of G Millman's cart, cut a Waistcoat for Hyne and a Smockfrock for J Crocker.

March 31. Cut a pair of trousers for Edwin Ellis and mended Coat and Trousers for Captain Bignell.

1838

May 2. Everlasting trousers for John Axworthy.

August 20. Coard trousers for Robert Lane Junr. Cut a Field of Barley beginning of Harvest.

November 16. Finished Everlasting Trousers for Smith's son. Cut a pair of Coard trousers T Wacome at Noss.

November 27. Made a Pair of Plush Trousers for William Crimp which settled his account up to this time.

November 28. Cut a Pair Cassimere Breeches for William Langworthy, heard of part of James Chinowath's Cargo washing ashore, being a Great Storm in which James Reeves' Cargo was all Lost and several Vessels wrecked – the *Eliza* of Cawsand and Cargo lost, Philip Kingcome, William Jenkins, T Langdon and James Hardy Drowned.

1839

May 28. Made Bed sacking for Joseph Penwill.

A week of entries in July 1839 gives a fair idea of the amount of tailoring work he could get through when he had no other activities to which to attend:

1. (Monday). Fustian waistcoat R[ichar]d Andrews.
2. Blk Coat Benj. Wyatt paid Ready Cash for.
3. At Wilburton to Work with Mr Lethbridge.
4. Mended trousers G Friend at Plymouth.
5. Mended Coat Benj Wyatt. At Noss evening.

6. Coat and w.ct Wm Crimp.

7. (Sunday). At Mothecombe Beach in a boat.

John employed William Stone, probably as an unpaid apprentice. William was the teenage son of a fellow tailor, John Stone of Mothecombe, and he would have been seventeen in 1836. It is possible that John Stone had trained John Evens and this was a *quid pro quo* – in any event, young William was with Evens for the whole of the period covered by the diary. John also records having help from John Cross and 'Mr Lethbridge [coming] to work with William Stone', but it seems as if they were occasional helpers, brought in at busy times, rather than regular employees.

Farming and gardening occupied some of John's time, and somehow he fitted them in with his tailoring work and his parish duties:

1836
February 27. ... at work in the Orchard, planted Cabbage Plants and Finished B Wyatt's [the innkeeper at the 'Union'] Smockfrock, wrote Crimp's Bill.
March 18. Gardening, planted Beans and Potatoes. Cut a Suit of Cloathes for Mary Easten's Boy, in the evening began writing Composition Rate ...
December 11. Finished Tilling of Wheat and Digging Potatoes ...

He records buying and selling a pony, and on 20 March 1836 he went to market, 'endeavouring to get Boars for working but could not.' He grew wheat, barley and potatoes, and spread his fields with fertiliser. He kept pigs and slaughtered them, tended his orchard and kept bees; in December 1838, for example, he 'made Bee Huts and shifted the Bees.' He picked his apples and made cider: '1839 May 10. Sold Candish a Hogshead Cyder.'

He also attended parish meetings at regular intervals. On 29 March 1836 he was re-sworn as 'Constable of the Parish ... this being the time that the new Highway Act takes place' and in April he was at the Surveyor's Nomination – presumably in connection with the new Act. He settled the accounts for Captain Bignell and a few days earlier had attended the meeting to inspect the overseers' accounts. It would seem that John Evens's mathematical abilities were much appreciated in his home parish. There were perks to this position. On 28 June 1838 the young Princess Victoria was crowned Queen and there were celebrations in towns and villages across the length and breadth of the British Isles. John Evens made 'the Colours' that were to be carried in a procession in which the 'greater part of the local inhabitants' of Holbeton took part. Jane Ellis was dressed to represent the Queen and Henry Millman was Albert – so it sounds as though Holbeton chose to create a replica of the Coronation procession. John recorded proudly that 'Myself headed the Procession with Drawn Sword, Mace; About 500 dined.'

Meanwhile his mother, Ann, lived with him and kept a grocer's shop, no doubt selling tea, coffee and other goods smuggled in from France and adding yet another stream of income to the family budget. John was probably glad of her presence, for in 1833 his first wife, Elizabeth Wyatt Evens, died aged twenty-six, leaving him with two small children: three-year-old Ann and baby Henry. If a young widow remarried quickly – or at all – she was seen as unfeeling and disrespectful to her late husband, but it was different for a man. Nineteenth-century society accepted that a young widower with children needed to find them a new mother as soon as possible; just two years after Elizabeth's death, in April 1835, John remarried. His new wife was Jane Jarvis from Blackawton near Totnes. John lost no time in getting her pregnant and there are some rather touching entries early on in the diary:

1836

March 10. A Daughter born about 11 in forenoon, in the afternoon spreading old thatch over the Orchard.

March 27. My daughter christened after Evening Service and named after my two wives, Elizabeth Jane (may she resemble them both for amiableness of Disposition)

June 7. Finished Henry's first suit of Cloathes. Hamlyn called on me wanting to go to France.

By then little Henry was five. John records the birth of Jane's second child – another girl – in 1839, but with much less enthusiasm than greeted Elizabeth Jane's arrival and he does not even bother to tell us her name; he seems much more interested in the £11 he received the same day from William Cudlipp for contraband items. The baby was in fact christened 'Mary King Evens' but died when she was just three years old. However, Jane went on to bear six more children: Rebecca in 1840, another Mary in 1842, Thomas in 1845, William in 1848, John Jarvis in 1852 and Michael in 1855. We know very little about the children, however. John Evens seldom mentions his family in his diary and, in any case, most of the children were born after he finished writing it early in 1840.

John Evens was a busy man but it was not all work and no play:

1838
August 16. At Wadum [Wadham] Fishing in Axworthy's Boat with Jane, Abram, Sarah and Henry.

John Axworthy was the miller at Holbeton, while 'Abram and Sarah' were members of Jane's family and they often visited. As well as fishing trips, John hunted, went on rabbit and pigeon shooting expeditions, attended local sales and fairs, and went to the theatre.

1838
February 14. At Plymouth at the Theatre, saw Mr Keane's King Lear.
November 5. At Plymouth Fair. Saw Wild Beasts.
1839
February 12. At Plymouth in G Millman's Cart about sending after Tobacco with Mr George Kirkin[s]. Then went to the theatre and spent the night in town.

Mr Millman went home early, so the following day John had to walk the nine miles home through heavy snow.

In July 1837 he and Jane visited Guernsey. This time he travelled legally on the steam packet, though when he arrived he may well have made arrangements with Guernsey merchants about shipments of tobacco; later in the diary he records taking delivery of cargoes of 'weed' from Guernsey.

Like many countrymen John was a practical man – he built cupboards in the house, repaired roofs and put up railings. In May 1836 Mr Rabbick's bake-house caught fire; it was a windy day and the wind funnelled the fire down the narrow street, destroying thirteen houses in the space of just two hours and making sixty-three people homeless. Next day John Evens was one of the men demolishing those parts of the damaged buildings that were in danger of collapsing.

However, far and away his most lucrative occupation was bringing in contraband. Smuggling was rife around the coast of the British Isles in the eighteenth and early nineteenth centuries, and few people saw it as a crime. Around a third of all imports into Britain were tobacco and foodstuffs – mainly tea, coffee, sugar, wine and spirits – and they carried a far higher import duty than other goods. In fact, of the total £22,962,610 the government received from import duties in 1839, £21,700, 630 came from duties on tobacco and foodstuffs.[6] The savings in buying goods duty-free were substantial; for example, tea cost around 7*d* a pound on the Continent but, duty paid, could sell at 8*s* a pound in England; smuggled tea was sold at around 5*s* a pound. There was a similar mark up on tobacco, wines and spirits. Even respectable people were quite happy to buy goods that they knew had been smuggled; indeed, it was estimated that up to half the spirits drunk in Britain were contraband. Few people objected to depriving the crown of revenue but the government took a different view. Smugglers, if and when they were caught, could face the death penalty, though in fact by John Evens's time only those smugglers who had caused death or serious injury to excise men were likely to be executed – and even then, local juries were often unwilling to convict.

Far and away the largest part of John Evens's diary is given over to describing his illicit activities; today it seems extraordinary that he saw no danger in writing a journal, naming his companions and his customers, and describing where he hid the smuggled goods.

John Evens may have stayed on land but he was still very much a hands-on member of the smuggling gang. The trade required careful planning and organisation. Orders had to be taken, voyages and terms agreed, ships and sailors hired. When a cargo was due a small army of men needed to be there to meet it, as a single vessel could carry several hundred 'things', and so timing and clear communication between ship and shore was essential. A system of hidden lights – in caves, in cottage windows facing the sea, visible from the sea but not from the land – would tell the sailors the coast was clear (a phrase that actually derives from smuggling) and it was safe to land. Alternatively, a series of bonfires on the cliffs would signal the presence of the excise men and warn that the ship should stay at sea for another twenty-four hours. A series of hiding places had to be arranged in advance and each group of men needed to know where their 'things' should be taken. According to the diary, many of these hidey-holes were several miles inland; the teams of unloaders would only have been able to make two or at most three return trips on foot apiece in the course of a night. Horses and carts also needed to be borrowed from sympathetic farmers and tradesmen, their hooves and wheels muffled with rags, while warning signals had to be agreed and roles had to be allocated. Arrangements then had to be made to move goods from temporary hiding places to buyers or to secure long-term storage. The whole business needed to be overseen by someone with a clear head and good administrative skills, and it seems that someone was John Evens.

One wonders how he managed to do his day jobs when so many of his nights were spent looking out for ships, landing cargo, moving it around and evading the excise officers. He seems to have been one of those people who can manage with very little sleep.

1836

March 23. At Borough [Farm] Sale received intelligence of 51 of the *Eliza*'s things being landed at Quarry Cove the night before.

April 9. Writing Bills and receiving Cash from Sale in the evening near Stoke Church and landed about 41 of the *Eliza*'s things about 4 O'Clock in the morning and brought 26 of them as far as Nedpenny Lane, placed them in the hedge and put R[ichar]d Andrews to look after them ...

April 10 Sunday. In the evening removed them to the store

April 16 Finished Mr S Hynes' Waistcoat in the evening finished landing the *Eliza*'s Cargo at Wadum [until] nearly daybreak and carried them all to Brownstone ...

Wadham Sands was a favourite landing spot, as it was far from a road and well-hidden – indeed, its seclusion is still valued as it is now a naturist beach. Even today it can only be reached on foot and the steep climb down from the coast path deters all but the most intrepid visitors. This particular cargo nearly landed John in serious trouble.

April 17 Sunday. Drove my Wife and Child to Brownstone [Brownstone Farm, near Luson] in Mr Rabbick's Car and remained there the whole day, went to bed there about 4 O'Clock was called again about 7 and told that the Officers had discovered our Landing, went towards the goods to caution Thomas Williams and met part of the Yealm Men who told me they had not met with Stafford in the road ...

The 'Yealm Men' were smugglers from Noss Mayo and Newton Ferrers on the River Yealm – an area notorious for smuggling.

...they then began to make a trench in the corner of the field to bury the things that were then in the Linhay ['the Linhay' was a field belonging to William Crimp] but had scarce commenced when Old Stafford came up to the place, on which we all ran off and he followed a short distance but soon returned and took possession of 44 things in the Linhay.

Richard Stafford was the head of the coastguard station at Mothecombe; he was an Irishman in his mid-thirties and so hardly deserved the dismissive soubriquet 'old'. The coastguard service was established in 1822, amalgamating three previous services: the revenue cutters that had chased smuggling boats at sea, the 'preventive water guard' that had patrolled the coast and the 'riding officers' who had attempted to intercept smugglers on land. The new coastguards were never local men, for fear that they would collaborate with the smugglers, and accommodation was provided for them and their families, usually in a purpose-built row of cottages, often with a boat house and lookout tower attached.[7]

The Mothecombe station had a chief officer and five 'boatmen'; the titles are misleading as they all worked both on land and at sea. However, they were usually the losers in any battle of wits with the smugglers. The smuggling gangs were large, well-organised and motivated by profit, and they had the active or tacit support of most of their neighbours. By contrast, there were just six coastguards (or 'excise men' or 'officers') at Mothecombe with two boats, and they were deeply unpopular. There were other stations nearby at Noss Mayo, Newton Ferrers and Cawsands, but they were similarly poorly staffed.

> ... our Men were by this time employed in carrying of[f] the remaining part from the corner of the Field which he had not discovered while I returned to my own House to secure what was within doors. On my return ran to Creacombe Cross met our party and remained looking out for them while they passed the road and returned to me again. I then went to Brownstone to ascertain whether any person had come to Stafford's assistance and found there had not, returned to the Cross and the party succeeded in securing Stafford and carried away all but three things, while at the Cross two Officers seized my Horse by the Bridle on which I called out murder as had been agreed on and then returned to Leuson [Luson] [and] told R[ober]t Nicholls the circumstance fearing I should be brought forward and then returned to my home and went to Bed.

Creacombe Cross is a small staggered crossroads hidden in the trees near Creacombe Farm. Robert Nicholls farmed Brownstone Farm,

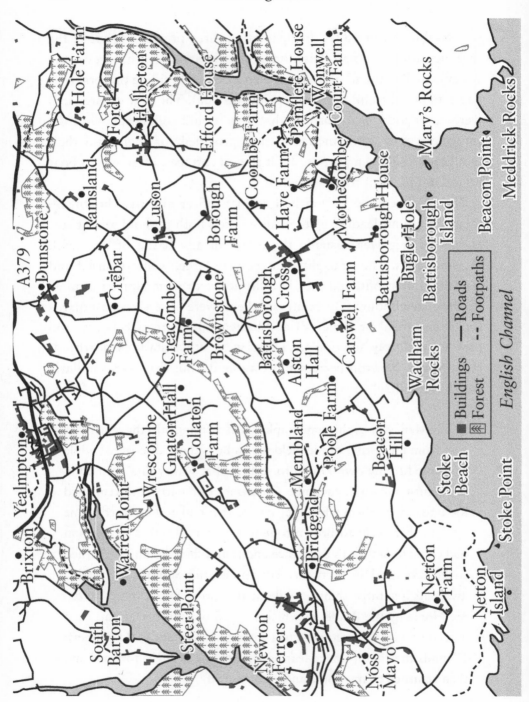

Map of the area between the Yealm and the Erme – John Evens's 'patch'.

which was where Jane and the baby were staying – presumably John expected him to break the news to them if he got arrested. The account is rather confused but it is clear that John covered a considerable distance in the course of that night. Wadham to Brownstone is about three miles and Brownstone to Holbeton by way of Luson is two, while Holbeton back to Creacombe Cross is another two-and-a-half (see map on facing page). It is not clear what the shout of 'Murder' was intended to signify. Was he calling for help or sounding a warning? How did he get his horse clear of the men who had seized its bridle? He had obviously had a very close call.

The following day, still keeping an eye out for the excise men, he set about securing more of the 'things', taking six from Luson Orchard and the remainder from Dunstone (a village two miles away to the north-east) and putting them in Whipples' Barn (at Westlake, just north of Luson). Some he left with 'P Luke in Yealmpton'. This was Philip Luke, who was a builder. The following day John calmly 'began making Smith's Waistcoat' and 'in the evening removed 9 things from Borough Hedge [part of Borough Farm, about a mile south-east of Holbeton] to the storehouse' (see plate 17). A few days later he removed the rest from the hedge and sold twelve 'things' to Mr Northmore for £30. The Northmores were a farming family in Buckland Monachorum. We do not know how much Philip Luke bought or paid – but John Evens had certainly made well in excess of £30 on the deal and still had at least £50 worth of stock. Given that he would have been lucky to make £1 a week from his tailoring and that most of his farm and garden produce was for home use, it is not difficult to see the appeal of smuggling. Such profits were not unusual. In January 1840, for example, his share of the proceeds of one of James Chinowath's ventures was '23 profit at £1-6s each' – £29 18s in total.

The episode at Creacombe Cross does not seem to have deterred John Evens in the slightest. Less than a week later he wrote 'Paid R[ichar]d Hamlyn for his Boat my Part cost £15-10s the Quarter'. We do not know whether this was a boat that made trips to France or a small boat used as a lighter. On 4 May he was in Plymouth making arrangements to send another boat – the *Hawk* – to France, and its goods were landed a couple of weeks later. On 30 May he was 'at Cawsand with J Elliott and J H Crocker and made an agreement for freight of [the] *Union* with T Warn (this was lost)'; on 4 July he was 'in Plymouth settling the *Eliza*'s voyage' and just two days later he went to Dartmouth for 'John Ellis to join the *Thetis* freight to Roscoff'. His tailoring skills sometimes came in handy as a way of paying off debts: 'July 13. Cut a Black Coat for Mr Lapthorne at Noss to make up freight of the *Hawk*.'

In September 1837 John Evens paid £20 10s into the bank from the sale of ten 'things' and later in the month he 'sent 8 large things and 1 flagon to Plymouth for Mr Cudlipp'. In October he got £15 from Mr Northmore at Buckland Monachorum for another '8 things' and bought himself a green coat with the proceeds; later in the month 'in the evening at Newton [Ferrers] sent for 14 things and 1 flagon at Cherbourg for J Jenkin and John Rowe'. 'Things' obviously came in different shapes and sizes for, on 27 October, he got £15 for just four items. On 15 December he lost another cargo and, unusually, he tells us what it was. 'Vessel and Cargo of Tobacco lost at Devonport'. On Boxing Day he did the final deal of the year, arranging the voyage of a ship called the *Three Brothers* with 'the Hanafords'.

For the next three years the diary records voyages and landings, and losses and gains in much the same manner, though John does begin to identify some of the cargoes as 'tubs' – presumably of wine or spirits – and 'weed', which must have been tobacco. Cargoes were bulky and creating safe hiding places was a constant preoccupation. One of the first entries in 1836 reads 'At Plymouth and Bought 3 Large Bottles at 3s each ...' and the next day he 'Fixed one Large Bottle in the Orchard' and on 19 February he 'fixed a Four Gallon Jug in the Orchard.' In November he 'Made an opening for a Private Place' on his land, though he does not tell us where, and in January 1839 he 'Began making a Private Place at Brownstone'.

What is clear is just how many people were involved in – or at least aware of – what was going on. To unload a cargo and hide it required a large body of men. Most of the men John records were local farm labourers, who would have earned a few shillings apiece for their night's work – not to be sneezed at when an average farm labourer's weekly wage was 8s – but after a night of heavy labour they cannot have been a great deal of use to their employers the following day. Presumably many of them worked for farmers who were themselves involved, or at least sympathetic. Cargoes were stashed, permanently or temporarily, on numerous farms, in hedges, barns and cellars, and all sorts of people provided carts in which things were transported. William Crimp was a butcher and victualler who kept the George Inn, Mr Rabbick (variously spelt 'Rabbich', 'Rabbick' or 'Rabbidge') was a baker, and Joseph Millman was a farmer; they all had vehicles that they made available to young Mr Evens. John lists a whole series of ships and individuals who owned, sailed or commissioned voyages – but James Chinowath, Robert Hamlyn, J. Elliott, J. H. Crocker, John Ellis, the Hanafords, George Kirkins and a group of people in Noss Mayo seem to have been his key contacts.

He was involved with cargoes arriving in a range of places, including Cawsands, Caulston, Noss Mayo, Stoke Beach (see plate 16), Wadham Sands, Bugle Hole and Mothecombe. He made occasional forays to Plymouth and further afield, but his 'patch' seems to have been a fifteen-square-mile area between the Yealm and Erme estuaries, stretching from the coast up to Dunstone and Yealmpton in the north. He had numerous contacts all across this district and would have known the tracks and fields like the back of his hand.

On occasion goods were sent further afield – his reputation must have spread.

1838
September 10. At Plymouth sent for 200 Weed with G Kirkins to be carried to Wales.

September 13. At Work on Mr Reeves Coat with William S[tone],
at 12 of Night to Stoke Point to look out for the Galley.
September 14. At Work on Coat with W[illiam] S[tone]. At Night
landed the Weed, brought 500 to Brownstone in Crimp's cart.

He apparently accepted losses to the excise men as an occupational
hazard; these losses were usually quite small – perhaps ten or twenty
items, a cartload. The customs men had as much difficulty transporting
large quantities of 'things' as did the smugglers. In February 1838 he
landed a cargo at five in the morning: 'Brought 27 Large ones, 1 Four,
2 Flagons to Brownstone'. However, the following day '21 of them
[were] taken by the Officers, sent 6 to Plymouth in Mr Hicks' cart in
the evening carried 2 to Fleet Mill for Mr Wacome.' On 12 July 1839
the Mothecombe officers got a larger haul than usual: '116 fours, 10
lost by me'. 'Fours' were four-gallon barrels. It is, therefore, quite
understandable that John was jubilant when in January the following
year he managed to acquire, and bring home as a trophy, an anchor
belonging to the Mothecombe coastguard.

Violence was always a possibility when so much was at stake, but
John Evens usually seems to have avoided confrontation. However, in
July 1839, he must really have lost his temper: 'July 9. At Yealmpton
sessions fined 5s and Costs for assaulting E. Lasky Collector of Tolls,
Laira Bridge. At Plymouth in evening.' He could well afford the fine
but he could have done without a criminal record.

Sometimes there were lucky accidents, as in January 1840, when,
in a storm 'The French Boat *L'Etoile of Marseilles* drove into
Mothecombe laden with Wine. Crew saved'. And from time to time
unlucky people got caught:

1839
October 10. ... both boats at Cawsand taken by the Cutter ...
October 18. At Noss Hockaday and Crocker taken.

The Crockers were a farming family, while William Hockaday
was a shoemaker. John had been very affected by the arrest of

two of his Plymouth customers, Mr Cudlipp and his wife, a year
previously. They ran a grocery business and were among his
'regulars' – in fact, just two months earlier, they had paid him
'£12 for 9 things'. Mrs Cudlipp was acquitted but, on 31 January
1838, William Cudlipp was 'sentenced to 6 months confinement
[with] Hard Labour in the Bridewell for obstructing the Officers
in the Execution of their duty.' John attended the trial and visited
Cudlipp before he was sent to the Bridewell, but there was no
hope of leniency as it was his fourth offence. William Cudlipp was
fifty-eight and prison broke him; by 1841 he was in the Plymouth
Lunatic Asylum.

John Evens could feel sympathy for his friend – tinged, no
doubt, with annoyance at the loss of a good customer – but he
had no qualms about upholding the law in matters other than
smuggling. He was not called upon to exercise his role as parish
constable very often but, when he was, he often recorded the event
in detail:

1836
April 4. Sent after in morning by H Tonkin Esq to remove his Servant
N Stone from his House on doing which he and I was [sic] serenaded
with Music on his departure from Pamfleet [Pamflete House] by all
the workmen and boys on the premises, rattling and beating old Tin
Kettles and Pans and marching after him across the meadows. Rec'd
a crown from H Tonkin for my trouble, cut a Waistcoat for Smith,
sowed Union Seed in the evening at Noss and got 2 of J[ohn] Rowe's
Spirit things which were brought home in the Car.

The workmen obviously disliked Nicholas Stone – a carpenter –
heartily, and were showing their disapproval in the time-honoured
way with 'rough music' intended to embarrass and humiliate the
person they thought was in the wrong. The last sentence of the
entry is a little difficult to interpret, however. He might mean 'onion
seed' – early-nineteenth-century spelling was often idiosyncratic – but
though he spent a lot of time at Noss Mayo John Evens does not

seem to have had any land there in which to sow seed. Given that we know the *Union* was a sailing vessel, the meaning is probably different. 'Sowing' or 'seeding' meant hiding contraband – usually barrels – by sinking it in the sea and marking the spot with some sort of line and buoy. The fact that John mentions collecting 'Spirit things' in the same sentence suggests that this is probably what he meant.

1837
May 18. Called by Thomas Alger to prevent William Lopes removing his goods without paying rent ...

Mr Alger (or 'Algar') was a painter and glazier and William Lopes was his tenant. William was trying to pull a fast one – if he had succeeded in doing a moonlight flit, his former landlord would have been entitled to keep any belongings left behind in lieu of rent. Lopes knew this and the following day many of his belongings were found hidden in a neighbour's house.

John was also called in to deal with unexpected deaths:

1838
October 1st. Mr Henry Friend hung himself. Fetched the Coroner.

On 11 June 1838 John was called to Gnaton Hall by Mr Lidstone, the carpenter who was working there and whose apprentice had tried to run away, and on the twelfth he was 'At Membland with ditto and Mr Walter's Girl at Alston. Girl acquitted. Boy Committed for 2 weeks.' Apprentices were often unhappy and frequently tried to run away. Most of them were young teenagers who were lonely and homesick; many masters were less than sympathetic, and some were downright cruel and exploitative. The saddest case John recorded was that of Elizabeth Smale, Mr May's apprentice, who was caught stealing fowls. Jonathan May farmed at Haye Farm in Holbeton, so Elizabeth was probably training to be a farm servant. She was tried at Exeter in January 1839; John Evens travelled there, at the parish's expense 'by Subscription Mail Coach' for the trial. Poor little Elizabeth was found guilty and sentenced to four weeks' hard labour, two of which were to be spent in solitary confinement. The trip to Exeter seems to have been exceptional but John attended local Petty Sessions at Modbury, Brixton and Ridgeway fairly frequently, to see local miscreants sentenced.

The diary comes to an abrupt end in February 1840. Perhaps John Evens realised that it could get him into trouble if it fell into the wrong hands, or perhaps he was just too busy to carry on keeping it – we have no way of knowing. However, he kept it safe and, in March 1863, when Michael, his youngest son, was nearly eight, there was a tea at the school to celebrate the marriage of the Prince of Wales. (A school had opened in the village in 1835.) Not a lot happened in Holbeton and it seems that young Michael was anxious to record what was – for him – a red letter day. One of his parents must have remembered John's old diary and suggested he write in that, and he did so, in pencil in a rather shaky childish script, proudly signing his entry 'Michael Evens'. Then, or at some later date, an adult added a note in ink to the effect that the tea had been held to commemorate the marriage of Prince Albert Edward to Princess Alexandra of Denmark.

John Evens may have ceased to write a diary, but he does not disappear from the record. Like Samuel Attwood, he does not seem to have enjoyed tailoring but, unlike Samuel, he did not really need the income it generated. When his first two children were christened, he is described in the parish register as 'tailor' and in 1841 that was the occupation he gave to the census enumerator. However, when his and Jane's younger children were baptised, he described himself first as a 'shopkeeper' and later as 'farmer and shopkeeper'. In 1851 he was still 'farmer and shopkeeper' but by 1861 he was 'farmer and innkeeper'. With so many occupations to choose from, the inconsistency is not altogether surprising.

Smuggling is a young man's game and perhaps John, with a growing family, decided that it was just too risky; besides, by the mid-1840s the trade was dying out. In desperation, the government had increased its forces. The coastguard, formed in 1822 with 3,000 men, had doubled in size by 1845, when it was amalgamated with the 'Coastal Blockade', a force hitherto controlled by the Admiralty, while the coastguard was managed by the Royal Navy.[8] More importantly, in the same decade the government began to adopt a free-trade policy, driven by the Whig, Charles Pelham Villiers, whose Committee on Import Duties was set up in 1840. The committee was more concerned with the effect high import duties had on food prices and the impact that had on the poor than with smuggling, but it reported that the whole import duty system was illogical and inconsistent and that the duty levied often varied according to the country from which the import came rather than in relation to the type of goods being imported:

> It will be seen that 17 articles, affording the largest amount of Customs Revenue, are articles of the first necessity and importance to the community; viz. sugar, tea, tobacco, spirits, wine, timber, corn, coffee, butter, currants, tallow, seeds, raisins, cheese, cotton wool, sheep's wool, and silk manufactures; and that the interests of the Public Revenue have been by no means the primary consideration in levying the Import Duties, inasmuch as competing foreign produce is in some instances excluded, and in others checked by high differential duties ...[9]

The best-known result of this report was the repeal of the Corn Laws in 1846, but the import duty on most other goods also began to fall – meaning that the profits from bringing in contraband were no longer worth the risks.

John Evens came to the trade late in the day; had he been smuggling in the period between 1780 and 1820 he would probably have died a rich man. As it was he made a comfortable income from his trade and he used the money to rent more land. By 1851 he had 50 acres and was employing two labourers; by 1871 he had 90 acres and a boy had joined the two men; by 1881 he had acquired a further 6 acres. His orchards were adjacent to his cottage on Brent Hill, but most of his fields, acquired piecemeal, were scattered across the eastern side of the parish. They included a strip of woodland on the south-eastern boundary and another nearby of 'waste' along the bank of a little tributary of the Erme – probably he originally saw them as good hiding places for illicit goods. Sometime between 1851 and 1855 he also took over the tenancy of the George Inn in the centre of Holbeton.[10]

He carried on working with the Parish Council and appears regularly in the minutes. By 1849 he was no longer the bright young man to whom the churchwarden gave a couple of sovereigns to write up the accounts; he was one of the people who checked those accounts and signed them off. His rates increased with his landholding – from the 4s 9d his father had paid in 1825, by 1869 John was paying almost a pound: 19s 7½d. He was a parish councillor and it was his pub, the George, that supplied the council with beer, with £1 2s 8½d worth in 1855, £2 11s 2d worth in 1876/7.[11] John Evens was becoming increasingly respectable, one of the village elders, a pillar of the community.

His children – most of them – married, and numerous grandchildren were born. Henry emigrated to Australia where he married and raised a family; William went to Ontario and did the same. John's daughters married and moved away from the village, but his other sons stayed. Thomas and John Jarvis continued to run the pub and farm his land; his youngest son, Michael, the one who as a little boy had been so excited by the celebrations for the Prince of Wales' wedding, farmed Ramsland Farm at Ford. Thomas remained a bachelor but both John and Michael married and had children.

John Evens died in 1885, at home in Holbeton with his sons, having outlived his wife by some three years. He would be remembered in the village for many years to come.

Noch Dem Oreman Shlept Zikh Der Shlimazel (Ill Fortune Follows the Poor Man): Adolph Kushner (*c.* 1868–1947), London

Adolph kissed the coroner's hand, tears of emotion streaming down his face. '*A sheynem dank, spasibo*,[1] tzank you, tzank you ...' Experience in his native Russia had given him a profound distrust of the state and here, in a strange land, unable to understand a word of the language, not knowing whether or not to trust the interpreter, the Coroner's Court had been terrifying. But things had turned out better than he could ever have dared imagine.

Adolph and Ella 'Cushneer'[2] had been married just eighteen months. To begin with they had found themselves a room in a tenement in Goulston Street with Bell Punzner, a fellow Russian Jew, and her five children, four of whom were tailors like Adolph – one or more of them may well have been Adolph's workmates at that time. They had probably told him the gory tale of how part of the bloodstained clothing of one of Jack the Ripper's first victims was found in a doorway in that very street, but it does not seem to have deterred Adolph from moving there with his young bride.

Adolph and Ella were poor but they were young and hopeful; he was twenty-two, she was twenty-one. Within a few months Ella was pregnant – that was to be expected, they would manage – but then, just four weeks before she was due to give birth, the worst happened. Adolph lost his job. We do not know why, but nineteenth-century employers did not have to give reasons. Perhaps trade was slack, perhaps one of the new wave of immigrants was more skilled than Adolph or desperate enough to work for a lower wage – we have no way of knowing. By then the couple had moved to a room in a tenement in Spelman Street and, one by one, they pawned their few possessions – sheets, blankets, baby things, their own clothes. Pawning Adolph's best trousers, for example, realised 1s 6d, enough for them to buy a boiling fowl that kept them in chicken soup for four days.

On Thursday 23 December 1891, Ella gave birth to a baby daughter – somehow Adolph persuaded a midwife to attend, though it is unlikely he was able to pay her. It was winter; they could not afford to heat the room and by then they had pawned all their spare clothes and blankets. Ella was weak and malnourished and could barely produce enough milk to feed the child, but somehow the little girl survived, hungry and wrapped in rags, for almost two weeks, though Adolph and Ella had so little hope for her that they never gave her a name. She died on Wednesday 6 January 1892. When it was clear she was failing, Adolph went to Brick Lane to fetch the surgeon – but Mr Dukes was old, a man in his seventies, and he refused to open the door on a cold winter night to an immigrant family who would be unable to pay him and to a case that he probably already knew would be hopeless. By the time he arrived the following afternoon the baby girl had been dead for almost twenty-four hours; she was painfully thin and lying stark naked on the bare mattress.

In court Mr Dukes agreed that it was a case of destitution – he saw many such. There was, he said, no food in the place, only a dirty glass of sour milk 'quite unfit for human consumption' on the table. He described Ella as 'a wretched, thin, emaciated woman. She had scarcely any clothing on and appeared starved.' He had given them 'a trifle to be going on with' – probably a few pence – and a referral to the Jewish Board of Guardians. Adolph acknowledged that they had then received 10s from the Board.

The jury returned the verdict 'That the deceased died from want of care and want of food owing to the poverty of the parents.' The Coroner ordered Adolph to apply immediately for admission to the workhouse and warned him that if he did not, and Ella also starved to death, he could be had up for manslaughter. Mr Wynne Baxter, the Coroner, was a middle-class official with little sympathy for the stream of hapless, hopeless, feckless humanity that passed through his courtroom, but the jury were working men, some of whom were themselves of immigrant stock. Even if Adolph had known of the existence of the workhouse – and he claimed he did not – the jury were well aware that going there would have been a dreadful experience. He and Ella would have been separated, and he would have been put to hard, humiliating work that would have coarsened his tailor's hands. It was a place where babies seldom survived, and the food they were given would not have been *kosher*. Better to sit it out and hope something would turn up; it was the sort of calculation many of them had had to make at some point in their lives. There but for the grace of God ... So they had a whip-round and presented the coroner with 12s 2d to be given to the Kushners – no wonder Adolph wept tears of gratitude.[3]

He had arrived in London in 1889, one of many thousands of Jews fleeing violence in Russia. Life had never been easy for the Russian Jews; for over a century they had been forced to remain within the 'Pale of Settlement', a broad strip of territory to the west of the empire, bordering Prussia and Austria-Hungary and running from the Baltic to the Black Sea, encompassing parts of the countries we now know as Lithuania, Poland and the Ukraine. Even within the Pale, Jews faced restrictions on where they could live and what work they were permitted to do. Most of them lived in their own townships or *shtetls,* and relations with their non-Jewish neighbours were at best uneasy.

Yekhezkel Kotik was born in 1847, two decades before Adolph Kushner, but his childhood in a Ukrainian *shtetl* was probably very similar to Adolph's.[4] It seems likely that Adolph also came from the Ukraine – he always identified himself as 'Russian', while those immigrants from further north usually described themselves as Poles or Lithuanians. Later writers make much of the charitable and self-help societies that existed in the Pale,[5] but Yekhezkel makes no mention of them. Instead he wrote of bleak lives and hardship. He describes the womenfolk keeping shops and sitting outside gossiping; they were only really busy at weekends, when the peasants came into town from the countryside. Most of the men were craftsmen – tailors, shoemakers, furriers, carpenters – but a few of them were employed by the local Russian landowners as advisers, gofers and general dogsbodies. They were ill-used and, like the peasants, they were subject to violent beatings if they incurred their master's displeasure; Kotik describes a particularly chilling form of abuse where the Jewish servant would be placed in the middle of a courtyard and baited with vicious dogs while his employer's family watched and laughed. Each *stetl* had its assessor and *ispravnik* (police chief), both Russians, who subjected the local Jewish-run businesses to the equivalent of protection rackets.

The food most people ate was poor and monotonous – mostly black bread, the staler the better, because then the family would eat less of it. Breakfast was *krupnik*, a barley and potato soup, to which occasionally was added a little butter or milk; lunch was *borscht*, bread and salt herring; supper was noodles or bread and milk. Little patties were made of small bony river fish, ground up and mixed with onions. Only on the Sabbath did the poor eat meat, and then very little of it; it was lean and tough because the butchers bought only old thin beasts that no-one else wanted.

Children, particularly boys, had a rough time. At the age of three they were handed over to the *Melamdim* or teacher with whom they would remain until they were well into their teens. Teaching centred on the *Talmud* and learning by heart, and beatings were commonplace. They worked seven days a week and had just twenty-six days' holiday a year, for the festivals of Purim, Passover, Shavuot, Rosh Hashannah, Yom Kippur and Succot. Jewish law said that, of the five duties of a parent, ensuring their children had a sound religious teaching was far and away the most important, and parents in the *shtetl* took this to heart. After school, many boys were conscripted into the Tsarist army for an obligatory period of twenty-five years – most of their working lives.

Wolf Kossoff recorded memories of his childhood in the Ukraine in a small *stetl* in the 1890s.[6] He spoke of single-storey houses with turf roofs on which animals grazed, of whole families sleeping together in a single bedroom and of schooling that depended entirely on the parents' ability to pay, with children whose families were late with the fees placed at the back of the class and ignored. For both Yekhezkel and Wolf, life revolved around the synagogue – in Wolf's town of around 1,200 inhabitants there were five synagogues and it was unthinkable that anyone in the community might not be religious. For Yekhezkel, such entertainment as there was centred on the synagogue, with travelling cantors and students, and *klezmorim* (dance musicians) and jesters at the weddings of the better-off.

Weeping and wailing were an important – probably cathartic – part of worship, and superstitions about demons and devils and evil spirits abounded. It was generally believed that misery did not end with death. The dead body was laid out on straw so it was pricked 'as with a thousand needles' and evil spirits surrounded it as it was carried in the funeral procession. As the body was lowered into the grave, the Angel Dawah would ask the corpse its name – and, as it would have forgotten, its guts were ripped out, and it was beaten with white hot iron rods and subjected to other excruciating tortures.[7] If Adolph and Ella had been brought up with these beliefs, they must have suffered unimaginable torment at the death of their baby girl.

The Russian Jewish and gentile populations in the Pale co-existed, though there was no legal protection for the Jews if their neighbours took against them. However, on 1 March 1881[8], Tsar Alexander II was assassinated by members of a revolutionary group, *Narodnaya Volya*, which was believed to have Jewish connections. Alexander was a popular figure and the assassination had a profound impact on attitudes to the Jews in Russia. The first *pogrom* after the assassination took place in Yelisavetgrad and the nearby villages in mid-April; then it was the turn of Kiev where Yekhezkel Kotik and his family were living. He describes how they hid in the attic, and then in the woodshed, and watched the killing, looting and raping going on around them: 'This must be how sheep feel when being led to slaughter', he wrote later.[9]

The *pogroms* spread across the Pale, though they were worst in the Ukraine. It is likely that Adolph's decision to emigrate was sparked by a *pogrom* or fear of one, though migration was also fuelled by poverty and the hope of a better life. In common with thousands of other Russian Jews he headed north and west; they travelled on foot, in carts and, if they could afford it, by rail. There were many obstacles in their way. If they were to leave Russia legally they needed a passport and other documents, all of which had to be paid for along with bribes to the various officials involved. People smugglers thrived. Inside the Pale there were agents who would sell would-be emigrants tickets to the US or South Africa via Britain but, when the travellers arrived, they would sometimes discover their tickets were not valid for their onward journey. The whole business was fraught with risk but, nevertheless, between 1881 and 1915 2 million people left the Pale; 150,000 of them settled in England but many more passed through on route to the New World and South Africa.[10]

By the mid-1880s the established Jewish community in Britain was providing aid to the newcomers. The boats carrying them were often met at the port of entry by representatives of Jewish organisations; there the passengers disembarking would be given a rudimentary health check and then accompanied up-river. Those who had no family or friends to greet them would be directed to the Poor Jews' Temporary Shelter in Leman Street for a brief respite – they could stay there for up to two weeks, paying only what they could afford – before embarking on the next leg of their journey or before they set out to find work and a home in London.

Adolph was probably luckier than most, as he arrived in 1889, the year of the tailor's strike; masters were desperate for workers to replace the strikers, so jobs were probably relatively easy to find. The strike, which lasted from 27 August to 2 October, was about reducing working hours, limiting overtime and allowing meals to be taken outside the workshop so that the workers got a breath of fresh air and the chance to move around. Many Jewish workers joined the strike – but in 1889 Adolph was probably prepared to tolerate any sort of conditions in return for the chance to work. For the first three months he would have been known as a 'greener' and paid a bare subsistence, surviving on 'a shake-down, a cup of coffee, a herring and a hunch of brown bread' and probably eating and sleeping in his workplace.[11] Thereafter he would earn somewhere between three and five shillings for a week of twelve- to fourteen-hour days. The 1889 strike was successful in that the official length of the working day was reduced to ten-and-a-half hours with limits on the amount of overtime any one worker could undertake; however, in small workshops the rules were frequently bent and broken. After a year or so the new worker's wage might double or treble, but there was always the risk of being replaced by one of the newer, cheaper immigrants. This is very probably what happened to Adolph in the winter of 1891/2. He told the Coroner's Court that he could earn between 16s 0d and £1 a week when he was in work – a respectable wage, which suggests he was a skilled worker.

There were various branches of the tailoring trade and various jobs within those branches. Unlike most gentile firms, the Jewish tailoring workshops ran on the principle of 'division of labour', as this essay by Levi Billig, a Jewish schoolboy, explains. He and his classmates from the Jewish Free School were taken to see a tailoring workshop – no doubt a very respectable one – in October 1911.

There are about twenty men at work and we notice that each man does a certain, separate kind of work. Let us watch this man 'fixing' a coat, which seems to us a medley of pieces of stuff. He is sitting on a bench with legs crossed. Look, he has done his work and is passing it to the 'plain' machinist. He is now taking another lot of stuff and begins 'fixing' that. Thus it is that he does only one part of the work and the coat begins to take shape. The machinist who has the coat now in his charge is putting a few delicate touches in. He passes it to a boy, only recently left school, who pulls out the bastings, and who then gives it to a man whose duty it is to put the lining in. The coat is passed to the under-presser, and then to the presser. There is, we notice, a chain of workers, who, as it were, each add a few links.[12]

Pressing and machining were distinct trades in their own right; the under-pressers worked on the inside seams and the pressers pressed the finished garment, banging the steam through the fabric with wooden 'cluppers'. Many workshops assembled garments that arrived ready-cut, but those that made garments from scratch were among the first to use the band-cutter, developed in 1858, which was a dangerous machine that cut a number of thicknesses of fabric at the same time. Jewish tailors were also quicker to adopt sewing machines than their gentile colleagues. The 'fixer', who tacked the pieces together ready for machining, was properly known as the 'baster'. It was a skilled job – the machinist could only do a good job if the baster had put the pieces together neatly and accurately. For a time at least, we know Adolph worked as a tailor's baster.[13]

Most of the work done in the East End was sub-contracted – making up pieces cut out by the fitter in a bespoke tailoring business 'up West', making up goods from ready-cut stock patterns, or making from scratch for less prestigious businesses that simply supplied the cloth to be used and an indication of which styles they required. Coats, trousers and waistcoats were different specialisations and tended to be made by different firms, and in many establishments the men were paid piecework rates. Workshops came in all shapes and sizes, from small businesses operating out of someone's living room to big, well-established firms. It cost very little to set up a basic tailoring workshop – around £5 for a sewing machine and a few benches.[14]

Adolph described himself as a 'ladies' tailor', which meant he made ladies' costumes, coats and jackets and worked in rather lighter materials than were used in the men's trade (see plates 6, 18 and 19). By the 1890s more and more women had jobs, and women's wear had become simpler and more 'masculine' – neat blouses worn with tailored skirts and jackets. Like many employees, Adolph probably moved from firm to firm as work dried up in one workshop, or as another offered a few pence more per week.

It seems that soon after the 1892 court case Adolph found work, and he and Ella stayed on at Spelman Street. Within a matter of months Ella was again pregnant, but she was no longer well – Adolph told the court she had always been too delicate to work – and she died on 6 February 1893 of '*albumniria*', which means kidney failure due to abnormal levels of protein in the urine. She went into a coma and never recovered consciousness. Adolph was with her when she died, while the doctor who signed the death certificate was old Mr Dukes, who had failed to visit the previous winter when their baby was dying. On the death certificate she is recorded as 'Eva', but the address and her husband's name and profession make it clear she and Ella were one and the same person. Adolph's English was poor – and Mr Dukes and the other officials who came into contact with him no doubt struggled to interpret his thick Eastern European accent.

Bad luck seems to have followed Adolph around. He next comes to our attention in October 1894. By this point he had moved to the Tenter-ground and was working for Youngs, a firm of mantle-makers in Booth Street. On Saturday 6 October – pay-day, so this must have been a gentile firm – he arrived at work to find a crowd of about fifteen men outside Youngs. One of them told him that he would have to hand over his wages when he came out – and when he naively asked why he was struck across the face. Sure enough, as he left work, he and three colleagues – Joseph and Isaac Fleishman and Joseph Abrahams – were attacked. Joseph Fleishman was

Above left: 1. Elizabeth Chaffard, *c*. 1865. Her dress is trimmed with crepe, so she is in the later stages of mourning, probably for one of her parents. (Courtesy of the National Library of Scotland)

Above right: 2. Fashion plate from *Petit Courrier des Dames*, 1853. Elizabeth Taylor/Chaffard would have worked on dresses very similar to this when she was in partnership with Mme Schoelcher.

3. 2 Castle Hill (now Castle Street) in May 2016. In the 1860s this was the shop of Chaffard et Cie. The façade probably dates from the 1930s; originally it would have looked more like the house on the right. (Valerie Hawkins)

4. Dress of brown and black striped silk, *c.* 1868. The bodice was machine-stitched using a chain-stitch machine (an old-fashioned machine, given the date). The sleeves were set in by hand and the seams of the skirt are also hand-sewn. Details: a) the inside of the bodice showing the heavy cotton lining, part of the 'diamond' back (formed by a dropped shoulder seam and seams to shape the bodice back where a modern dressmaker would use darts), the basque and the neatly finished seams and button holes; b) the front of the skirt showing the 'pinked' trimming; c) detail of a sleeve showing the curved cut and kilted inner trimming; d) detail of the hem showing the 'brush braid' – a coarse braid that protruded a millimetre or two below the hem and took the wear as the skirt brushed the floor – and the tacking stitches holding the trimming in place. (Courtesy of Leicester City Council Arts and Museum Service)

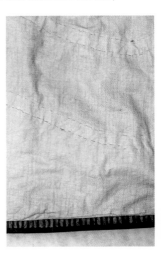

5. Wedding dress of lilac and grey silk, *c*. 1875. This dress is entirely machine-sewn using a lock-stitch machine, and is most beautifully cut and finished. Details: a) the inside of the bodice showing the coarse lining, kilted trimming and delicate shaping – and a repair or alteration to the lining; b) detail of the sleeve showing the elaborately kilted cuff; c) detail of the skirt showing how the flounces are set and the tacking stitches that hold the trimming in place. (Courtesy of Leicester City Council Arts and Museum Service)

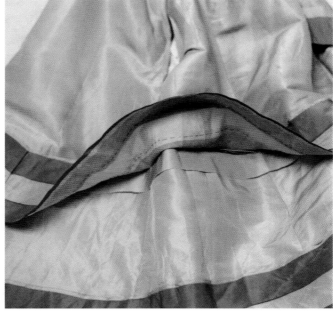

DEW DRESSES.

6. Fashions of 1882 from *The Girls' Own Paper*. The figure on the left wears a tailored walking costume. Adolph Kushner would have made similar garments. The other two dresses show the elaborate trimming made possible by the increased use of sewing machines. All would have been worn over bustles. Rebecca Thomas's firm would have made dresses like these in the 1880s.

7. Mrs Pattinson's shop on the corner of Upper Brook Street. It now forms part of the larger carpet shop next door. (Author's photograph)

8. The Promenade, Cheltenham, in 1865. (Copyright The Francis Frith Foundation)

9. Low House, Cleabarrow, where the Fentons lived in the early 1890s. The house is just a mile-and-a-half from Bowness-in-Windermere, but is surrounded by woodland and feels much more isolated. (Author's photograph)

Above left: 10. Plate from *Costumes Parisiens* showing the fashions of 1816. The man wears the sort of garments that were in fashion when Samuel Attwood started in the tailoring trade – note the tight knee-breeches and cutaway coat. (Courtesy of the Victoria and Albert Museum)

Above right: 11. Plate from *Petit Courrier des Dames* showing a man's overcoat of 1825 – men's coats at this date were very long. Note the elaborate collar and the full sleeves. (Courtesy of the Victoria and Albert Museum)

Above left: 12. Fashion plate showing evening dress of 1829 from *Costumes Parisiens*. Note the man's tight trousers, fancy waistcoat and pleated shirt, and the huge sleeves, high waist and elaborate trimming of the woman's dress, along with the large, showy headdress she is wearing. Samuel Attwood would have made menswear like this for his more fashionable customers, and Elizabeth Chaffard probably worked on equally complicated evening dresses when she was an apprentice. (Courtesy of the Victoria and Albert Museum)

Above right: 13. Plate from *La Mode* showing 'country wear' in 1834. (Courtesy of the Victoria and Albert Museum)

14. Holbeton. (Christine Endacott)

15. Two sketches of country folk by William Johnstone White, showing the sort of garments John Evens made for his poorer clients. There would have been few changes in the style of their garments between 1818 and the 1840s. Note that one of the men is wearing a 'smockfrock' and three of them are wearing knee breeches. From White's *Sketches of Characters consisting of Whole Length Portraits ... Illustrative of the Counties of Norfolk, Cambridgeshire and Middlesex* (1818).

16. Part of Stoke beach, seen from Stoke Point. John Evens unloaded cargoes of contraband there. Most of the beaches and coves he used are still only accessible on foot. (Christine Endacott)

17. Sunken lane near Borough Farm, showing the high, steep banks in which the smugglers dug 'private places' to hide contraband. (Author's photograph)

Above left: 18. Tailored garments from 'Fashions for February' in *Cassell's Magazine*, 1889.

Above right: 19. 'Fashions for October' in *Cassell's Magazine*, 1891. The figure on the left wears the sort of tailored costume Adolph Kushner would have helped make. The figure on the right wears the softer sort of garments Mrs Pattinson would have made for Mrs Fenton, and they both wear elaborate hats like the one described in Mrs Fenton's letter.

20. Tailoring workshop in the East End, 1910–14. Adolph Kushner would have spent much of his working life in conditions like this. With the coming of the sewing machine, tailors no longer sat cross-legged at their work as they had earlier in the century. (Courtesy of the Jewish Museum, London)

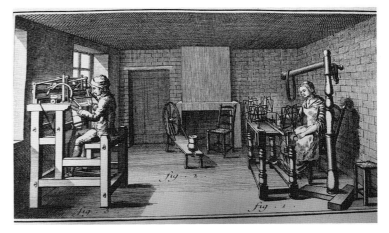

21. Framework knitter and woman winding thread from Diderot's *Encyclopaedia*, 1751–1780. Joseph Burdett and Joseph Moss would have used machines very similar to this one, though the rooms they worked in would have been much more cramped.

22. Church Street, Lambley. Note the large upstairs windows to light the knitting frames. (Courtesy of PictureThePast)

23. Brampton Bryan *bron* or horse fair in 1906. James Edwards's cottage, with its postbox and large shop windows, is in the centre of the picture. It would have looked very little different when he lived there. (Courtesy of Leintwardine Local History Society)

24. James Edward's workshop as it was when it was opened up in 1961. It had lain undisturbed since 1924 when James's son, Arthur, died. (Courtesy of Herefordshire Archive Service)

Above left: 25. Photograph of George Odger. After his death, £30 was raised for his family from sales of signed photographs like this one. (Private collection)

Above right: 26. Cartoon relating to Odger's attempts to enter Parliament. (Private collection)

Right: 27. Another. (Courtesy of Plymouth City Council Arts and Record Service)

28. James and Sarah
Symington, *c*. 1850. (Courtesy
of Leicestershire County
Council Environment and
Heritage Services)

29. Robert Symington in his
Volunteer uniform. (Courtesy
of Leicestershire County
Council Environment and
Heritage Services)

30. Perry Gold Symington.
(Courtesy of Leicestershire
County Council Environment and
Heritage Services)

31. William Henry Symington.
(Courtesy of Leicestershire
County Council Environment and
Heritage Services)

32. Two corsets – an embroidered black corset of 1880–90, and the 'Pretty Housemaid', the design of which was registered in 1886, becoming one of Symington's best sellers. (Courtesy of Leicestershire County Council Environment and Heritage Services)

Above: 33. Ida Allen at the door of her
lace shop in the 1930s. (Courtesy of
Norman Lambert)

Right: 34. Mrs Woodgate Low, aged 82,
making Honiton lace on a lace pillow.
(Courtesy of Norman Lambert)

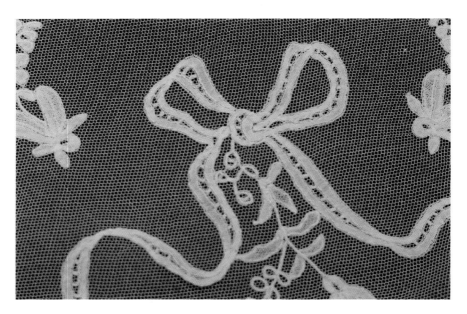

35. Detail of a Honiton lace veil sold by Mrs Ida Allen. Each motif was made separately and stitched to a base of machine-made net. The sprigs are neatly made, but use only the most basic stitches, while the net has not been cut away behind the open parts of the design – so this is not a particularly high-quality piece. (Courtesy of Allhallows Museum, Honiton)

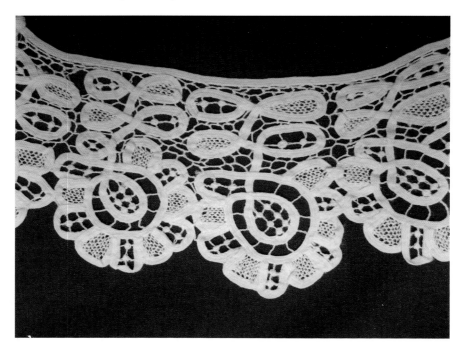

36. Sample of Branscombe Point lace, the type of needle-made lace described in 'Primrose's' competition essay. (Courtesy of Allhallows Museum, Honiton)

thrown to the ground, and one of the assailants bit his fingers to make him drop the money he was clutching in his hand; he lost six or seven shillings, possibly his entire week's wages. Joseph Abrahams received a black eye but did not lose any money, and it seems Adolph and Isaac Fleishman got away shaken but unharmed.

Joseph Jones, Isaac Goldstein and David Alexander appeared in court two weeks later; Joseph Jones, the only non-Jewish member of the group, was acquitted, the other two were referred to Crown Court. 'Beyond the getting money by menaces, there did not appear in the evidence, any other motive for the strange proceeding; but the Magistrate said he should send the case to a jury, and leave the mystery of it to be unravelled there,' the *Standard* reported on 18 October. To modern eyes, there does not seem to be any mystery – when times are hard and people are desperate some will resort to crime – but language may have been part of the problem. The newspaper report explained that, as both prosecutors and defendants were Jewish, most of the case was conducted through interpreters. It would seem Adolph still had not learnt much English.

In the spring of the following year he remarried. His new wife was Rosa Sweet, and she had lived just across the road from him in Anthony Street in Mile End Old Town, where he must have moved some time after the incident in Booth Street. People in the East End were constantly on the move from one set of rented premises to another according to the fluctuations in their wages, or because they were evicted from properties when they were unable to keep up with the rent or when a more desirable tenant appeared on the scene. At the time of the marriage Rosa gave her age as twenty-one, perhaps for legal reasons, for if the later records are to be believed she was in fact only eighteen. From the marriage certificate we learn that her father was called Woolf Sweet and that Adolph's father was Gershon Kushner, but both men were dead and the column for 'rank or profession of father' is blank in both cases – perhaps neither of them remembered their fathers. The couple married at the East London Synagogue on 17 March 1895 and the marriage certificate gives us one other snippet of information: both Adolph and Rosa were illiterate and signed the certificate with a cross.

Rosa must have got pregnant almost immediately for, by census time in 1901, she and Adolph had a six-year-old son, Aaron, known as Harry, and a baby girl, Annie. By then they were sharing 4 Garden Street in Mile End Old Town with another young couple, Simon and Melia Reece, and their baby daughter. Despite their English-sounding names, Simon came from Russia and Melia from Germany. Adolph's brother, Barnet, was also part of the household. His age is given as thirty-two, like Adolph's, so they may even have been twins. Barnet was a gentleman's tailor but, whereas Adolf described himself as a 'workman', Barnet claimed to be an 'employer'.[15]

So what was their life like? We do not have Adolph and Rosa's own accounts of life in London's East End, but there are many other sources of information. Conditions were grim. As early as 1885 the *Report of the East End Enquiry Commission of the Council of the United Synagogue* found 'At present, the houses occupied by the Jewish poor ... are for the most part barely fit, and many utterly unfit, for human habitation ...'. Conditions worsened as more and more refugees crowded into the area, and the family that had a room to themselves, let alone an apartment, was considered fortunate. Men like Adolph left their damp, dilapidated, bug-infested, overcrowded homes to work in equally desperate conditions. In 1893 the factory inspectors reported that over a third of the tailoring workshops in Mile End Old Town – where Adolph spent much of his working life – offered less than the 200 cubic feet of space per worker that the law required. Surviving photographs show workers crammed together in windowless rooms with flaking plaster – and presumably these images were arranged to show the workshops at their best (see plate 20)! We do not know whether Adolph joined the mantle-makers' union, which was established in 1890, or whether he ever participated in strike action to improve conditions; there were strikes in the East End in 1896 and 1912, largely orchestrated by the Jewish clothing workers.

Despite the best efforts of the unions, Adolph would have worked long hours – eight in the morning to six at night were the set times but working through the night to finish an order was still commonplace. The proprietor of the workshop that the Free School boys visited in 1911 was careful to explain the regulations about how much overtime individuals were allowed to do and to show them the charts and rotas – but the reality in many smaller workshops was very different. In an overcrowded labour market, employers had the whip hand and workers feared for their jobs if they did not do as they were told, regardless of the risks to their health. Exhausted men working in rooms steamy from the pressers' irons, with no air conditioning and poor lighting, had frequent minor accidents with their machines.[16] Things would have improved slightly after the establishment of the Trade Boards in 1909, which, in theory, regulated wages in the sweated trades; however, for most of his working life Adolph would have worked hard and long for low wages, and his lack of English made him particularly vulnerable to exploitation.

However, the great advantage for Adolph and Rosa was that they were living among their own people. The East End – at least until the Second World War – was almost a foreign country. Zangwill[17] describes people in the streets:

[The men were] strange, stunted, swarthy, hairy creatures, with muddy complexions illumined by black, twinkling eyes. A few were of imposing stature, wearing coarse, dusty felt hats or peaked caps, with shaggy beards or faded scarfs around their throats. Here and there, too, was a woman of comely face and figure, but for the most part it was a collection of crones, prematurely aged, with weird, wan, old-world features, slip-shod and draggle-tailed, their heads bare, or covered with dingy shawls in lieu of bonnets — red shawls, grey shawls, brick-dust shawls, mud-coloured shawls. Yet there was an indefinable touch of romance and pathos about the tawdriness ... The majority wore cheap earrings and black wigs with preternaturally polished hair.

Shops catered for the tastes and needs of Jews from all over Europe, and there were gentile bakers who would cook the Sabbath meals overnight on Friday so they were ready to eat the following day. Friday afternoons before sundown, the official start of the Sabbath, saw women scurrying through the streets to the bakers, carrying joints and large pots of *cholent* (stew). The Jewish calendar was full of fast days and feast days – the fasts were easier for the poor to celebrate than the feasts, though no doubt Rosa Kushner did her best.

> *Seder* [Passover] night was a charmed time. The strange symbolic dishes – the bitter herbs and the sweet mixture of apples, almonds, spices and wine, the roasted bone and the lamb, the salt water and the four cups of raisin wine, the great round unleavened cakes with their mottled surfaces, some specially thick and sacred, the special Hebrew melodies and verses with their jingle of rhymes and assonances, the quaint ceremonial with its striking moments, as when the finger was dipped in the wine and the drops sprinkled over the shoulder in repudiation of the ten plagues of Egypt cabalistically magnified to two hundred and fifty ...[18]

Did Rosa and Adolph manage to afford meals like this and the special set of dishes that each household was supposed to set aside for use at Passover? If they did, it is probable those dishes spent much of the year in pawn.

When Adolph arrived in the East End there was a *chevra* (small synagogue, usually in a private house) on every street corner. Zangwill describes one of these little *chevras* and captures beautifully the appeal of religion to people whose lives were drab and colourless:

> ...[T]wo large rooms knocked into one, and the rear partitioned off for the use of the bewigged, heavy-jawed women who might not sit with the men lest they should fascinate their thoughts away from

things spiritual. Its furniture was bare benches, a raised platform with a reading desk in the centre and a wooden curtained ark at the end containing two parchment scrolls of the Law, each with a silver pointer and silver bells and pomegranates ... The room was badly ventilated and what little air there was was generally sucked up by a greedy company of wax candles, big and little, stuck in brass holders ... [the worshippers] dropped in, mostly in their work-a-day garments and grime, and rumbled and roared and chorused prayers with a zeal that shook the window-panes, and there was never lack of *minyan* – the congregational quorum of ten ... They prayed metaphysics, acrostics, angelology, Cabalah, history, exegetics, Talmudical controversies, menus, recipes, priestly prescriptions, the canonical books, psalms, love-poems, an undigested hotch-potch of exalted and questionable sentiments ... It was a wonderful liturgy, as grotesque as it was beautiful ... Their religious consciousness was largely a musical box – the thrill of the ram's horn, the cadenza of psalmic phrase, the jubilance of a festival 'Amen' and the sobriety of a work-a-day 'Amen', the Passover melodies and the Pentecost, ... all this was known and loved and was far more important than the meaning of it all or its relation to their real lives ... if they did not always know what they were saying they always meant it ...[19]

The East End of the 1880s and 1890s[20] had Yiddish newspapers, concert halls, and ritual bath houses; there was even a theatre – the Temple on Commercial Road – that put on plays in Yiddish. Cantors came all the way from Germany and Poland to perform to huge open-air audiences. There was the Jewish Free School that had been founded in 1817 and was for many years the largest school in Europe, with over a thousand pupils. There was also a range of *heders*, or religious schools. Even the local board schools catered to their Jewish pupils, observing all the Jewish festivals and allowing the boys to leave early on Friday afternoons in winter when the Sabbath began before the official end of the school day.[21] There were Jewish maternity homes and clinics, *mohelim* who would circumcise baby boys, and corpse-watchers who would help busy families observe the lengthy rituals for mourning the dead. From 1919 there was a Jewish hospital providing *kosher* meals and an environment sensitive to Jewish practice. A range of societies sprang up to enable the wealthier members of the community to support their poorer neighbours – *tzedekah*, charity towards the poor, is one of the duties of the observant Jew. In theory at least, the community supported its destitute members; there were soup kitchens where they could eat and clothing exchanges where they could find presentable clothes. However, as Adolph and Ella discovered in 1892, practice did not always match theory.

The Jewish Board of Guardians was founded in 1859 and had offices in Middlesex Street off Petticoat Lane. The workhouse did not cater for Jewish dietary and religious needs, so the Jewish Board of Guardians created their own form of welfare. It was based on loans of items like sewing machines, which would enable people to earn a living, not cash, and concentrated particularly on providing education and apprenticeships for poor children. The numbers they supported were comparatively small and the Guardians were always short of money and very selective about who they would help. In court in 1892, Adolph explained that he had not applied to the Guardians himself when his child was ill because he had approached them the previous year when he was out of work and been refused help because he was young and fit. Poverty was endemic. In 1883 Joseph Jacobs's survey in the *Jewish Chronicle* found that 25 per cent of the East End population survived on under £50 a year – less than the regular £1 a week that was seen to be the respectable minimum wage for a working-class family throughout the nineteenth century. However, to set this in context, Samuel Attwood in Basingstoke, working for the family firm, seldom made more than 15s a week, though admittedly he had a house and garden, kept pigs and had various money-making sidelines.

Presiding over all these Jewish groups and organisations was Beth Din (the House of Judgement) on Mulberry Street, which ruled on all things Jewish – which foods were and were not *kosher*, the correct rituals for slaughtering animals, the licensing of *mohelim* (circumcisers) and *mikveh* (ritual baths), mourning and burial practices, whether or not an individual could call themselves Jewish, how state legislation might affect religious practice and a whole host of other issues. Alongside it was Beth Midrash (the House of Study), a hall and library devoted to intense study of the Torah. We do not know how observant Adolph was, or to which sect he belonged, but if he cared about such things he would have known his religious welfare was in the safe hands of dedicated scholars. For Adolph and Rosa, for all its privations, life in the East End was more secure than the life they had known in Russia – and a good deal less foreign than they might have feared.

By 1911 the Kashners, as they were calling themselves by then, were living at 183 Fieldgate Mansions. Harry was fifteen and the couple had another son, one-year-old Louis. Little Annie, their second child, had died as a toddler and there seem to have been several other children who died in infancy – the infant mortality rate in the East End of London was shockingly high in this period. A third son, Saunder, was born in December 1914. After years in down-at-heel tenement blocks, Fieldgate Mansions was definitely a step up. It was built in 1906, initially as a private venture, but it was soon taken over by the LCC and was a series of huge, four-storey, brick blocks of purpose-built flats with running water and indoor sanitation. Over time they degenerated into slums and, by the 1970s, they were scheduled for demolition,[22] but in 1911 they were still modern homes. The Kashners must have been reasonably happy there for they were still at Fieldgate Mansions in 1939.

It is likely that it was Harry who filled in the 1911 census form – the first census completed by the householder rather than by a visiting enumerator – and he described himself as a 'ladies' tailor' like his father. Harry would have gone to school so, unlike his parents, he was literate in English. He does not appear in the registers of the Jewish Free School, so he probably went to one – or a series – of local board schools. He would have started work as a 'shop boy' at the age of eleven or twelve, delivering great piles of finished garments to the firms that had ordered them, and would have moved on to various other jobs as he got older. He was still a teenager when England went to war. It seems that Harry was in no rush to join the army, but he did sign up at the end of February 1916, aged twenty; however, six months later he was discharged as 'unlikely to become efficient' because of heart problems. Not only did those problems probably save his life, but he was also given a grant of £20 in lieu of a pension[23] – a huge sum for a family like the Kashners – and went back to what he knew: ladies' tailoring. Like his father, Harry became a tailor's baster. He married in 1920 and his wife Ida – or Ada – Greengross was a hat machinist. They had two children, Betty and Louis; a third child, Martin, died in infancy. Harry's heart defect does not seem to have shortened his life, as he lived to be nearly eighty and had two wives.

Adolph and Rosa's second son, Louis, also became a ladies' tailor. In 1933 he married Beatrice Joseph and they had a son. In 1939 they were living at Rectory Road, Hackney, and Saunder, the youngest Kashner brother, was staying with them, working as a 'ladies' machinist'. He had married Lily Chaytow in 1938 and they had two daughters. Adolph's sons were among the last generation of Jews to go into the tailoring trades as workers. In the 1930s roughly a quarter of the Jews in England worked in the clothing trades – when Adolph arrived in London, the figure was nearer 60 per cent[24]. However, by the 1970s, although there were Jewish-owned clothing businesses (some like Moss Bros, Montagu Burton and Cecil Gee became household names), most parents who had themselves been garment workers had higher ambitions for their own children. Menial jobs in the clothing trades became the preserve of the next wave of refugees, Bangladeshis and Pakistanis.

'Kashner' was suspiciously foreign-sounding, and a name of Germanic origin was a grave disadvantage in 1914–18; however, at that stage none of the family chose to change it, though many East European Jews did find it expedient to change their names to something that sounded English and was easy to say and spell. However, during the Second World War, Louis changed his name from 'Kashner' to 'Kaye', perhaps in a bid to avoid internment as an enemy alien; when Adolph died in 1947 of diabetic gangrene in his right foot, in Hackney Hospital at the ripe old age of seventy-eight, it was 'L. Kaye, Son' who signed the death certificate.[25] That death certificate also tells us that by then Adolph and Rosa had left Fieldgate Mansions and moved to Navarino Mansions, where Harry and his family lived – although by then, Ida, their daughter-in-law, was dead, killed in the Blitz in 1941. Navarino Mansions was a group of four huge brick apartment blocks that had been erected by the Four Percent Industrial Dwellings Company, a philanthropic association started by Lord Rothschild to build homes for artisans. It kept rents low by capping shareholder profits at four per cent as the rather cumbersome name of the organisation implies.[26] By contrast, rents in Fieldgate Mansions had risen dramatically, which may be one of the reasons why Adolph and Rosa decided to leave. In fact in 1939 sixty-four of the tenants in their old buildings staged a rent strike, which lasted twenty weeks and eventually succeeded in getting the rents reduced by up to 3s 0d a week.[27]

Neither Rosa nor Adolph ever became naturalised citizens of their adopted country, though they spent nearly fifty years in the East End, enduring two world wars and seeing the area change out of all recognition. Rosa outlived her husband by some twenty years and died of pneumonia in 1967 in Wandsworth, while staying with her son Louis. She was eighty-eight and was survived by her three English sons and five English grandchildren. The Cushneers and the Sweets from the Russian Pale of Settlement had been completely assimilated, their history all but forgotten.

PART 3

OTHER TRADES

The Two Josephs: Joseph Burdett (*c.* 1796–) and Joseph Moss (1798–1881), Stockingers, Lambley, Nottinghamshire

Joseph could hear branches snapping in the orchard and he knew all too well what his stepfather was doing. He was fashioning something with which to thrash Joseph – 'I'll larn thee ter go off and leave me by mysel' in future,' the old man had hollered when he caught sight of his stepson that morning. Young Joseph Burdett had endured his stepfather's beatings before and he had no intention of staying around for another one. He turned on his heel and ran as far and as fast as his legs would carry him.[1]

He'd been expecting trouble. He knew he should never have gone off the previous afternoon – but excitement had got the better of him. A group of village lads were walking into Nottingham to watch Mr Sadler fly his balloon; they'd urged Joseph to join them and before he knew where he was it was too late to turn back. It was a beautiful bright day for November and, though none of the boys could afford the five-shilling charge to get into the main arena, there was a good view from the Meadows. A crowd had assembled there and they all watched the scarlet-and-white balloon float up into the sky, 'splendidly and majestically'. It flew 'right over the thousands that were feasting their eyes to see it amidst the most deafening shouts and clapping of hands as it is possible ... to describe.' It was Mr Sadler's twenty-eighth ascent, but for most of the watching crowd it was hugely exciting, the first time they had ever seen a human being airborne. The ascent started at 2.30 p.m. and the balloon was visible for over half-an-hour, drifting slowly north-west. It would eventually come down near Grantham.[2]

As it disappeared from sight, Joseph began to realise the enormity of what he had done and the probable consequences. He headed into Nottingham and wandered round for an hour or two, looking in shop windows at things he could never afford to buy, and putting off the inevitable confrontation with his stepfather; but it was November, and as darkness fell it grew cold, and Joseph was hungry. There was nothing for it but to go home and face the music. He arrived back in New Radford at about 8.30 p.m. only to find his punishment had begun. The house was locked, his parents had deliberately gone to bed early and he did not dare knock and wake them; but he was in luck, as a neighbour, Mrs Hicklin, took pity on him and let him sleep with her sons. She had no food to spare, however, so he went to bed supper-less. He had hoped that his stepfather would see that as punishment enough, which was why he had tried to sneak into work unnoticed the following morning, but clearly he had miscalculated. He does not tell us what that work was, but it was in the neighbouring village of Bilborough, probably on a farm.

However, Joseph had a plan. This was not a one-off incident; life at home had been miserable ever since his stepfather came into his life and his mother seemed unable or unwilling to defend her son. Joseph determined to head for Newarke and appeal to the overseers for a place in the workhouse. In 1813 the workhouse was not the dreaded institution it would become after 1834, when the government in its wisdom decreed that the only way to deter the poor from becoming a charge on the community was to make life in the workhouse as wretched and humiliating as possible. Nevertheless, few people would have preferred the workhouse to home. Joseph was desperate.

He retraced his steps towards New Radford but left the road and cut across the fields from the windmill to avoid his mother seeing him. He reached Newarke at four that afternoon and went to the Pack Horse, where he knew the overseer would be. We do not know what story he told – perhaps he bore scars of previous beatings, perhaps his brutal stepfather was already known to the authorities – whatever the reason, the overseers were happy to admit him. The master and his wife gave him a good meal of bread and cheese and beer, a clean bed, and a few days later he was set to work in Seale and Bamford's bleach yard. Joseph acknowledged that it was cold, wet work, but 'our masters was good tempered' and he was delighted to discover how short his working day was: 8 a.m. to dusk, which in November would have been about 4.30 p.m. The master of the workhouse and his wife were Mr and Mrs Taylor, and they seem to have run a surprisingly benign establishment. Joseph's account suggests that for a time he was actually happy: 'I was never so comfortable before,' he wrote. He went to Sunday school and in the evenings after work the inmates sat together telling stories and singing – it seems Joseph had a fine singing voice. He tells us that 'there were no wants and scants' and that 'the inmates were all cheerful and happy.'

His mother did go looking for him, checking with the local recruiting sergeants to see whether he had enlisted; this was the period of the Napoleonic wars and the army was constantly on the lookout for fresh cannon fodder. However, having ascertained that he was safe and well in the workhouse, she seems to have been content to leave him where he was, out of her husband's way. We do not know when Joseph was born, but he was probably about fourteen or fifteen at this point and it was the overseers' duty to give him a future. Joseph remained in the workhouse for almost two months but, immediately after Christmas, he and three other boys were summoned to the master's office.

Two men, master stockingers from Lambley, wanted prentices. They gave a very flattering account of the trade prospects so at last two of us agreed to go and the next day, December 27th 1813, we was bound prentice. The masters gave us lads me and my mate a shilling apiece for good luck before we started. My master's name was Arthur Kirk. I understood the premium to be three pounds ten shillings each, and two suits of clothes. We reached Lambley about ten o'clock. I went to bed with the other prentice who had been there about a year, he asked me if I was bound, I said 'Yes', then says he 'You will repent it'. I was afraid I should for I did not like the looks of anything about the place.

Joseph was right to have misgivings. In the eighteenth century, stockingers had earned good money: in 1714 the average wage in the hosiery trade in Nottingham was 10*s* 6*d* for a four-day week, and the makers of fancy silk stockings could earn double that. The masters probably still hoped those days would return, and so their 'flattering account of the trade' was perhaps optimistic rather than deliberately untruthful.[3]

However, as early as 1778 the knitters had petitioned Parliament for a Bill to regulate their wages because hosiery prices were going down. Part of the problem was the development in 1776 of wide knitting frames, which used more needles in a row than the earlier ones. Whereas the narrow frames created a ready-shaped piece of knitting for making into a garment, the wider frames produced a breadth of knitted fabric out of which garments could be cut ready for making up – these were known as 'cut-ups'. The wide frames were easier and quicker to operate, so the workers who used them were paid less than the knitters using traditional narrow frames. From the masters' point of view, this was clearly the most economical method of production, but the workers were understandably aggrieved to see their standard of living fall (see plate 21).

In commencing to learn the art and mysteries of making stockings I was given to understand that I should have to earn ten shillings per week in a 24 gauge frame for my master and all I earned

more than that I should receive for pocket money. I understood
my indentures to say that the master should provide me with
food, lodging and clothing till I was 21 years of age, and with this
engagement I commenced on the 3rd of January 1814 with a firm
determination to fulfil the same. I therefore began to work and the
progress I made far exceeded all expectations for I learned my task
in nine weeks from commencement, a thing quite unprecedented in
the village.

Joseph was justifiably proud of his achievement. The terms of his
apprenticeship were still quite generous – his master would make
10*s* a week out of the boy and Joseph would make around 6*d* for
himself – though he tells us that for every shilling of his own that
he earned he had to pay 1*d* for 'seaming' (making up), which was a
separate trade and was usually women's work.

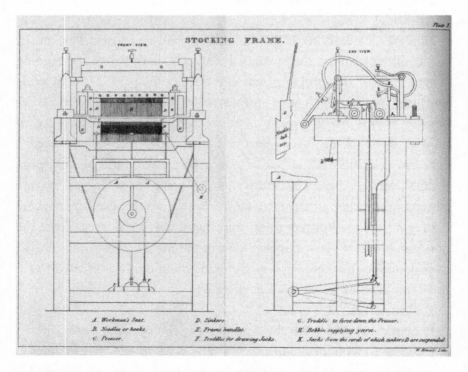

Diagram of a knitting machine from Felkin's *History of the Manufactures of
Machine-wrought Hosiery and Lace*, 1867.

However, by the time Joseph was apprenticed, the hosiery business really was in decline. The trade was over-subscribed; four-day weeks were a thing of the past; and the wholesale buyers were paying less and less. Things would get steadily worse throughout his career – but, in 1814, Joseph was still hopeful:

> I also began to get overwork and after I had worked several weeks I expected he, the master, would reckon with me and pay me up. He did give me the shilling at the nine weeks end but what I got after I had to wait for. As for reckoning, he could not reckon with anybody only by thought. He kept no books for he could not even write his own name as he was no scholar at all. But he could drive a bargain. He was possessed of that shrewd low cunning and selfishness which made him very clever in his own estimation ...

Another problem was that Mr Kirk was a farmer as well as a stockinger and the boys were expected to help on the farm at busy times. In fact, on his first morning Joseph was sent off at the crack of dawn with the maidservant to walk a mile through ice and snow to learn to milk the cows. Arthur Kirk was apparently well-known for his skill as a cattle farmer, but the boys also had to help with the hay and corn harvests and to go to market with him to sell his pigs. All this ate into the time they could spend at their frames and meant that some weeks they were unable to make their ten shillings' worth of stockings, let alone earn anything for themselves.

Joseph's poor impression of Lambley was probably influenced by the weather. In fact, it was a pleasant enough village with around a thousand inhabitants, set in a deep valley and surrounded by fine agricultural land. There were a number of large farms but the majority of the villagers were framework knitters and many of the cottages had enlarged windows to light the frames (see plate 22). They were served by five pubs, and two windmills ground flour from the grain produced on the farms. There was an area of woodland known as the Dumbles, where cowslips grew in abundance each spring, and people flocked from miles around to gather them to make wine. The village was also noted for the fine quality of its water; there was a spring opposite the Robin Hood that was said never to have run dry.[4]

But that first winter the ice and snow lasted for fourteen weeks and, when the thaw came, around Easter, the cracking of the ice on the Trent was so loud that Joseph said it sounded like gunfire. Easter also brought the boys' first holiday. Arrangements had been made when they were apprenticed that they would return to Newarke for a few days to see Mr Taylor and tell him how they were getting on; another indication that life in the workhouse before the 1834 Act was quite a pleasant affair. They enjoyed themselves hugely and returned to Lambley in high spirits to a sheep roast and celebrations for Wellington's victory over Marshal Soult at the Battle of Toulouse on 10 April.

At some point – Joseph does not tell us how or when – he got back in touch with his family. He records gifts of clothes, taking garments home to be mended and what sound like fairly civil conversations with his stepfather about things that happened in the village. Things were looking up and might even have been good 'if we had had a more punctul [sic] master and more plentiful rations'. In fact it is questionable whether Arthur Kirk would ever have been a good master but, as his profits declined, he did less and less to fulfil his obligations to his apprentices. The new clothes he was supposed to provide never materialised and the boys were ill-fed. There was a bad harvest in 1816 and for months most of the poor had only barley bread to eat 'and we apprentices [were] very short of that,' Joseph wrote grimly. The boys were 'wearing our clothes out and getting no new ones' – and no doubt, as teenagers do, they were also growing, though when the recruiting sergeant came to Lambley in the spring of 1815 both James and Joseph considered joining up but found they were not tall enough.

Joseph may well have known of the activities of the 'Luddites' a few years earlier, but he was then only a child and probably barely understood what it was all about. The situation was this. In March

1811 the framework knitters had made a desperate attempt to negotiate higher wages and force the hosiers stop using cut-ups – but their arguments were futile because the masters were never going to abandon a system that was so much to their economic advantage. As talks failed, groups from across the county gathered in Nottingham's marketplace. In response, 12,000 soldiers were brought in to control the situation in the town, but they were unable to prevent widespread destruction elsewhere. Sixty-three frames were smashed at Arnold (north-east of Nottingham and very near Lambley) and, over the following three weeks, 200 frames were destroyed across the county. In total, over 800 frames were destroyed in Nottinghamshire in the course of 1811/12 and the riots spread to the neighbouring counties of Derbyshire and Leicestershire.[5] Things had quietened down by the time Joseph's apprenticeship indentures were signed at the end of 1813, but they would not remain peaceful for long.

Payment for the work that Joseph, James Peat and Jacob (we never learn his full name), his fellow apprentices, had done for themselves was constantly deferred. 'Masters in the town, as a general rule, settled with their hands every week but ours was a continuous running account and nothing said about it,' Joseph grumbled. A series of meaningless chalk marks on the pantry door were supposed to record what they were owed, though the boys themselves had calculated their earnings to the last halfpenny. They were always told they would be paid next time Kirk went to Nottingham, but they never were; they were simply given a few pence from time to time 'on account'. Their master was also aggressive, particularly when they came back from time away, 'and would sometimes lunge us very severely and we did not know what for'.

Eventually, James Peat ran away and got work at Shepshed in Leicestershire, but he was brought back after a few weeks. Mr Kirk seems to have pursued him himself without recourse to the parish constable. A few weeks later Joseph himself ran away – the catalyst seems to have been that he asked Kirk for his money, which by this point added up to 15s, and was given 4d to be going on with. Three other local apprentices went with him, even though Joseph's 4*d* was all the cash they had between them. Setting off into the blue with no money and no food, relying on luck and the kindness of strangers, seems to have been very much part of working-class life. They slept in barns; people took pity on them and shared meals with them; and they earned the odd penny or two by helping passers-by. One of Joseph's three runaway companions earned 2*d* by helping an old gentleman carry his disobedient dog, for example. The money was spent on bread to share.

It is not clear how long the four boys were on the run, but Joseph describes how they would accost men going to work and ask where they were; there would have been few milestones or signs. They had no clear sense of where they were headed, and he lists Codnor, Swanwick, Pentridge, Alfreton, South Wingfield and Nessington as places they visited in search of work. Eventually they found themselves at Whitwick in Leicestershire. Joseph found work there for a time 'and was quite content'; he does not tell us what happened to his three friends. Somehow, Arthur Kirk discovered where he was and came to collect him – news of boys on the run seems to have been quite easy to come by – and took him back to Lambley. Again, there seem to have been no real recriminations. It almost seems to have been accepted that hosier's apprentices would run away from time to time.

However, Joseph's story takes an unexpected twist at this point, for the mother who would not protect her son from her violent husband was quite happy to step in and remonstrate with Arthur Kirk about his non-payment of Joseph's wages, 'which was very unpalatable to his dignity'. She intervened to good effect, for Joseph was paid 13*s* 8*d* and James Peat also got the money owing to him, 'which he [Kirk] paid like a man in the public house sign of Sir John Warren, Milk Street, Nottingham.' In fact, as Joseph recorded with some surprise, his parents and his master seem to have become good friends. This was obviously to his advantage, though his descriptions of his master remain uncomplimentary: 'Arthur Kirk was a fussy bragart [sic], [a] crafty and consequential sort of man, very domineering to those under him, but rude and vulgar in respectable company'.

The latter part of Joseph's memoir is devoted to the frame breaking and lawlessness, which began anew with an attack on the lacemaking factory of Heathcote and Boden in Loughborough on 28 June 1816; it resulted in £6,000 worth of damage. The rioting soon spread. 'When Ned Lud first began to break frames in 1811 there were some people thought the hosiers really did oppress their workpeople. Hosiers, some of them getting enormously rich while the workpeople were starving,' Joseph admitted, but he saw the Luddites of 1816/7 as a different breed. Not only did they damage frames, they attacked people who got in their way, and stole, plundered and damaged property. Joseph had first-hand experience of such men.

On Saturday October 12th 1816 we three apprentices went to bed about ten o'clock. Soon after midnight we was woke by some people coming up the road making a great noise we thought at first it was the club men coming home rather fresh and merry.

But next I heard a very gruff voice shout or rather growl 'Open the door, we are come to break all Rodgers and Shaws Frames.' The master we could hear was at the window and he answered and said 'We have none of Rodgers and Shaws Frames here, sir.' 'Oh be damned you've summat' he growled again, others we could hear was flocking up the steps to their door. One of them said, very sharp, 'Break it open! Break it open!' The hammer man then gave two blows and the door flew open. 'Bring the light', growled the growler, he it appeared was coming toward the shop door which was but a few feet from the house door, the others was flocking into the house. The master kept shouting but one of them fired a pistol upstairs and the master spoke no more. There was two of them breaking the frames and while they was doing that the others were plundering the house. They took all the groceries, some pots of preserves, stripped the clothes lines so that we had no clean linen for Sunday.

They then went to Needham's and destroyed eight frames, there they also stole a pair of men's new boots and a great many other articles. Then they went to Mr Robert Godber's and soon destroyed seven frames and stole a guinea hat with lots of other valuables.

Many of the men, Joseph tells us, had been involved in other incidents. He lists a number of them by name. 'Big Sam', for example, got into a fracas with Dick Green, the local gamekeeper, in which Dick lost an eye. John Blackbourn was one of twenty men from Basford who attacked Mr Cook, Lord Middleton's gamekeeper. Fights between gamekeepers and desperate men poaching game were not uncommon – but the Basford men crossed the line. Cook was at home minding his own business, when they broke in, robbed him and beat him up. It was not self-defence but an unprovoked attack on someone they perceived as the enemy, a lackey of his wealthy employer. David Diggle seems to have been the ringleader and was hanged, but Lord Middleton stepped in to plead clemency for the others. Joseph obviously felt he was misguided, for he goes on to tell us at length about other crimes the men committed; two of them were later transported, the one for attacking and robbing the Loughborough carrier, the other for shooting pheasants. Violence, lawlessness and draconian punishments were very much part of working-class life when Joseph was a boy.

Joseph Burdett is a lively informant, but unfortunately we know almost nothing about him. His *Reminiscences of a Journeyman Stockinger* come in the form of a typed manuscript donated to the Nottingham Archive in 1985 by J. Bugg and allegedly created from some photocopies of original documents that were lent to him. There is nothing in the document to suggest it is a forgery – it is not of sufficient importance to warrant that interpretation – and no doubt for some reason the person who lent the papers wanted to protect the anonymity of the owner of the originals, but the lack of information about the source does call it into question.

It is therefore to our second Joseph that we will turn for corroboration. He was Joseph Moss, born in Boston in Lincolnshire in 1798, and he too found himself in Lambley as a stockinger's apprentice in 1817.[6] We know his family called him 'Joe' and, to avoid confusion, so will we. Joe Moss and Joseph Burdett would almost certainly have known each other and in later life both men seem to have felt the need to record their experiences. They had lived through turbulent times and both were very affected by the frame-breaking and lawlessness of 1816/17. While Joseph Burdett ends his record with a long account of those episodes and the men involved, Joe Moss begins with a description of them. The accounts differ slightly in detail and both differ in some ways from contemporary newspaper reports, but it is clear that for both men these were traumatic events, ones to be reflected on and remembered for years to come.

The outbreak of frame-breaking had various causes. Fashions were changing – in particular, men were beginning to wear trousers rather than knee breeches, and so no longer needed long stockings. Demand was less but, as a result of the stockingers' earlier prosperity, the trade had become over-subscribed, and over-supply drove prices down. A series of poor harvests caused the price of bread to rise, so men who had gone into the trade expecting to make a decent living now struggled to feed their families; and, on top of all that, the Napoleonic wars created a climate of fear and uncertainty.

On 1 April 1817 a group of men appeared in court in Leicester before Sir Richard Richards. John Blackbourn had shot John Asher, intending to murder him, in the course of breaking frames in his shop. Joe Moss lists Thomas Savidge, William Withers, John Amos, John Crowder, Joshua Mitchel, William Towle, James Watson, John Clark 'alias Little Sam' and Samuel Caldwell 'alias Big Sam', and all were charged with being accessories to the attempted murder. These may well have been the men Joe knew personally, for others were sentenced with them whom he does not name. The riots of 1811/12 had caught the judiciary by surprise and many of the rioters went unpunished; in the end just four of the ringleaders were sentenced to transportation to Australia. However, an Act was rushed through in 1812 making frame-breaking a capital offence; the second wave of Luddites were taking much greater risks than had their predecessors.

'Big Sam' was a good deal less brave in court than he had been when he and his cronies were assaulting gamekeepers in the woods, and the trial was delayed for two hours because he seems to have had some sort of fit of nervous convulsions. We have no way of knowing whether he was really ill or whether it was a ploy to evade the gallows. The doctor was called, and he was bled and given restorative drinks – a parody of care for a man facing the hangman's noose. In the end, his case was deferred to the next Assizes. When the trial resumed, the accused were all sentenced to hang, together with two men named Barker and Gate, and Thomas Babbington, who was convicted of rick burning. Only Clark and Watson were eventually reprieved and a man named John Slater was transported to Australia for life. The newspapers tell us that they were all fit young men in their thirties and early forties, and several of them left wives and families. Joe Moss tells us that Thomas Savidge left six children; John Amos and John Crowder left five apiece; and William Towle and William Withers each had a wife and baby. Joseph Burdett tells us of others, some of whom were sentenced to death at Nottingham: they were Daniel Diggle, Jim Towle, Thomas Barker and Thomas Henfrey who came from Basford, Chris Blackbourn who came from the Burdett's home village of New Radford, and others who all came from Nottingham. Small wonder that the horror of seeing so many people they knew sentenced to hang or transported to the other side of the globe haunted the two Josephs for the rest of their lives.

The newspapers tell of other episodes, but they do not seem to have impinged on Joe and he does not mention them. 'The people of Lambley were now in hope that all Luding was at an end', he wrote of the period after the trials, and 'The people in general was sorry that a lot of young men should come to such an untimely end.'

For his own part Joe seems to have had little sympathy with the Luddites. Their activities were 'a great drawback and a hindrance' and 'It was a very bad job for the hands having to toil very hard to get the frames to work again,' while the most seriously damaged frames had to go to frame-smiths in Nottingham to be rebuilt, which could take several weeks. Like Joseph Burdett, Joe had personal experience of the Luddites' handiwork; his own master's shop suffered £40 worth of damage.

Joe Moss is less outspoken in his criticism of his master than Joseph Burdett, but it is clear that things were not good. His big grievance was that he and his 'fellow prentice' – we never learn his name – had no new clothes and were so ragged that they were ashamed to go out. He seems to have been a religious young man, and feeling his clothes were too shabby for him to go to church caused him a good deal of distress. Perhaps because of this, he was attracted to 'the Ranters' – probably Methodists – who visited Lambley from time to time and preached in the streets. 'I took great delight in going to hear them myself although I was almost naked,' he wrote. The non-conformists often attracted people like Joe, who were too poor to have respectable clothes for church. They knew their audience and used 'language so simple it was irresistible' – unlike the preaching of many university-educated Anglican clergy – and they played on feelings of guilt. 'I became deeply convicted that I was a great sinner,' wrote Joe. He even claimed to have had a religious revelation as a result of the ranters' preaching, although he admitted the feeling did not last long: 'a spel [sic] came over me and all at once I felt peace and comfort to my soul and I wished every person in the world the same ... I have never been so happy since'.

He, too, seems to have been able to make money for himself over and above what he earned for his master, and he tells us proudly that, in 1817, despite business having been poor all summer, he managed to save enough to buy himself a new 'smockfrock'. It would probably have cost three or four shillings.[7] That August there was a meeting of framework knitters from 'the three counties' (Nottinghamshire,

Derbyshire and Leicestershire) and the workers agreed to go on strike. Frame-breaking had proved a dangerous strategy; they would now try withdrawing their labour. Joe was not happy but felt he had little option but to do as he was told. '[S]trict orders were given to the delegates at the meeting to see that the order was punctually carried out.' His master despatched his apprentices to go gleaning to earn their keep while the frames were idle, but the corn had not been carried away and the harvesters would not let them into the fields, so they returned home empty-handed. The master's wife was unimpressed. 'No work, no supper!' she decreed, so the young men went to bed hungry.

At this point Joe seems to have decided to use this time of enforced idleness to take an unofficial holiday. His own boots were worn out and he had been going barefoot, but his master had lent him a pair in which to go gleaning. They were several sizes too big but Joe decided they would have to do. He borrowed an old hat and set off, with just a halfpenny in his pocket, to 'have a Tramp to Boston' to see his family. He went through Southwell and Kelham to Newarke, where he stayed the night with his 'old friend' Mr Taylor. It may well be that this was Mr Taylor at the workhouse who had been so kind to Joseph Burdett, but we cannot be sure. The Taylors gave him food to take with him – like the runaway apprentices Joe had made no provision for his journey – and after breakfast he headed to Boston via Ledburn and Sleaford, arriving in Boston just as the church clock was striking eight, and made his way to his grandfather's house.

His aunts Jane and Fanny, cousin John and uncle Jim seem to have been delighted to see him; the family rallied round, came up with bundles of old clothes for him, including a second-hand suit and a tailor to alter it to fit, and his uncle even gave him some pocket money 'so that I was quite a new man'. Grandfather, however, seems to have been a grumpy old man who scarcely looked up from his newspaper to greet his prodigal grandson's arrival.

Working-class families could not afford idle guests and so, despite the old man's lack of enthusiasm, Joe was sent to work with his grandfather in 'the garden'. This was not the family's garden; it would seem that the old man was gardener to Thomas Fydell. The two Thomas Fydells, father and son, were MPs for Boston from 1790 to 1812, and they had a large property, with the abbey ruins in one corner. For a day or two Joe worked with his grandfather and 'gave satisfaction'; one gets the impression that it was grudgingly acknowledged. Then he volunteered to brick up a window in a building (part of the abbey ruins) where the old man kept rabbits and pigeons. Presumably these were for the table and it seems rather doubtful whether Thomas Fydell knew of this sideline; the rabbits must have been caged, but pigeons and gardens are not a good combination. Joe completed this task satisfactorily too, but then his grandfather set him to pick plums from a tree and advised him to shake it to dislodge the ones at the top. Joe obeyed his instructions rather too enthusiastically and broke a branch – he tells us it was quite a thin one. This was the excuse the old man had been looking for – 'he raved like somebody crazy' – and the rant went on and on. No doubt had Joe been smaller and younger he would have got a beating, but he was almost a grown man and his grandfather was elderly. Joe downed tools and left the garden.

When he got home he announced that he was not staying any longer and, though his uncle urged him not to go and told him he need not do any more work in the garden, Joe was adamant. Two days later, on Thursday 28 August, he set off for Lambley. He arrived back on the Saturday to find that, after three weeks, the strike was over and so – fortuitously for him – his master was delighted to have him back and made no comments about his unscheduled absence.

The strike had been a complete waste of time, for stockings were still paid for at the old rate. His master urged the boys to work at double speed to make up for lost time – but then, capriciously, took Joe away from his frame to go to Nottingham Goose Fair to help him sell his pigs. While Joseph Burdett's master specialised in cattle, Joe Moss's master was a pig farmer. 'I did not like it, so hindering to us,' Joe grumbled, but he had little option, and

reported proudly that, while his master went to the warehouse
to sell their stockings, he sold three pigs in the space of twenty
minutes – for which he got his 'old allowance'. We may deduce
that this was not very much, for a few days later Joe and the other
apprentice lay in bed 'talking of our grievanises [sic]' and Joe
made a decision. 'I shall Bolt on Monday Morning' and his friend
promised, 'I will not betray you.'

That is the last sentence at the bottom of the last page of the
hand-made exercise book in which the *Memoir* is written, so we do
not know what happened next. Did Joe Moss 'bolt'? Did his master
fetch him back? At the age of nineteen Joe must have been nearing
the end of his apprenticeship – perhaps they let him go. What we
do know is that, five years later, in March 1822, at Heanor in
Derbyshire, he married Mary Ratcliff, a fellow framework knitter.
The couple settled at nearby Smalley, some six miles north of Derby
on the Mansfield road, a village with around 600 inhabitants. It was
an industrial village, in that there were coal mines and an ironworks,
and many of the inhabitants were framework knitters like the
Mosses; there were 150 frames in the village in 1844.[8] Joe and Mary
had seven children there: Robert, born in 1823, then Elizabeth,
Mary (who died young), William, James, Fanny, Martha and Sarah.
Sometime in the late 1830s they moved down the road to Horsley
Woodhouse, where two more daughters, Sally and Georgiana, were
born in 1840 and 1844.

At some point in the mid-1850s it seems that Joseph Moss began
to keep a diary. The first entries are dated 1855 – that may well be
the date he wrote his memoir, and writing that may have decided
him to keep a further record. In any event, he carried on writing it
until 1881, the year of his death. Unfortunately for us, that diary
has not survived; we only know of it from a history of Smalley,
written by Charles Kerry and published in 1905. Charles Kerry was
a retired clergyman, a bachelor, who had been born in Smalley and
had retired there to die. He was born in 1834 and as a boy knew
Joe Moss – he tells us that Joe was a violinist, who often performed
at local events and had a fine singing voice. Joe's repertoire included

his own version of the 'Beggar's Rambler', with various local variations on the words – such snippets of information make us wish we knew more.

Sadly, the only quotations Charles Kerry uses from the diary relate to local events – the presentation of a subscription portrait to John Radford of Smalley Hall (21 October 1856), the theft of prayer books and vestments from the church (2 April 1857), the celebrations for Edward Dagge Sitwell's eightieth birthday at Stainsby House (28 February 1858) and his death two years later (21 July), and the deaths of various other notable people in the locality – including ninety-three-year-old Joseph Caley, a coal higgler, who had outlived six wives. He records Lord and Lady Palmerston passing through the village in a carriage-and-four (1 September 1862) and an ancient yew tree being blown down in a gale (19 February 1860), and spends a good deal of time describing the restoration of Horsley Church and the collapse of part of it in July 1858 during the rebuilding. Apparently this was due to the digging of a grave, which undermined the foundations: 'a loud shout was made, and the workmen had only just time to scamper out of the building before the roof and top windows and all came down.' It finally reopened on 11 September 1860, when 'A collation [was] served in the schoolroom afterwards – something after the fashion of electioneering: the wealthy and proud were filled with good things, but the humble and poor were sent empty away.' Joe may have recorded the doings of his wealthy neighbours but he was no sycophant.

There are only two entries recorded by Charles Kerry that are at all personal to Joe. On 28 March 1859, he wrote that 'The Glebe at Smalley was let out in allotments to industrious cottagers' to alleviate the desperate poverty many of the framework knitters were experiencing. By this point Joe himself was living in Horsley Woodhouse, but some of his children were back in Smalley – perhaps they were among the 'industrious cottagers'. On 20 December 1860 Joe wrote that he and 'Thomas Burgogne' provided the music at the Rose and Crown for the ball held to celebrate the christening of 'Thomas Bateman's son and heir'. This was Frederick Osborne

Fitzherbert Bateman, son of Thomas Osborne Bateman of Hartington Hall, Deputy Lieutenant of Derbyshire.

It would be fascinating to know what the rest of the diary contained. Joe and Mary would have seen conditions in their trade deteriorate as the years went by, and would probably have looked back on the days when an apprentice could make ten or eleven shillings worth of stockings in a week as a golden age. By the 1830s the average wage for a stocking knitter who worked long hours, six or more days a week, was less than a labourer earned. Payment depended on the quality of the work and the material used – finer gauge items were paid for at a proportionally higher rate, as they were slower to make. It was estimated that the weekly wage for workers like the Mosses making cotton hose was 4s 0d to 7s 0d, while those working in worsted earned 3s 0d to 6s 0d and those working in silk made 6s 0d to 12s 0d. Workers on wide frames making cloth for 'cut-ups' did rather better, making 10s 0d to 24s 0d, but to earn those amounts they would all have been working sixty- to seventy-two-hour weeks.[9]

By 1843 conditions in the trade were so bad that over 25,000 framework knitters signed a petition and submitted it to Parliament – Joe and Mary may well have been among the signatories. The petition complained about wages, unemployment, new machinery, frame-rents and imports of knitted goods. The government responded by setting up a Royal Commission to report on the industry. Over a period of several months, the commissioners interviewed knitters, hosiers, masters, local officials, doctors and clergymen in the East Midlands. The report was published in 1845.

Thomas Holland and Thomas Henderson from Joe's village of Horsley Woodhouse were among the interviewees. They told the commissioners that there were 204 frames in the village and all but one were used for making cotton hose. The one exception was used for making gloves. The chief employers were Ward's and Brettle's in Belper and 'Mr Morley' in Nottingham, and an average week's work would result in nine pairs of stockings. Thomas Holland gave a very detailed breakdown of prices in the village. The worker would receive 8s 7½d for his nine pairs of stockings, of which 1s 0d would go on frame-rent, 10d on paying for seaming, 3½d on needles, 4½d on heating and lighting, 3d for 'standing' and 3d for 'taking-in' – that, is for delivering goods to the master. Altogether, this made a weekly wage of 5s 7½d. 'Standing' was an addition to frame-rent – the payment for the right to supply a place for the frame to stand.[10]

Frame-rent and 'standing' were the cause of much complaint. Most knitters rented their frames from the master hosiers and, over the life of the frame, they would pay out in rent several times the amount it would have cost when new; in the 1840s the rental for a frame was between 9d and 3s 0d a week, while the price of a new one was between £19 and £34, and a second-hand narrow frame could cost as little as £4 7s 0d. Thomas Wright of Lambley told the commissioners that 'Men most experienced in the trade, think that frames pay better interest than any other property in the kingdom. If I had a frame recruited, which cost perhaps £10 for a 36-gauge, I could work it ten years and should [receive] £25 rent for it ...'

Gone were the days Joe would have remembered, where he and his master went to Nottingham market, dropped off the finished stockings at the wholesaler's and were paid on the spot. By the 1840s knitters could not spare the time it took to walk to town and back to deliver their goods and collect their pay. Instead the hosiers employed 'bag men', who went from house to house collecting goods and delivering wages. Disputes between the knitters and the bag men about under-payment and missing wages were frequent. The situation was made worse because there was no clarity about what rates were due or what deductions would be made, and the hosiers paid as little as they could in any given week.

Workers also complained about the 'truck' system. Many of the hosiers owned the shops where the workers were expected to buy their food. Sometimes they had to pay for their purchases in kind, but even when they paid cash the hosiers had a monopoly and charged more than the market price – however, if knitters dared to patronise other shopkeepers 'there would soon be a frown upon them and very little work for them', as Thomas Kerry of Smalley explained to the commissioners. One of the local bagmen, Joseph Ogden, was prosecuted several times for truck offences but clearly the penalties were insufficient to deter him from what was a very profitable practice.

The truck system was less of a problem in Horsley Woodhouse than in Smalley, which may have been one of the reasons the Mosses moved – though there were disadvantages too, one of which being that there was no free school. There was a Sunday school but what that offered the children was 'trifling as compared to what they ought to have,' according to Thomas Wright, another interviewee. However, even when education was available for free, many parents did not send their children to school once they were old enough to help at home, so the children's education probably did not play a big part in the Mosses' calculations.

The commissioner's report described the problems but did little to solve them, concluding that the trade was oversubscribed and too easy to get into, criticising the low quality of much of the work produced and acknowledging that between 1814 and 1844 wages had fallen by almost 40 per cent. They highlighted several other problems, including competition from knitwear manufacturers abroad. But they concluded that the biggest evils were frame-rent and the unfair practices of the employers.

While wages remain, as they have done for years past, almost at the minimum of existence to the workman; while custom sanctions, and his defenceless poverty forces him to submit to pay an exorbitant and disproportionate weekly rent for the machine in which he works; while the mode of conducting the business remains in force ... and while at any time the employer can, at little sacrifice to himself, lay down his one, or his ten, or his hundred frames ... there must be great advantages clearly manifested as derivable from any new system of production ...[11]

In fact, the days of knitting as a cottage industry were numbered. After the mid-1840s, an increasing amount of work was produced in factories on the newly developed circular, rotary and warp machines. But the Mosses stuck to what they knew. In 1851 William, James, Fanny and Martha were all working at home with their parents. Robert, the eldest son, was married and living in Smalley with his wife and children, and he, too, earned his living as a knitter; the three younger girls were 'scholars'. Nonetheless, if the adults were earning even the average wage of 5s 7½d a week, and fifteen-year-old Martha was making a bit less, the family income would have been around £1 12s after deductions – a perfectly respectable sum, albeit one that had to support a family of nine. As the decade progressed William and James both married and started families of their own, and Sarah died; but, by 1861, there were still six workers in the family home. They may have given up two of their frames, for Mary and Georgiana, the youngest daughter, are listed as 'seamers'. Two fewer frame-rents to pay and a saving of a penny for seaming on every dozen hose probably left the family reasonably comfortably off on just four wages, for Sally was now knitting alongside her father and sisters.

As the 1860s drew to a close, however, Joe and Mary must have begun to feel the pinch. Their daughters had all married and left home, though Fanny and Georgiana stayed close by in the village. The couple were getting old and, even if you were used to it, working a knitting frame was a strenuous occupation. The worker had to use both feet to operate the treadle and both arms to move the heavy iron carriage on its wooden frame – it was no job for the frail or the arthritic.

Their sons were all knitters, so there was little hope of financial help from them, and none of the sons-in-law had well-paid jobs. On top of that there were increasing numbers of grandchildren for Joe and Mary to help look after. At census time in 1871, for example, thirteen-year-old Laura and nine-year-old Fanny were staying with their grandparents. Of course, it worked both ways. A decade later, by which time both Joe and Mary were over eighty, and still describing themselves to the census enumerator as 'framework knitters', which implies that they had not retired – probably because they could not afford to – their seventeen-year-old grandson, Joshua, was staying with them. He worked in one of the local coal mines and was probably there to help support the old couple. Few working people lived to be over eighty and, given the hard lives they had lived, their longevity is almost miraculous. Joe died in October 1881, with Mary outliving him by three years.

Knitters like the Mosses were a dying breed, however. In 1871 in Horsley Woodhouse there were forty households that contained at least one framework knitter; by 1881 there were just twenty-seven such households and by 1891 there were a bare half-dozen.

Climbing the Ladder: James Edwards (1823–1898), Shoemaker, Brampton Bryan, Herefordshire

'That'll be threepence if you please, Sir.'

'There you are, my boy, and a ha'penny for yourself.'

'Thank you kindly, Sir.'

Beaming, James touched his forelock and ran to open the gate for the gentleman on the horse. This was what could happen if you were quick and lucky – the seven Edwards children all competed to be the first at the gate to open it for travellers because, every once in a while, a kindly individual would give them a halfpenny or a farthing tip.[1]

The Edwards family lived at 'Toll Bar' – the toll keeper's cottage at Brampton Bryan on what was then the turnpike road between Ludlow and Knighton and is now the A1113. It seems likely that they had the cottage rent free in return for collecting tolls from passing traffic, and Thomas Edwards, James's father, may also have been paid a small salary. Tolls were a lucrative business, especially on busy roads, and the right to collect tolls on various routes or groups of routes was sold at auction. The price related to the annual sum of the tolls collected on the route or routes and often amounted to several hundred pounds. The owner then paid the toll-gate keeper, organised repairs to the stretch of road the tolls covered – and usually also made a handsome profit for themselves.

Many toll-gate keepers also had regular jobs – Thomas Edwards was a farm labourer – and left the task of manning the gate and collecting the money to their wives and children. There were disadvantages, as they could be roused several times a night by passing travellers and attacks on gate keepers by irate road users were not uncommon, but there were also perks, one of which was probably that the family made a wide range of friends and contacts. Thomas Edwards was anxious to do his best for his family and, when they were old enough he apprenticed his boys to useful trades, very probably through friendships forged at the toll-gate. Son Thomas became a wheelwright, son James a shoemaker, and son Herbert a coachman. It is James who concerns us here.

Brampton Bryan lies in a landscape of steep rolling hills and ancient trees and hedges. On a fine spring day it is idyllic, with ewes and lambs grazing the hills, and bright yellow drifts of daffodils in the woods and hedgerows; however, in a cold, wet Welsh winter it presents a very different picture. The parish straddles the border between Herefordshire and Radnorshire and is made up of a series of hamlets: Brampton Bryan, Upper and Lower Pedwardine and Boresford in England and Stanage Lordship in Wales. The population of the five hamlets was 500 in 1871.

The village's main claim to fame came during the English Civil War. Sir Robert Harley, owner of Brampton Bryan Castle, and his wife, Brilliana, were staunch Parliamentarians and, in July 1643, while Sir Robert was in London, the Royalists laid siege to the castle. Brilliana held the castle for seven weeks, sending repeated messages to her assailants when they begged her to surrender that 'My Lord bids me hold out' – meanwhile, around her, the Royalists destroyed the church, forty houses and mills, and installed a gun in what had been the church tower. Fortunately this did little damage and eventually the siege was abandoned; nevertheless, Brilliana's health was broken and she died a few weeks later. The following year the castle was again besieged and this time it was destroyed.

Sir Robert eventually rebuilt the church, as a plain, Puritan 'preaching box', which is not surprising, as his role during the war had been 'to receive information as to idolatrous monuments in Westminster Abbey and London churches with power to demolish same'.[2] Brampton Bryan Church was completed in 1756, a matter of days before his death, and was one of only six English churches to be built during the Civil War. The Hall was built in 1666 and 'improved' a hundred years later; the village as a whole never really recovered. The Edwards may have been dimly aware of the history of their village but it had little impact on their day-to-day lives. Like most working families in the nineteenth century, they were mostly concerned with making ends meet and securing a future for their children.

By the time he was seventeen, young James Edwards was a journeyman shoemaker, working with William and Joseph Brown in Eign Street in Hereford. He may well have served his apprenticeship with them but, by 1841, another young boy had taken that role – eleven-year-old Stephen Davies. The 1841 census lists young Stephen as an apprentice while James is simply a 'shoemaker', though at just seventeen he cannot have been long out of his time. James Devlin in *The Shoemaker* of 1839[3] painted a rosy picture of the life of the shoemaker's apprentice:

> The shoemaker's boy ... is generally a very happy urchin, acquiring the first beginnings of his art with scarcely any pain; except, occasionally, in consequence of the points of his threads not being properly formed, [they] come off in being pulled through the hole made by the awl – and then the hands fly into a perspiration, the cheeks get red, the ears burning, and he knows not what to do ...

Shoemakers did not always use needles; they attached points, called 'hairs', to the ends of their sewing threads and these could come loose. James Devlin admitted that he had been apprenticed to his father so he probably had a rosier view of apprenticeship than many boys in the trade. His book is a curious mixture of little vignettes that could almost come from the pages of a novel and descriptions of shoemaking processes using terms that are so detailed as to be virtually incomprehensible to the lay reader. He acknowledges that his book is not a manual of instruction – which it clearly is not – but it is really not at all obvious who he intended the audience to be.

Making footwear, Mr Devlin tells us, was divided into a series of distinct trades: clickers (who cut out the leather pieces that would be made into uppers), shoe closers (who stitched the pieces together to make uppers), blockers (who set the wet insole on the last and moulded it to shape), shoe-men (who attached the soles to the uppers), boot closers and boot-men who worked only on boots, jobbers and cobblers who mended shoes – and a whole host of others. However, he went on to explain that an apprentice would have been expected to become proficient in all the processes because, if he became a shoemaker in a small way of business, he would have had to do them all himself.

He described how a boy would have to learn the names of the tools of the trade – the 'grindery' – and would be taught how to make the various pastes and waxes his master needed. He would learn to 'close' shoes using clam[p]s 'those two tall nipping pieces of stave-like timber which he holds, pressed hard together between his knees; or on the block – that somewhat half round clump of wood, which he lays along his left thigh, held down by the stirrup.' He describes 'stabbing' – the process of making stitch-holes in leather with an awl. This was hard work, done with a dangerously sharp tool, and the interviews carried out by the Children's Employment Commission in 1863/4 tell us that it was often done by quite young boys. Mr Bostock of Northampton explained:

> The stabbing was laborious, requiring great attention, and was even dangerous, for [the children] often sat so close that in drawing the thread with both hands, the awl, which was always held point outwards, in the right hand, not unfrequently struck the next child in the face or eye; many have lost an eye in this way …

The Commissioner added a rather shocking note of his own to the entry. 'I had noticed, before seeing Mr Bostock, that several persons of both sexes, whom I had met in the town, had lost an eye; but thinking it merely an odd coincidence, had not enquired about it ...'[4] By 1864 the stabbing machine had largely replaced hand-stabbing, so fewer children were risking their eyesight for the pittance of 1s or 1s 6d a week that had been the average wage for this work. However, James would have started his career as a stabber and it may be that his apprentices did too – the photograph of his workshop does not suggest it was a particularly high-tech operation, so they may have continued to use the old techniques rather than expensive, new-fangled machinery (see plate 24).

Of course, James Devlin does not mention the dangers, and there is no mistaking his passion for his craft as he describes 'blind stabbing' – piercing the leather from the outer to the inner surface 'from whence the left hand hair should be at once protruded, the right-hand hair being put in afterwards, and then the stitch smartly drawn in.' This he thought was 'the most beautiful process in the whole trade; regular, easy, and rapid, and to the eye of the spectator a matter even of marvellous description.' It was not as rapid as all that, however, for he goes on to tell us that it took a quick worker half-an-hour to stab the four side rows and two back rows of a boot, depending in part on how closely it was to be stitched. A fine quality boot might have twenty stitches to the inch.

He also waxed eloquent about

Stitching, [which] when performed with ease and certainty, is a handsome operation and, and especially when the work is light, the performance, too, is rapid, the adept workman going round the entire welt of a thin-edged shoe or boot in something about an hour.

Perhaps writing of his own experience, he described how an apprentice might carry his practice pieces of finely stitched leather in his pocket and proudly show them to his friends. There was a great deal else the young apprentice had to learn:

the names of the entire kit; the difference between a shoe and a pump, between those of a channel or galosh shoe; between women's and men's work; the greater perfection of the boot; the terms of the whole trade – vamps, quarters, boot-legs, boot-tongues; boot fronts and backs; counters, tops, top-linings, straps; in-soles, welts (closing and making), rands, bottom-fillings, out-soles, split-lifts, lifts, top-pieces; the sewing stitch, fore-part stitch, rand stitch; the seat, heel, fore-part, feather, channel-clicking, hammering-stuff, blocking in-soles, pegging, fitting welts, levelling bottoms, rounding-up, jiggering, taking-off, glazing or balling heels, buffing bottoms, stamping; all these things he will have learned ...

The apprentice would also learn to block leather over a last, to round soles, to stitch using a protective hand-leather and to rasp and glass heels and foreparts. He would practise finishing by running the jigger and shoulder iron 'over some inferior shoe, the excited perspiration meanwhile dropping lustily from his forehead, so busy and sanguine is he during these his first attempts to become a finisher.'

The lay reader is unlikely – and does not need – to understand all this detail and one gets the distinct impression that sometimes Mr Devlin was trying to blind his readers with science. However, young James Edwards would have understood *The Shoemaker* perfectly, for, some time in the late 1840s, he returned to Brampton Bryan and set up in business on his own account. It may be that he would have preferred to remain in the city but circumstances conspired against him.

James Edwards's father had died at Christmas 1845 of jaundice, probably caused by a damaged liver, and, three years later, almost to the day, his mother also died, of 'congestion of the brain' – a catch-all diagnosis covering anything that caused the brain to swell, ranging from a clot, to meningitis to an accidental blow on the head. The care of the two youngest Edwards children, Eliza and George, then fell to James. Eliza was ten in 1848 and George was eleven – a heavy responsibility for James who was himself only twenty-five. We have no way of knowing how Mary Edwards had supported herself and the children in the three years between her husband's death and her own – was the toll-gate keeper's salary sufficient, did she take another job, did the older children send money home, did friends and family help, or did she become dependent on the parish? It is unlikely that she and Thomas Edwards had been able to save, as the couple had had nine children and raised seven of them. Nor do we know who cared for Eliza and George in the immediate aftermath of their mother's death or how the family decided that it was James who should move back to Brampton Bryan to look after them.

It seems probable that it fell to his lot because, of the three adult brothers, he was the one whose trade was most likely to enable him to make a living in the village – there was no other shoemaker there. His brother Thomas would have been unable to establish himself in business because the village already had a wheelwright and, though the Hall and Rectory families both employed coachmen, it would seem neither had a vacancy for his brother Herbert. For a time James, George and Eliza lived in the old family home, presumably continuing to collect tolls from road users, and James seems to have supported them all by making and mending shoes. He had probably acquired some tools while working in Hereford, but again it is not clear how he could afford to set up in business on his own account at such a young age. It is the minutiae of lives like James's that is fascinating – and so often missing.

James's first business records[5] date from the summer of 1849 so it seems likely that is when he returned to the village to live. The first account in his first day book is for Mr Edward Stedman (NB: patches and pieces are types of repair):

June 23	pr boots soled and heeled	3s-6d
July 5	pr heeled and 2 pieces	1s-4d
Oct 29	Mrs a pr boots	7s-0d
	Mrs a pr galoshes and 2 pieces	1s-8d
1850		
March 23	Fanny a pr boots	3s-3d
Jan 16	Mr a pr repaired	8d

July 3	Martha a pr boots	7s-6d
July 6	Mr a pr soled	2s-6d
July 17	Caroline a pr boots	7s-6d
Sept 11	Martha a pr 3 pieces	6d
	Ellen a pr 4 pieces	8d
Nov 1	Caroline a pair Galoshed boots	7s-6d
Nov 7	Ellen a pr sold 1 patch	2s-0d
Nov 7	Martha a pr soled and vamped	2s-6d'

Edward Stedman was a tailor in Bucknell, a few miles from Brampton Bryan, over the border in Shropshire, and he had a family of daughters. In January 1851 James married one of them, Caroline. The business seems to have flourished and even by 1851, James had sufficient work to warrant taking on an apprentice. Apprentices lived with the family and were paid pocket money, if they were paid at all, so employing young John Evnall did not cost James very much. John was nineteen in 1851 and probably nearing the end of his apprenticeship; perhaps he had begun his training with someone else.

James and Caroline's first child, Constance, was born in December 1851. She was followed by Evelyn in 1853, Herbert – who died at the age of three – in 1856, Jessie in 1858, Arthur Henry in 1860, Horace in 1861 and Alice Caroline in 1866. Given that he was responsible for his two young siblings, and a wife and growing family of his own, James needed his business to succeed and he must have been on the look-out for other ways to make ends meet; it was common practice for a village tradesman to have more than one string to his bow.

In 1851 Brampton Bryan had a little grocery store run by a middle-aged widow, Elizabeth Price, but in or around 1853 she seems to have ceased trading, and James and Caroline decided to open a grocery shop of their own. At that point the family left the toll-gate and moved into the village proper, to a cottage owned by Lady Langdale, for which James paid £12 a year in rent and about 6d a week in rates. In fact the 'village' was little more than a hamlet consisting of a handful of pretty cottages, many of them half-timbered, that were clustered around the church and the entrance to the Hall grounds. James's cottage was in the middle of a row and the ground floor windows were enlarged for his shop (see plate 23). Directly opposite was the high yew hedge, which runs for over 300 yards around the hall and churchyard. Today it is the most outstanding feature of the hamlet, sculpted into uneven, almost phallic, humps and bumps, though in James's day its contours were apparently much more normal.

The Edwards sold anything and everything the villagers might need, from bread, barm, flour, tea, sugar and bacon, to soap, washing soda and hearthstones, sewing cotton and paper, candles and matches, nails and tin tacks. The firm's daybooks survive and show that, in 1853, their first part-year of trading, their turnover was around £70 – though it is hard to know how much of that was profit. What it does mean, however, was that the family would have been able to buy all their own household requirements at cost. In 1863 the business turned over £259 or £5 a week, though by 1883 the figure was down to £150 or £3 a week. If we compare those figures with what James was making in his shoemaking workshop, we can see that the grocery business made a significant contribution to the family income.

It seems that the shop was largely Caroline's responsibility, despite the trade card for 'James Edwards, Tea Dealer and General Grocer', and as well as selling to her neighbours she seems to have tried to broaden their culinary horizons. The grocery daybooks are full of recipes cut from newspapers; these included fried chicken à l'Italienne, gooseberry cream, cucumber 'catchup' (cucumber juice with wine and anchovies), 'artistically' poached eggs, stewed cabbage with herbs and bacon, duck with olives, Palestine soup (made from Jerusalem artichokes), minced kidneys and macaroni, pilaff 'a famous Turkish dish' and a 'nightcap' recommended by 'Dr Kitchener', which consisted of a heated mixture of table beer, brandy, brown sugar, nutmeg, ginger and lemon peel and rejoiced in the name of 'tewahiddle'. There were also recipes for household cleaners, cough syrups, cures for consumption, 'brown flour for browning gravies' (basically burnt flour), advice on turning sheets sides-to-middle and instructions on how to tell the difference between butter and 'oleomargarine'. Knowing of her interest, Major Murray, the vicar's

JOHN TOMKYNS AND ARRY BLOATER
(Time of Queen Victoria, 1862. Not at all scarce.)
ARRY, *(in the boots of the period).*—"Yes, they're dooced comfortable, and they give one a Military and rather Sporting appearance, I fancy."

When is a fellow's eye like a barrel ?—When it's bunged up.

James Edwards,
Tea Dealer and General Grocer,
Brampton Bryan.

Trade card advertising James (and Caroline) Edwards's grocery business. It is probably no coincidence that the cartoon he chose to illustrate it relates to boots! (Courtesy of Herefordshire Archive Service)

brother from Leintwardine, presented Caroline with a handwritten book of recipes from his own family, including how to make barm (from water, malt, hops and sugar), how to brew beer and ginger wine, and how to make distemper pills for dogs (a kill-or-cure compound of calomel, tartar emetic and soap). Caroline's shop was an advice centre as well as a grocery store, and she probably served her husband's customers as well as people in the village.

Many of James's customers came from Brampton Bryan itself, but others came from as far afield as Clulow, Leintwardine, Hopton, Bache, Charnock, Bucknell, Stanage, Letton and numerous other small towns and villages within a ten-mile radius of Brampton Bryan. They were farmers, labourers and small tradesmen, but James's business was also patronised by the vicar, his brother, Major Murray, the schoolmaster, the post-master, Major General Staunton at Brampton Bryan Hall and the Harley family who returned to the Hall when the General and his family moved on – even Lord Ruthven when he was in the area.

James Devlin created a scenario in his book to describe the sort of task with which a village cobbler might be presented:

He scratches his head, a carter's old shoe is in his hand, gaping like an oyster between sole and upper leather, and with a rent in the upper-leather stretching half-way across the vamp, and running into various sinuosities. What is he to do? He himself wants his 9*d* or his 1s-0*d* for the job, and the carter wants his shoe, and will call for it in his dinner hour. It won't do to scratch long, he must begin; and with a good patch, a good thread, and a good awl, the upper is made, as it were, whole again – no rent in it. The huge ripping at the welt is drawn tightly and closely together, so that no mud can get in, and the carter may go forth again in his two shoes, neither of which, without the achievement of the cobbler, would have been of service.

James Edwards certainly did a good many repairs – even well-to-do customers expected their footwear to last. A lot of his work was repairing and patching, which could cost as little as 2*d* or 3*d*, though heeling a pair of boots usually cost around 1s 6*d* and soling them cost 2s 6*d*. James charged between 3*d* and 7*d* for putting new buttons on a pair of boots and 1s 9*d* for new soles for a pair of slippers.

He also sold boots and shoes, though the daybooks do not usually tell us how many of them he made himself and how many were bought wholly or partly ready-made. In November 1850, however, he does record 'closing and making' a pair of Wellington boots for Mr Plant of Leintwardine, which suggests in this instance he was using ready-cut uppers but doing the rest of the work himself. In the early 1850s he charged between 7s 6d and 11s 6d for a pair of boots; galoshes were 7s 6d; a pair of men's black shoes was 10s 6d; while a pair of women's slippers cost 4s. Prices rose gradually as he became more established. High boots cost 17s to 18s in the 1870s, as did a pair of 'calf Balmorals', though cloth ones were just 10s 6d. He supplied 'underlays', which are what we would call inner soles. Unsurprisingly, waterproof boots of various qualities, costing between 15s and £1, were his best-sellers.

James trained his younger brother, George, and by 1861 twenty-four-year-old George had become his assistant, while John Evnall had been replaced as apprentice by sixteen-year-old James Goodwin from Aymestrey. Within a few years, however, George married and set up a successful shoemaking business of his own on the High Street in Clun, and James was again dependent on hired help.

He kept detailed daybooks throughout his career but the content is very repetitive. The accounts of a handful of customers in the 1860s, when he was at the height of his career, will give a better idea of the range of James Edwards's work.

Thomas 'Trailer' of Pedwardine

Thomas Traylor was a forty-five-year-old unmarried farm labourer who lived in the hamlet of Pedwardine. It is unlikely that he ever earned more than 8s a week – small wonder that he had his boots repaired one at a time and took so long to save up for a new pair.

1866		
Sept 20	Pr Waterproof boots	15s-6d
Oct 4	1 underlay	4d
Dec 1	1 underlay and half a heel	8d
1867		
Feb 20	1 boot underlay and boot mended	6d
25	1 boot mended	3d
March 18	1 boot soled	1s-6d
May 4	a pr soled and heeled	4s-0d

| June 17 | 1 boot soled and 1 patch | 1s-9d |
| Dec 12 | A pr boots | 16s-0d |

General Staunton

Major-General George Staunton lived at Brampton Bryan Hall for several years from the early 1860s to the early 1880s. He had married late in life and his wife, Henrietta, was some twenty-five years his junior. They eventually had eight children, of whom 'Master G' (George) was the eldest. He was five in 1866. The 'little boots' were probably for one of the younger children.

The family lived in some style with a live-in butler, housekeeper, upper housemaid, kitchen maid, nurse and two under-nurses. 'Mrs Cooper' was Henrietta's mother. It looks as if they were happy to entrust repairs and the occasional purchase of children's shoes to the village shoemaker – but new shoes for the adults in the household seem to have been purchased elsewhere.

1866

Oct 15	Master G a pr soled and 2 patches, and	2s-0d
	a pr and 4 underlays	1s-0d
Dec	Mrs Cooper a pr soled and repaired	1s-2d
1867	ditto a pr heeled and 2 underlays	1s-0d
Feb 7	Mrs Staunton a pr repaired	3d
Feb 16	ditto a pr heeled	9d
Feb 20	One boot underlay	3d
	A pr slippers toe capped	4d
March 8	Mrs Staunton a pr boots heeled	1s-0d
March 27	A pr little boots and 4 pieces	1s-0d
March 27	Master G a pr button boots	7s-6d
June 25	Mrs Staunton 1 boot repaired	4d
	2 prs slippers toe capped	10d
July 22	A pr boots soled and heeled	4s-0d
Aug 10	Master G a pr soled and heeled	2s-4d
Oct 10	Mrs Staunton a pr soled and heeled	2s-6d

Dec 2	3 pairs slippers toe caped [sic]	
Dec 31	Mrs Staunton a pr soled and	3s-0d
	heeled and 2 patches	
	Leather for carriage	8d

Lord Ruthven

No doubt it was flattering for James to work for such an august client but, like the Major-General, Lord Ruthven seems only to have used the village cobbler for essential running repairs. He was Walter James Hore-Ruthven, the ninth[6] Lord Ruthven, who had inherited the title in 1864 from his grandmother. He was a career soldier, who served in the Crimea, Abyssinia and Afghanistan, and was a descendant of the Ruthvens of Freeland in Perthshire. He does not seem to have lived in the area, though for some reason he was a JP for Herefordshire as well as for Perthshire and Lanarkshire; however, his mother, the Honourable Mrs Hore-Ruthven, and sister, Wilhelmina, lived in Bucknell for some years and it seems he visited them from time to time.

This particular account added up to just *7s 6d* – but James had to wait a year for his money.

1867		
Oct 3	A pr of shoes nailed	6d
	New buttons to a pr boots	6d
Nov 6	Strap to hunting boot	4d
1868		
May 5	Pr boots heeled	1s-0d
May 24	Pr boots soled and heeled	4s-0d
Sept 2	Pr shoes nailed	2d
Nov 11	2 prs shoes repaired	8d

Mary Ann Luggar

Mary Ann was in service; by 1871 she was working as cook to a wealthy lady in Great Malvern. She was Caroline Edwards's niece, which may be why she was allowed to run up such an extensive bill: £3 6s 10d over the course of three years.

1866		
Aug 30	A pr boots	10s-6d
	A pr mended	9d
1867		
Jan	A pr boots mended	3d
Jan 29	A pr boots soled and heeled	2s-6d
Aug 26	ditto	2s-3d
Sept 25	A pr heeled, 1 piece	1s-0d
Nov 1	A pr elastic sided boots	10s-6d
1868		
Feb 12	A pr soled and heeled	2s-3d
April 28	A pr boots repaired	8d
June 13	A pr side spring boots	10s-6d
Oct 1	ditto	10s-6d
1869		
Jan 4	A pr heeled and underlay	1s-0d
March 13	A pr soled	1s-9d
April 24	A pr soled and underlay	1s-0d
June 10	A pr elastic sided boots	10s-6d

Working people were seldom allowed credit, but well-to-do people could leave their bills unpaid for months or even years. William Knill of Letton ran up a bill of £5 6s 7d between July 1867 and October 1870, for example. It covered twenty-four separate transactions, ranging from 6d for repairing leggings to payment for two pairs of waterproof boots at 15s 6d each. He paid £2 on account partway through the period and another £2 in April 1871 but, four years after the account was opened, £1 6s 7d was still outstanding. Similarly, Mr Winstone Cane of Ludlow owed £5 8s 8d, built up over a two-year period from July 1867 to June 1869, which included boots for seven different members of his family; however, when he did pay, he paid in full.

Keeping a family decently shod was an expensive business, as the following account shows.

Mrs Hughes, Wordells

The Hughes family were farmers in Brampton Bryan. Robert was twenty-three in 1865; Edward was sixteen and obviously very heavy on his boots; and 'Miss' was Elizabeth, aged twenty.

1865		
Feb 23	Edward, a pr boots	13s-6d
May 10	Robert, a pr best laced boots	16s
Aug 13	Miss, a pr laced boots	9s-6d
Nov 29	Edward, a pr strong boots	14s
1866		
Jan 29	Miss, a pr soled and heeled and 3 patches	3s
April 16	Edward, a pr soled and heeled	4s
May 15	Edward, a pr best light boots	16s
May 23	A pr 3 patches and soled	10d
Oct 30	Edward, a pr strong boots	14s-6d
Nov 31	Miss, a pr boots	9s-6d
1867		
July 6	Edward a pr soled and heeled	4s
Oct 3	Edward, a pr waterproof boots	15s-6d
Dec 9	Edward, a pr soled and heeled and 3 patches	4s-9d
1868		
March 9	Miss, a pr best laced boots	10s-6d
Oct 1	Edward, a pr Balmorals	17s
Oct 1	Miss, a pr soled and heeled and 3 patches	3s-3d
Total	£7-15s-10d	

In 1841, following on from his treatise on shoemaking, James Devlin wrote a book called *The Shop* because, in his rather condescending view, 'few commence shoemaking with large capitals; and fewer still are qualified to commence at all.'[7] He wrote about buying leather, cutting up hides and measuring customers, and paid particular attention to the need for careful account keeping. He recommended keeping an array of books – an invoice or Bills of Parcels book, an order book, a work book, a wages book, a number book, a last book, a daybook, a ledger, inward and outward cash books, a 'bills delivered' book and a stock book. Few small tradesmen had time, energy – or even the need – to record so much. James Edwards is unusual in that his accounts are really quite full, but even he confined himself to keeping detailed daybooks and customer account books.

From these we learn that he had between thirty and fifty customers listed in his customer accounts book at any given time – but if we read those books in conjunction with the daybooks we find that the number of people who used his services was considerably higher. The customer account books list those regular customers who paid their bills at intervals, while the daybooks show that many of Edwards's customers paid in cash on the day. Poor people could not afford to run up bills and tradesmen could not risk allowing them to do so.

It must have been quite difficult to budget when so much of the family income was tied up in bills that might not be paid for months and, though most people paid for their groceries on the spot, some ran up accounts for those, too. As with grocery sales, the shoemaking daybooks only tell us about turnover, not profit. In 1854 this was just £48 4s 3d – we can be accurate because that year James kept a running total. In 1863 it had increased to £144; it was £160 in 1875; £164 in 1885; and £172 in 1891 – a fairly consistent total of +/-£3 a week, of which probably no more than a third was profit.

As time went by James seems to have sold increasing amounts of footwear and, though some of this must have been bought ready-made, books of customer measurements and photographs showing the workroom full of lasts are evidence that he also made boots and shoes. These may not all have been built from scratch, however, as by the 1860s it was possible to buy ready-closed shoe uppers, which could be adjusted to fit in the process of attaching them to a sole. The *Man of Ross*, a local paper, carried an advertisement in May 1866:

> TO SHOEMAKERS
> JUST ARRIVED FROM LONDON, a very large
> Assortment of GENTLEMEN'S and LADIES'
> CLOSED UPPERS of every quality, variety and
> Price
> Also all kinds of Shoemakers' Kid, and Messrs
> Ullathorne's Grindery at lowest terms for cash
> WM SMALL'S
> ROSS LEATHER STORES
> *Kyrle Street, near the Gas House*

We do not know whether James took up their offer; indeed we know nothing about his suppliers, though we do know that by the early twentieth century James's son, Arthur Henry, kept catalogues from a range of suppliers located all over the country.

Measuring customers' feet for bespoke footwear followed a similar format to the way in which tailors measured for coats – the foot was divided up into a series of 'points', round which measurements were taken and recorded in strict sequence. Edwards had a measurements book: 'RWD Harley Esq. A7¼, 9¼, 13⅝, 10¼, 9⅛ Derby Brogues (Only a 10s upper required for the foot)' and 'Florrie Jones, Lingen 13A, 8, 7¾, 11¼, 8½, 7½ Pair strong lace boots sprigs or small nails' are typical entries. Robert William Daker Harley JP was a cadet member of the Harley family, who owned Brampton Bryan Hall, and he lived at Brampton Bryan Cottage; Florrie Jones was a maid-of-all-work in the nearby village of Lingen.

The range of goods James was able to supply was considerable. In 1884 Mrs Griffiths of Poston bought a pair of 'Jockey Boots' for £2 6s 0d; Miss Gower bought high calf lace boots for 11s 6d and Harry Humphries acquired some silk-topped boots for 18s 6d. Mr Marlow's Oxford shoes cost 14s 0d in 1885 but a few months later Amy Swan's pretty kid lace-up shoes were just 9s 6d.

By 1881 James was employing two men. The only other shoemakers in the parish were twenty-three-year-old James Scott, the son of the gamekeeper at The Hendrie, and William Jones, so they were almost certainly James's two employees. William was a married man in his thirties with a wife and a young son. She was a dressmaker. William described himself as a 'cordwainer' (the old-fashioned term for a shoemaker) and he was also the local Baptist preacher. James's sons, Arthur Henry and Horace, had also trained as shoemakers and were living together in a cottage, which was a few hundred yards from their parents' home and next door to William Jones – no doubt they, too, worked with their father. Arthur was twenty and Horace nineteen in 1881, so they would have completed – or almost completed – their apprenticeships. Certainly they would have learnt enough to be useful. This means that in the 1880s James was paying four lots of wages out of his takings.

Perhaps the boys had moved out because the family home was becoming overcrowded. Constance, the eldest daughter, had left home and was working as a nursemaid to a banker's family in Bishop's Castle, over the border in Shropshire, but the three younger girls were still at home. By 1871, Caroline's eighty-one-year-old widowed father, Edward Stedman, was also living with the family.

By the 1880s General Staunton and his family had moved away and the Harleys were back at the Hall. However, like James's wealthier clients twenty years earlier, they patronised him for running repairs rather than purchases – although in 1884 R. D. Harley's bill did include two pairs of 'livery boots' for his servants. For the most part, however, James repaired bits of harness, cartridge bags, whip-holders and the like for them at a few pence a time, and in 1884 he charged 3s 3d for 'fitting pieces of leather to yard hose'; the hose was obviously deteriorating, as patching it up the previous year had cost just 6d.

While we know a good deal about James's business, we know much less about him as a person. He was obviously hardworking and successful, which suggests he was good at his job. He and Caroline were enterprising and aspirational – Caroline's collection of recipes suggests as much. So do the names they gave their children. For generations Edwards children had been baptised with traditional names – Thomas and William, Mary and Eliza – but James and Caroline chose 'modern' names with no apparent family connections: Jessie and Evelyn, Horace and Arthur.

James was, for a time, an overseer of the poor in the parish, and a respected local patriarch, albeit in a very small community.[8] He was also a Freemason – his membership card for the Leintwardine Loyal Perseverance Lodge for 1883 survives, as do several 1860s rulebooks for various lodges.[9]

The Edwards were literate and, unusually for a village family, they had books. We cannot be sure which belonged to James and which belonged to his son, Arthur, who took over the house and business, but it seems likely that several children's prayer books, *The Juvenile Missionary Magazine for 1863, The Little Merchants, The Old Missionary Box* and *The Way to Honour* (all mid-nineteenth century) – belonged to James's children. Meanwhile *Sermons and Homilies in the Time of Queen Elizabeth* (1818), two early-nineteenth-century *Guides to Health, Life Health and Disease* (1859), *Gardening for the Millions* (1862), Adam Smith's *Wealth of Nations* (1858), the *Manual of the Rudiments of Theology* (1830) and *The Life of Dr John Tillotson, Archbishop of Canterbury* (1752), among others, belonged to James himself.[10] It also seems likely that James attended, or at least was sufficiently interested to acquire the transcript of, a lecture about the Civil War siege in Herefordshire, given at Leominster Town Hall in 1866.[11]

In many ways James Edwards was a Victorian success story. He came from humble beginnings, worked hard and built a thriving business. He supported his younger siblings, saw them educated, and gave his younger brother a training that enabled him to build a business of his own. He saw his sister Eliza through school; she then moved to Ludlow to work with their married sister, Mary Howard, who was a dressmaker. Arthur and Horace moved back in with the family when their grandfather died and worked with their father in the little workshop in Brampton Bryan. In addition, in 1890 Horace became the village sub-post-master.

Arthur expanded the business, becoming an agent for sewing machines and bicycles. James's eldest daughter had a career as a children's nanny; he left the grocery business to his wife and his second daughter, Evelyn. Jessie, the third daughter, might have shared it with them but she married in 1886, moved to Tapenhall near Droitwich where her husband worked on a farm, and raised a family. Alice, the youngest, went to training college and became a teacher. Slowly but surely the family was moving into the middle classes.

Horace died in 1892, and James died six years later, aged seventy-four, leaving savings of £434 0s 6d – a very respectable sum for a village tradesman. Arthur then took over both the post office and the shoemaking workshop alongside his cycle business. He had married in 1883, and he and his wife, Mary Ann, had four little girls but no son to carry on the family firm. Arthur looked after his widowed mother until her death in 1909 and remained in business for another fifteen years. On his death in 1924 the workshop and its contents were abandoned, and survived, gathering dust, as a little time capsule until 1961, when the contents were divided between Hereford Museum and Herefordshire Record Office.

'The Beacon Star of the Working Class': George Odger (1820–1877), Shoemaker and Trades Unionist, London[1]

Failing to 'know your place' was a cardinal sin in Victorian society. The writer Henry James reflected the snobbery of his adopted country when he described George Odger's funeral:

> The element of the grotesque was very noticeable to me in the most marked collection of the shabbier English types that I had seen since I came to London. The occasion of my seeing them was the funeral of Mr. George Odger, which befell some four or five weeks before the Easter period. Mr. George Odger, it will perhaps be remembered, was an English Radical agitator of humble origin, who had distinguished himself by a perverse desire to get into Parliament. He exercised, I believe, the useful profession of a shoemaker, and he knocked in vain at the door that opens but to the refined.[2]

To others, George was a working-class hero. On his death in March 1877, his friends and colleagues set up a testimonial appeal that raised over £1,130 in donations from across the UK, from Europe and from America. Once his funeral expenses had been paid, the remainder was invested to provide an income for his widow and James, his youngest son, who was crippled. They were to receive 25s a week. In financial terms it is almost certain that George was of more use to Jane and her children dead than he had been when he was alive (see plate 25).

George had trained as a shoemaker in the early 1830s, and for the rest of his life that is how he described himself but, in reality, he can have done precious little shoemaking because George Odger was, first and last, a politician. The numerous organisations with which he was involved paid his expenses, in cash or in kind, for he was a poor man and the only money he had was what he could earn. How Jane and their five children managed is open to question.

While a certain amount has been written about Odger the politician, a good deal less is known about Odger the man. George Bennet Odger was born in 1820, the second son of James and Mary Odger, who had recently moved to Roborough from Plymouth. Roborough is near Torrington in North Devon, and for some reason it was then known as 'Jump'. Their eldest son, John Hocken Odger, was born in Plymouth in 1817 and they had also had a daughter, Emilia, born in 1815, who died as a toddler. James appears in the records variously as a miner and as a labourer. We are told that young George was apprenticed to a shoemaker at about the age of ten because of his family's poverty and, though we cannot trace his father's death with any certainty, it seems likely that he was the James Odger who died in Roborough in 1826, aged fifty-two. George would then have been six and his brother would have been nine; it may well be that they had to work to support, or at least not to be a burden to, their widowed mother. We do not know with whom George was apprenticed but it may well have been with John Isaacs in Roborough; when George was ten John would have been a man of twenty-five, and a decade later he was employing two young assistants. However, George did not stay in Roborough when he finished his apprenticeship – perhaps at that stage John Isaacs was not well-established enough to take him on.

George's experience up to this point was no doubt very similar to that of James Edwards but, while James had a settled job and then worked for himself, George's career was much more varied and insecure. Traditionally, when an apprentice completed the term of his apprenticeship – which George would have done when he was about seventeen – he became a 'journeyman'. In other words he went 'journeying', looking for work and gaining a little experience here and there by working for a number of masters over periods that ranged from a few days to a few months. He would eventually be aiming to find a permanent post, hone his skills and, perhaps, to become a master in his own right. In fact, many apprentices went straight into a permanent post, either with the firm that had trained them or elsewhere, but George became a 'journeyman' in the original sense of the word. This process was known as going 'on the tramp' or 'tramping'. It was a precarious way of making a living, and, understandably, tramping workmen (the system was common to most trades) were often viewed with suspicion.

We have no way of knowing where George's 'tramp' took him. His eulogists airily suggest he travelled 'all over the country' but there is no evidence to suggest that this is true. He seems first to have headed west into Cornwall. In 1837/8, we know he was in St Mabyn because it was there that he met Jane Blewitt, who became his wife. He was eighteen, while she was a couple of years older and already had a two-year-old illegitimate son, Henry. We do not know when, where – or indeed whether – she and George married, but she seems to have joined him in his wanderings. They were at Southsea in Hampshire in 1840 when their son William was born, and in Woolwich at census time in 1841, but then they seem to have headed back to Plymouth where they settled for a while – their daughter, Mary, and second son, John Henry, were born there in 1843 and 1846 respectively. In later years George recalled walking the thirteen miles from Plymouth to Tavistock just to hear a speech about Chartism by John Bright – that probably happened during this period.

George Odger seems to have been an attractive personality. 'Social, convivial, full of anecdotes, good at repartee, never out of temper ...'[3] but he could give as good as he got both verbally, and, so we are told, physically, for he was a competent wrestler. Other accounts suggest he was stubborn and hot-tempered. One thing is certain; he was not a man to be ignored.

By 1851 the family had settled in London, in Holborn. The Odgers' second daughter, Jane, was born in 1854 in St Pancras parish and their youngest son, James, arrived in 1859 and was registered in St Giles. George was making shoes and Jane is listed as a 'shoe binder'. We also know that George specialised in making ladies' shoes, for he became a member of the Ladies' Shoe and Bootmakers' Union. Inevitably his obituary writers described him as a 'fine craftsmen'[4], though there is no evidence for this assertion and he does not ever seem to have set up in business on his own account. We are told that one of his employers was Mr Goodyear of Leicester Square, who patented a range of rubberised waterproof footwear, and George is credited with helping him with the process.[5] Again, this may or may not be true – but it is clear that, though George Odger had received very little formal education, he was a shrewd and intelligent man, the sort to whom others turned for help. His friend and associate, George Howell, described him thus, 'as a friendly critic in revising – that was his forte ... for a clear statement of a case or a deputation Odger was almost unrivalled. We could trust him on all occasions. Only just give him his brief – that is just the main points – George did all the rest.' Howell was talking about his skill in a political context but no doubt it was equally useful when drafting a patent application.

The focus in this chapter is necessarily on George Odger the politician. He was not the only clothing worker to have tried to improve wages and conditions for his fellow workers; from the Luddite frame-breakers onwards, the trades had seen strikes and agitation, particularly in the big cities. They were nearly always unsuccessful but they played an important part in the development of the clothing trades, and so it is appropriate to have at least one chapter of this book devoted to an activist.

We are told that George Odger was part of a delegation that protested to the House of Commons about the importation of French silks, laces, fancy shoes and other goods in the 1840s, and it would seem he acquitted himself well. Robert Peel is said to have asked, 'How is it, that you shoemakers are ever foremost in every movement? If there is a plot, or conspiracy, or insurrection, or political movement, I always find there is a shoemaker foremost in the fray.'6 Odger's answer is unrecorded. However, the anecdote does suggest that he was already politically involved in his early twenties, though it was not until the builders' strike of 1859 that he came to prominence.

In August 1859 the building masters staged a lockout of workers who belonged to the building trade unions. The unions had long been asking for a nine-hour day and a worker at Trollope and Son's Belgrave Works in Pimlico presented a petition to his master requesting that their hours be so reduced. Mr Trollope allegedly sacked the unfortunate man on the spot. Other masters were so nervous of the implications of their men working shorter hours that they attempted to persuade their employees to sign a document renouncing their union membership and organised a lockout against those who refused. It was a serious miscalculation. Other unions recognised the infamous document as a direct attack on the right of trades to form unions – something that had been legal since 1824 – and expressed their sympathy and support, both moral and financial, on a grand scale. George is recorded as conveying 'his strong sympathy with the movement which the boot and shoemakers felt they ought to have commenced themselves many years ago' and on 30 August he made a £10 donation to the lockout fund on their behalf. Other unions followed suit – the Amalgamated Society of Engineers astounded both the building workers' unions and the employers by presenting £3,000 over a period of three weeks, a totally unprecedented sum. The lockout was by no means universal, however, as out of around a thousand builders' yards in London only the eighty-eight largest were closed.[7]

The lockout lasted until February 1860 when the employers finally agreed to re-employ union men. It was only a partial victory in that the builders had not won the nine-hour day they had hoped for, but it was important psychologically as it showed that determined working men actually could defeat a powerful, wealthy association of employers. It also proved the value of unions supporting each other. The direct result was the establishment of the London Trades Council (LTC). George Odger was on the executive from the start; Tom Jones of the Operative Tin Plate Workers' Union was the first secretary, followed by George Howell, who was a former Chartist, an active member of the Operative Bricklayers' Union and a close associate and would-be biographer of Odger's; then in 1862 George took over himself, remaining in post for the next ten years and on the Council's executive until a few weeks before his death. It is at this point that one begins to wonder how he continued to provide for his family; in 1862 his youngest child was a handicapped three-year-old and he also had a six-year-old daughter and two teenagers at home. No one in 1862 expected a working man to be a hands-on father, but it was expected that he would spend his time earning money to feed his family.

The LTC had various objectives, notably to support any trade whose members were in dispute with their employers, and:

> Rule 8. That the duties of the Council shall be to watch over the general interests of labour, political and social, both in and out of Parliament; to use their influence in supporting any measure likely to benefit Trades Unions; also to publish (if necessary) an annual Trades Union Directory.

George Odger was largely responsible for writing Rule Eight, though if he had had his way the reference to Parliament would have been much more specific, for he firmly believed that the best way to improve the lot of the working class was by having working men in government.

Over the next twenty years the LTC was involved, directly or indirectly, with almost every movement that sought to improve the lot of the working class – and so was George Odger. There were numerous spin-offs. In October 1861 a weekly newspaper specifically aimed at working men with unionist sympathies – *The Beehive* – was founded. It was financed by five shilling shares in a company called the Trade Newspaper Company, which were purchased by various trade unions. George was on the Board of Directors from the start, and in fact the newspaper died with him in March 1877.

The LTC was also involved with the movement to extend the franchise to working men, but George was so disappointed by the lacklustre compromises made in their discussions in 1862 that he determined to take matters into his own hands. He put out an appeal in *The Beehive* that October, and in November the Trades Unionists' Manhood Suffrage and Vote by Ballot Association was formed, with George Odger as President – catchy titles were not his forte. George's summing up of the aims of his organisation tell us a great deal about the man:

> Let our advocacy be firm, intelligent, and persistent; not a sowing
> of the seeds of discord, but a promise of the growth of union; not
> an excitement of class against class, but an endeavour to promote
> the welfare of all; by moderation in our demands, forbearance to
> our opponents, and while earnestly contending for our own rights,
> by the sacred maintenance of the rights of others.

He was ever the moderate, deprecating any form of aggression, convinced that reason and persistence would carry the day. He also had a gift for oratory that even his opponents acknowledged, and a facility with language rare in a man with so little formal education. Some writers opined that he had studied Shakespeare and spent time with a company of players[8] – but, like so many assertions about George Odger's background, there is no evidence to back it up.

What we do know is that he sometimes wrote poetry. One example survives in a published collection of *Rhymes for the People*. It is called 'Paul Copse the Poacher' and begins:

Twas one night, when the rain down the mountain came pouring
A famed poacher, Paul Copse, seized his gun while 'twas low'ring ...[9]

It does not improve greatly as it goes on to detail a fight between the poacher, a gamekeeper and their dogs, in which everyone is killed in a welter of blood: 'And the groans of the dying were hushed by the gale'. Even the poacher's faithful dog is shot as it sits by its master's body ...

Poetry may have been a hobby but politics was George Odger's life. Under his guidance the LTC garnered the support of the National Association for the Promotion of Social Science, a mainly middle-class group containing a number of prominent academics who were able to put forward a credible case for the existence of trade unions. It was also associated with the Universal League for the Elevation of the Industrious Classes, which had the Marquis of Townshend as a sponsor and was supported by Lords Shaftesbury, Brougham, St Leonards, Elcho and Lichfield – aristocrats who felt genuine concern for the working class. A meeting was held in December 1863 and the objectives of the League were established as:

- the reduction of working hours
- a general extension of the franchise
- provision of educational institutions for members
- 'to establish fraternal communication with the industrial populations of all countries ...'

However, relations between the classes were always a little uneasy. Working men were often resentful and suspicious of people who they

perceived as wealthy do-gooders; Thomas Hughes has the narrator of
Tom Brown's Schooldays articulate this:

> I don't think much of you yet – I wish I could; though you do go
> talking and lecturing up and down the country to crowded audiences,
> and are busy with all sorts of philanthropic intellectualism, and
> circulating libraries and museums, and Heaven only knows what
> besides; and try to make me think, through newspaper reports,
> that you are, even as me, of the working class. But, bless your
> hearts, we 'ain't so green', though lots of us of all sorts toady
> you ...[10]

George Odger was no toady but, when the League was formally
constituted in January 1864, he was the second speaker after the
Marquis and claimed that 'during a long life of political activity
he had attended the formation of many societies, promoted by
those who sought to elevate the working classes. None was as
good as this one.' Naturally, he added membership of the League's
council to all his other activities. In March 1864 the League
held a soirée, attended by around 250 people, and here we see
another side to George Odger. He performed a series of songs and
readings, obviously designed to impress the great and the good;
The Beehive commented on the 'high and pure character' of the
entertainment.[11] The extension of the franchise was one of George's
main preoccupations, and we shall return to it, but there were many
others.

The League's commitment to international affairs chimed with
Odger's own interests – and events in Italy, America and Poland
galvanised support among working men in the UK and were a
significant factor in keeping the League alive. It may come as
something of a surprise to those who have not studied nineteenth-
century labour history to realise just how aware many working men
were of what was going on abroad.

Garibaldi's success in uniting Italy in 1861/2 had been much
applauded, and there was a good deal of excitement when it was

rumoured that the great man himself planned to visit England, which led to the formation of a Workingmen's Garibaldi Demonstration Committee. The formation and dissolution of guilds and leagues and committees of working men is very much a feature of this period, and the plethora of acronyms and similar titles can be quite confusing. The purpose of the Demonstration Committee was to ensure that Garibaldi received a rousing welcome from the working class, was presented with a testimonial, and met as many of them as possible. The visit was postponed and postponed, but eventually Garibaldi did come to London on 11 April 1864, by which time a number of other welcome groups had been formed. *The Times* was scathing:

> There are signs that a certain sort of people want to thrust themselves forward and help their little names to notoriety by demonstrations connected with him ... Garibaldi can be very sincerely welcomed by Englishmen of all classes without the parade of absurdities. (24 March)

Odger was one of the deputation who met Garibaldi at Nine Elms station and the working men of London turned out *en masse* to fete him. However, as ever, class struggles intervened; Garibaldi cancelled his planned tour of the provinces and left the country after little over a month on the pretext of ill health, disappointing the many who had hoped to see him.

Discontent about this affair rumbled on and, after the successful Working Men's Shakespeare Celebration – another event that comes as something of a surprise – at Primrose Hill on Shakespeare's tercentenary, there was a protest meeting about the government's handling of the Garibaldi affair – and the police arrived to break it up. This raised a whole series of questions about the rights of working men to assemble in public parks, an issue that would not be resolved satisfactorily for some years.

The American Civil War of 1860–5 was widely reported in the British press and the issues were much debated. By and large the aristocracy supported the South; the working class supported the North; and the middle class was divided. George Odger was a vigorous supporter of the anti-slavery Republicans and is credited with helping shift the editorial line of *The Beehive* away from supporting the Confederate States of America in the conflict. He himself claimed to have given three years of his life to 'averting so sad a calamity'.

The Polish insurrection of 1863 also caught the imagination of British working men. The LTC presented a petition to Palmerston asking him to support Poland's right to independence and to withdraw the British ambassador from Russia if he was refused, and the LTC pledged its own support for Polish workers. Palmerston ignored the request and the pledge of support did not amount to anything that helped the Poles in practical terms – but it is yet another example of how outward-looking the labour movement was at this date. They were not alone. A French deputation of workers visited England to solicit support for Poland, and Odger wrote and delivered an *Address to the Workmen of France from the Working Men of England*. It was stirring stuff. 'We are proud to welcome the representatives of the liberty-loving French people, who came forward to initiate what has long been delayed, a grand fraternity of people,' he declaimed in his clear, slow voice with its distinctive Devon burr:

> We say again 'fraternise'. Let us have a perfect understanding with all men whose prospects are in peace, in industrial development, in freedom and in human happiness all over the world. Do this, that the strong and brave, instead of being led forth with fire and sword to kill and destroy, to satisfy the craving desire of traders for gold, ministers for place and despots for conquest, may live to make their homes happy, and use their strength to assist the weak, the aged, the destitute, with the consolation of being free from the miseries produced by war ...

The result was that, on 28 September 1864, a meeting was held at the St Martin's Hotel in London to launch an international association bringing together trade union leaders from Great Britain and Europe. George Odger not only attended this gathering but was a prominent speaker at the event. The resulting organisation was the International Workingmen's Association (IWA), remembered today as the 'First International'. George Odger was on the governing General Council of this organisation from the first until his resignation in 1872.

It would take him to the first IWA conference in Geneva in 1866; the culture shock of foreign travel to the miner's son from Devon can only be imagined. When the Franco-Prussian war broke out in July 1870, George's sympathies were originally with Prussia but, when Napoleon III fell and a Republic was declared, working-class sympathies went over to France. A Workmen's Peace Committee was formed, at which Odger gave speech in favour of the Republic, and there was a great rally in Hyde Park on 10 September. Odger went to Paris to see things for himself – and was seized as a Prussian spy on his return – though he was soon released. However, the actions of the French Commune in March 1871 proved a bridge too far; George could not support such violence and, indirectly, this spelled the death knell of the First International.

There is no space here to detail all the issues with which George Odger occupied himself, but they were many and varied. One thing that particularly concerned him was the repeal of the Master and Servant Law. As time went by and the unions grew stronger, employers resorted to the courts rather than lockouts, invoking the Master and Servant Law, which criminalised recalcitrant employees. George Odger was one of the people called before the Parliamentary Select Committee in 1866 to discuss the issue. Of particular interest to us is his explanation of why the projected new law would be unworkable in his own trade of shoemaking – and many others – because of piecework. Work was given out by masters and the worker had to return it within eight days; however, there was no obligation on masters to distribute work regularly or fairly. This system is familiar to us from other trades; it would seem that it also applied to shoemakers in the big cities.

George had strong opinions about how labour should organise. He favoured the development of large, amalgamated unions, which would have more clout than the small, local and specialist ones to which most men belonged. His own trade set an example with a Conference of the London and Provincial Societies of Boot and Shoe Makers convened in London in January 1863, and agreed the objectives of protecting wages, providing help for tramping journeymen, and establishing sick funds and burial funds. It also urged members not to oppose the factory system and the increasing use of machinery – more and more workshop trades were going over to factory production and George was wise enough to see that this was the future and that resistance would be counter-productive.

He also argued for the creation of arbitration and conciliation boards to mediate between masters and men; at a meeting with the Sheffield ironworkers in 1867 he compared 'strikes in the social world to wars in the political world'. His ability to mediate was much in demand that year – after a period of relative prosperity, 1867 saw a bad harvest and an economic downturn – and George seems to have spent a lot of his time touring the country, meeting workers and arbitrating in disputes. Probably the worst case he had to deal with was when he and Robert Danter were sent to Sheffield to enquire into the various violent outrages orchestrated by William Broadhead, TU representative of the Saw Grinder's Union, who expressed his disapproval of opponents by having them shot or blowing up their houses.[12]

In 1867 a Royal Commission was appointed to report on the trade unions – partly as a result of the violence in Sheffield – and Odger was one of the people interviewed. The Commission resulted in the Trades Union Bill, which was passed in 1871; it was a deeply unsatisfactory piece of legislation that recognised the legality of unions but criminalised all sorts of actions like picketing and remonstrating – however peacefully – with strike-breakers.

There was no limit to George's involvement in issues that affected working men. For instance, he was elected to the committee of the

Land Tenure Reform League, which was formed in September 1869, and in January 1867 he was even invited to a conference with clergy and working-class leaders to investigate why working people did not go to church. Odger seems to have had little interest in the church himself and flirted with secularism, but that did not stop him being invited. Unsurprisingly, that meeting concluded that the 'Church's greatest weakness is its own lack of conformity between its preaching and its practice'!

However, his main focus was always on parliamentary representation. Under Palmerston this was an unrealisable dream, but Gladstone's speech of 11 May 1864, arguing for the extension of the franchise, offered a ray of hope: 'We are told that the working classes do not agitate for an extension of the franchise,' Gladstone argued, 'but is it right that we should wait until they do agitate?' A few days later on 17 May, there was another rally about the right to hold meetings in public parks – and Odger ensured that part of it was taken up by discussing the extension of the franchise.

In May 1865 the National Reform League issued an *Address to the Working Man of England,* which alluded to the American dictum of 'no taxation without representation' and urged 'Let us contrive to act an example of respect for law and thereby give a dignified answer to all calumniators ... Above all let us sink our individual differences in presence of our common grievance and thereby prove how earnest we are in the struggle for our rights.' Odger spent much of this period travelling and drumming up support for the cause. He also gave a series of lectures on Palmerston, which were, by all accounts, lively and very uncomplimentary.

That gentleman's unexpected death in October intensified the campaign for extending the franchise – everyone knew reform would now be on the agenda. There was an endless programme of meetings to raise awareness and soirées to which sympathisers from the middle and upper classes were invited. Publicity was of the essence. In 1866 the Industrial Newspaper Company was formed, with Odger as president and sometime editor, and it acquired the

Miner and Workmen's Advocate (founded 1861) and renamed it the *Commonwealth*.[13] Issue 1 laid down their agenda:

> Starting from the position (1) that the people are the only legitimate source of political power (2) that government is invested with authority by the people to use it for the protection of the people's interests (3) that to the people it properly belongs to judge and express their judgement as to whether or not the objects of their trust have been secured, the *Commonwealth* will stand for manhood suffrage, the ballot, equal electoral districts, direct taxation, the acquisition of land for the people through legislation, co-operative industry, reduction in the hours of labour and working class Political, International and Trade Associations ...

However, as with so many political movements, there were disagreements and breakaway groups, the chief of which was the Working Men's Association (WMA), formed by Odger's arch-rival, George Potter, which was much more militant than the Reform League.

On 12 March 1866 Gladstone introduced the bill for the £7 franchise; it was a very moderate reform and did not involve any redistribution of seats. While both the Reform League and the WMA had accepted the bill as a step in the right direction, they knew it was woefully inadequate, and they were quite unprepared for the vehemence of Robert Lowe's speech in response: 'If you wanted venality, ignorance, drunkenness – if you wanted impulsive, unreflective, violent people – where would you look for them?' he thundered. Others agreed with his assessment of working-class would-be voters and the bill was defeated. This was followed by two huge demonstrations in Trafalgar Square: 10,000 were there on 27 June, and by 2 July the number had risen to 80,000.

A third demo in Hyde Park on 23 July 1866 narrowly escaped turning into a riot because the terrified government insisted on providing a military presence. The movement was gathering strength, and numerous other meetings took place both in London and the provinces. The number of branches of the Reform League increased from seventy to 238. The League appointed a series of lecturers to travel around the country drumming up support – Odger was one of them and for a time was relatively well-paid. The lecturers received £2 a week, which included £1 for personal expenses, plus 20 per cent of the money they collected for League. To celebrate their success, the League then held a ball on 23 November. Odger recited a poem called 'A Rough Ride' and his daughter Jenny (Jane) sang 'Through the Woods'. This is one of the very, very few occasions upon which a member of George's family is mentioned.

The campaigning continued and, for the next few months, both sides put out a huge amount of propaganda. They had an enormous constituency. In 1866 there were 22 million individuals identified as members of the working class – two-thirds of the entire population – and they had just 25 per cent of the vote; 11 million of them were workers, roughly half-and-half labourers and artisans. The Reform Bill was presented in March. One issue that caused a good deal of debate was the position of lodgers; many working men and their families were not rate-payers because they lodged with others and the initial draft disenfranchised them. However, that restriction was partially removed and the bill was finally passed in August. *Punch* could not resist the fact that 'lodgers' rhymed with 'Odgers'.[14]

> Enfranchised are lodgers,
> Be quiet then, Odgers
> And you noisy codgers,
> Beales, Bradlaugh and Bright ...

It was not yet full manhood suffrage but the electorate had increased by 88 per cent. Two pieces of legislation came about as a result, both of which should have pleased George Odger, though neither went far enough for his taste: an amended Master and Servant Act and a Conciliation Act to enable arbitration in disputes.

For a brief period some of George Odger's attention was taken up by the education question. School provision in the 1860s was patchy at best, despite the best efforts of the National School movement, which was established in 1811 with the laudable but unfulfilled aim of establishing a church school in every parish. The situation was at its worst in the manufacturing towns and one of the issues Odger and his fellow trades unionists had to deal with was the ignorance of many of the workers they were trying to help. What is more surprising, however, is how many working men like George Odger himself were self-educated and highly literate. Forster's Bill, making schooling compulsory for all children between the ages of five and ten, was passed in November 1870. Education was not free, however, and the penny-a-week charge per child was a stumbling block for large families. The TUC did not campaign on that issue, however; their objection was to Clause 25, the compulsory religious element. True to form, they established an Education League to get working-class members on to the school boards that oversaw the new 'board schools' that were being set up, but in this they were largely unsuccessful.

George Odger soon returned to government reform. Having got much of what he wanted in relation to the extension of the franchise – the idea that this might one day be extended to women never seems to have occurred to him – his ambition turned to getting a working man, preferably himself, elected as an MP. The first stage was to persuade working men to use their newly acquired vote to support Liberal candidates and unseat the Tories, and to this end the Reform League despatched fourteen pairs of men to travel round the regions to publicise the policy. George Odger and J. Coffey were allocated Devon and Cornwall.

In 1868 – the first election after the passing of the bill to extend the franchise – George Odger stood for the newly created Chelsea seat, stating proudly that 'he would not go there simply as a labour representative, but as an unflinching supporter of the great Liberal party'. His platform was that he would sweep away the remaining restrictions on lodgers voting and the limits on rate-payers, vote to disestablish the Irish Church, support education for all and argue for conciliation and arbitration boards as 'strikes and lockouts were a thing of past'. However, there were two other Liberal candidates and he was persuaded to withdraw, so as not to split the vote. There were a handful of working-class candidates for other seats at the same election but none of them got in. The *Illustrated London News* reported:

> So ends, we trust, the terror which certain amiable but weak-minded persons owned lest the artisans in a body should storm the House of Commons; and other persons will probably feel with us that here, again, is a matter for regret, as the presence of some of the class is desirable, both for the information of the House on sundry details which ought to be known, and as witnesses for the House to the artisan class that their interests are respectfully and earnestly considered.[15]

However, 'the amiable but weak-minded persons' could not relax for long. In June 1869 George Odger was one of four Liberal candidates competing for two seats in Stafford. Edmond Beales, a prominent member of the Reform League, wrote a letter of commendation to Stafford for him, saying he was, 'One of the foremost champions of your rights in that contest, one of the most zealous, undaunted and indefatigable combatants, under the banner of the Reform League.' There was a test ballot to choose two candidates out of four; Odger came third so he again withdrew. The fight to get a working-class MP elected to Parliament was becoming fiercer and in August 1869 the Labour Representation League (LRL) was formed – an amalgamation of various smaller groups – with the specific purpose of getting a working man into Parliament (see plates 26 and 27).

In October 1869 A. H. Layard, MP for Southwark, was appointed British ambassador to Spain and in the ensuing by-election in February 1870, the LRL put Odger up against Sir Sydney Waterlow, a wealthy city man who had made his money in printing, as the Liberal candidate. The *Telegraph*, once so scathing about working-class ambitions, opined that 'of all the working men in England ... [George Odger] is the best qualified

SOUTHWARK ELECTION.

ODGER

AND

VICTORY

Now all you gallant Southwark men
Who does require protection,
Just mind, I say, your p's and q's
At this Great Grand Election;
Never don't elect a man
Who your wages will be stinting,
And never have a covetous man
Like one who lives by printing.

The act like men, you Southwark blades,
Have neither a printer nor a 'sodger',
Vote for a man who will protect your trade,
And sing, Southwark, lads, and Odger.

Long enough the poor man has been crushed,
Now is your time or never,
Come, now with me lads, nimble be,
Here's Odger, lads, for ever.
Don't you elect a Waterlow,
Whose principles are stinting,
He knows as much about the poor man's rights
As a donkey knows of printing.

There has lately been some glorious fights,
In Southwark, says Ben Fagan,
It beat the Battle of Bunker Hill,
And the glories of Copenhagen;
An old lady stood by London Bridge,
Bawling, lick me you shall never,
She jumped complete to Tooley Street,
Bawling, Odger, boys, for ever.

In Bermondsey there was glorious fun
Among the girls and sailors,
It put the Borough all in mind
Of the devil among the tailors.
A grocer's wife, full of spleen and spite,
Doffed her chignon so clever,
Pulled her petticoat off and went aloft,
Singing, Odger, boys, for ever.

Oh Colonel, Colonel Beresford
You are a rum old codger,
Neither you or Waterlow
Can ever cope with Odger; -
Odger is a working man,
And as clever a man as Pompey,
Odger is a gentleman,
And you're a pair of donkeys.

When Odger is returned, my boys,
To the brim we'll fill our glasses,
We will drink success to the tanners' wives
And the blooming Kent Street lasses;
From the Bricklayer's Arms to London Bridge
There will be such a hustle
Aye, and all the way from Cotton's Wharf
To the Elephant and Castle.

Put the right man in the right place
Keep out the aristocratic sodger,
Tell old Waterlow it is no go -
It is victory and Odger;
The working man must have a friend,
Who against tyranny is clever,
With heart and glee sing liberty,
Odger, my lads, for ever.

Odger we know is a working man,
If he's not rich, he's noble-minded,
He will understand how the working man
Has been crushed down and grinded.
Then send him into Parliament,
To put a stop to their capers,
And tell them we want a good beef steak,
Instead of herring and taters.

Keep out the printing gentleman,
Banish the tyrant sodger,
Strive with all your might to do what's right,
And plump, my lads, for Odger.

to represent his class in the House of Commons.' It was a popular seat – at one point there were nine candidates for it, though eventually they were whittled down to three: Odger, Waterlow and a Tory, Beresford. Odger had considerable support as the broadsheet on the facing page shows.

Waterlow eventually retired in favour of Odger after a preliminary vote – but he did so too late and Beresford was returned, though Odger only lost by about 300 votes out of more than 9,000. At that point the *Telegraph* offered him a job as a reporter, but he turned it down, preferring the cut-and-thrust of debate to the quieter – and better-paid – task of writing. A month later he agreed to stand for Bristol but came third in a test ballot and so withdrew. He was also invited to stand for Stafford again but it seems his heart was not in it and he scarcely visited the town – to the extent that his enemies began asking questions as to whether he had been paid to lose. He was criticised by the LRL for dodging from seat to seat. His argument was that 'It is not the work of getting a man to parliament, it is the work of principle' – but nevertheless, as a result of the criticism he resigned from the LRL executive. Family issues may have played a part; his married daughter, Mary Jordan, died that year, and George and Jane Odger took in her baby daughter.

George's final foray into electioneering came in 1874. That year fifteen working-class candidates went to the polls and two of them, Alexander Macdonald in Stafford and Thomas Burt in Morpeth, both miners, were successful. Odger contested Southwark again, but his health was failing, his campaign was lacklustre and once again the Liberal vote was split and he lost. It was his last election.

In later years he became increasingly attracted to republicanism. It was a period when the Royal Family, and the Queen in particular, were not at all popular, partly because of Victoria's long period of seclusion following Albert's death. Despite this, George's views caused a rift with many of his former friends, particularly George Howell, and marred his later years. In 1872 John Mortimer of the

London Figaro began to wage a campaign of abuse against George Odger, largely because of his republican sympathies. It started in April:

> Know all men that Odger the cobbler rules the government of England ... We do not like the cobbler. We abhor his principles. We regard him as an enemy of order. We hold him to be a demagogue of the lowest and most contemptible type – half booby and half humbug; a political Cheap Jack who would be a political sharper if he had brains enough.

The campaign continued for several months and eventually George Odger was ill-advised enough to bring a case for libel against Mortimer. The case came to court in February 1873 and the fact that George had publicly spoken and written of his republican leanings told heavily against him. He lost the case; appealed; and lost again. Costs of £500 were awarded against him and he was forced to declare himself bankrupt with assets valued at just 15s – though his friends launched a Defence Fund to help him out. He was not a man to give up, and in May he called a national republican conference in Birmingham. It was not a resounding success and republicanism gradually lost its following.

George continued with other aspects of his political life, giving his support to Joseph Arch's agricultural union and trying to mediate in the ensuing lockout of farm labourers. One of his last acts was to go to Newcastle in 1876 to arrange a meeting there of the TUC, but he became so ill that he had to return to London. It was the beginning of the end. In September the TUC agreed to send £20 to support him in his illness – Odger replied that, 'No letter I received in my life touched me more closely', and though he rallied for a while he died in March 1877 of heart disease, diabetes and dropsy.

He was survived by his wife, Jane, three of his children – John Henry, Jenny and James – and his two grandchildren, William and Ada Jordan, who were the children of his late daughter, Mary. Jane died in 1882, leaving almost half her annuity to be divided between the surviving children. Jenny married a solicitor's clerk and went on to have a large family; James died in his thirties; John stayed at home with his mother until her death and worked as a shoemaker. Ada went on to become a chorus girl and appeared on stage with Marie Lloyd – it is hard to know what George would have made of that.[16] Some of them lived to see universal adult suffrage and the birth of the Labour Party, and some of George's grandchildren would see the first Labour government come to power in 1924 – events of which he could only have dreamt.

Sadly, despite his years of dedication to the cause of the working man, George Odger is today little remembered. He has entries on *Wikipedia* and in the *DNB* but, given his origins, his was an extraordinary life and he merits much more in the way of a biography.

The Tales People Tell: The Symington Family (*c.* 1840–1923), Corsetry Manufacturers, Market Harborough, Leicestershire

Families create their own myths and legends. This is especially true when the family in question establishes a successful business – people ask questions about how it started, and there is a tendency for the owners to exaggerate or elaborate the little that they actually know. Half-remembered conversations are reinvented, facts are reinterpreted, inconvenient details are forgotten. This is what happened with the firm of R. & W. H. Symington, corset manufacturers of Market Harborough. By the time Christopher Page wrote his history of Symingtons, *Foundations of Fashion*, in 1980, the narrative describing the creation of the firm was well-established. Two talented and enterprising brothers from Scotland had arrived in the town in the early nineteenth century; one set up a grocery business, and the other became a draper and married a young woman who worked with her mother as a stay-maker in a cottage adjacent to his shop. Seeing his future wife at work allegedly gave James Symington the idea of setting up a corset factory – and bingo! – Symingtons was born. It is a good story – but it is only a story.

The two Scottish brothers were William and James Symington, the sons of Robert Symington, a grocer in Sanquhar in Dumfriesshire. Robert had five sons and one daughter, with four of his boys following him into the grocery trade. William, James and their youngest brother, Samuel, all travelled south and attempted to earn their livings as travelling tea and coffee salesmen; they all eventually settled in or near Market Harborough. William, the eldest, seems to have arrived there first, sometime in the late 1820s. He had the agency for 'Howqua' tea and his advertisements appeared regularly in the Midlands press. In 1852 he developed a type of flour made from dried peas that could be used as the basis for soups and stews. It made his fortune – the troops used 'Symington's high pressure steam prepared pea flour' during the Crimean War, and Scott took containers of it to the Antarctic.[1]

We do not know when James Symington, the second brother, left Sanquhar but it was some time before he came to Market Harborough. In the early 1830s he was living in Warwick, and it was there that he met and married Sarah Gold (see plate 28). She was born in 1809, the sixth of the eleven children of Robert Gold and his wife Ann, née Perry. Robert Gold was a tailor with premises on Market Street in Warwick and, as young adults, Sarah and two of her sisters, Elizabeth and Lydia, set up as dressmakers on the Market Place. It is quite likely that the Gold sisters made corsets – many dressmakers did – so it is possible that James Symington did see Sarah stitching stays. However, this was in Warwick, not in Market Harborough, and years before he went into the drapery business himself. The couple married in 1834.

Corsets were known as 'stays' up to the 1850s, and the two terms are interchangeable. Whatever they called them, corsets or stays were an important part of a woman's wardrobe throughout much of history. Heavy corsets made of leather or layers of stiffened fabric, with bones and a detachable busk (a broad strip of wood, metal or whalebone at the centre front), gave women the conical upper-body shape we see in so many portraits of the sixteenth, seventeenth and eighteenth centuries. Even in the early nineteenth century, women in their simple, floaty, high-waisted dresses of silk and muslin were wearing stays underneath them. As the century progressed, the fashionable silhouette changed, but a small waist remained the ideal. By the 1880s and 1890s, narrow hips and a flat stomach were also needed to show dresses of the period to their best advantage – and corsets became more and more constricting.

However, corsets were expected to last. They were never worn next to the skin; they were instead put on over the top of the chemise – a loose, short-sleeved, knee-length undergarment that must have puckered and pleated into uncomfortable ridges as the corset was tightly laced. The rationale was that, unlike the corset, the chemise could be washed at reasonably frequent intervals. After a while, corsets moulded to the shape of their wearer, so an old pair of corsets was much more comfortable than a new pair, and as corsets were comparatively expensive most women did not buy new ones very often.

'Sarah Gold' still appears as a dressmaker in *Pigot's Warwick Directory* in 1835; it may be that she continued to work under that name after her marriage or it may be that the information for the directory was gathered while she was still single. Either way it seems the young couple remained in Warwick. Their first child, Janet, was born there in 1836 and by then Sarah may already have been beginning to question her choice of husband. On 23 April 1836 'James Symington of Warwick, tea dealer' appeared in the *Leamington Spa Courier* as a conditionally discharged bankrupt. This was bad news for his creditors. It meant the receivers had sold all of his assets and that those to whom he was still in debt could wave their money goodbye.

We do not know what happened next but, by 1838 when James and Sarah's second child, Robert, was born, the family were in Kenilworth, perhaps staying with Sarah's elder sister, Mary Ann. Mary Ann Gold had married Samuel Pratt, a maker of agricultural implements in the town. The Symingtons were not there long, however, for their third child, Sarah, was born in Hinckley in Leicestershire a year later. By then James was describing himself as a 'draper', though we do not know whether he was working for himself or for someone else. Finally, in 1840, they moved to Market Harborough.

In October that year advertisements began to appear in the *Leicester Mercury*:

GREAT BARGAINS
Ready-made Clothing, Hats, Caps, etc. etc.
MAY BE HAD AT

SYMINGTON'S UNRIVALLED ESTABLISHMENT
CHURCH STREET, MARKET HARBOROUGH

J. SYMINGTON
Having recently entered upon the Shop recently occupied by MR A. WOODWARD, has provided an immense stock of
MEN'S and BOY'S
READY-MADE CLOTHES, HATS, CAPS, MACKINTOSHES, BROAD and NARROW CLOTHS and all kinds of
MATERIAL for
MEN'S APPAREL; also a large amount of Carpet Bags, Hat Cases, Umbrellas, etc., etc.
Ladies' French and English Stays of Superior Quality made to order
EXAMINE THE PRINTED LIST OF PRICES which may be obtained at the Shop gratis
READY MONEY

It seems that James Symington's brother, William, provided the money to set him up in business. There are no records of them making a formal agreement but, in February 1848, the local press reported that the partnership of 'W. and J. Symington, drapers' had been dissolved.[2] Presumably this meant that James's business no longer needed William's backing. Four months later, over in Warwick, James's father-in-law, Robert Gold the tailor, went bankrupt and James was one of the three people to whom his bankruptcy was assigned, which suggests that by then he was seen as an established tradesman. By 1851 James could identify himself to the census enumerator as a 'tailor, stay-maker and draper (master) employing sixteen hands' – his business in Market Harborough was obviously thriving.

With her knowledge of the dressmaking, stay-making and tailoring trades, it seems quite likely that it was Sarah who was responsible for at least some of Symington's success; for, far from being the visionary entrepreneur of family legend, James Symington actually seems to have been a man who did not stick at anything for very long. Sarah also seems to have persuaded her husband to employ her younger brother, Henry Gold, as a 'shopman'; in 1842 Henry gave evidence in court when a customer walked out of the shop without paying for a waistcoat he had tried on.[3] Henry must have got a good grounding in the business; he married Hellen Symington, James's sister, and by 1851 had returned to Warwick, where he was running his own clothing business and employing a staff of eight.

It is clear from the 1840 advertisement that stay-making was an integral part of James's drapery business from the start but we do not know how important a part it was. Nor do we know who made the corsets. There is a family story that Sarah Symington headed the stay-making workshop attached to the shop herself and had three assistants. This might be true, though given the size of her household it seems unlikely that she worked there full-time. Between 1841 and 1853 she gave birth to seven more children: William Henry in 1841, Eliza in 1842, Perry Gold (named after her two maternal grandparents) in 1845, Agnes in 1848, Julia in 1849, Edward Johnston in 1851 and James Lindsey in 1853, by which time Sarah herself was forty-four. It is possible that her sister, Elizabeth, helped with the stay-making for a time – the Gold sisters' dressmaking business in Warwick was wound up in 1836 when Lydia Gold married – and Elizabeth certainly spent time with the Symingtons, for she married the youngest Symington brother, Samuel, in 1842. However, we have no way of knowing who the other assistants were, particularly as trained stay-makers seem to have been thin on the ground in Market Harborough. In the 1841 census the only young woman who described herself as a maker of stays was twenty-year-old Elizabeth Claypole, and we cannot be sure that she worked for Symingtons. She married in 1843 and a decade later there was still only one corset-maker in Market Harborough, according to the census: twenty-six-year-old Mary Cox. Of course, it may be that the 'three assistants' is an exaggeration and that one stay/corset maker, with supervision and occasional help from the boss's wife, was quite sufficient to fulfil the corsetry requirements of the ladies of Market Harborough.

Until the middle of the nineteenth century, corsets were all made by hand – lines of meticulous stitching formed channels into which bones and busks were inserted, and heavy-duty thread and strong needles were needed to create garments robust enough to withstand tight lacing. Stitching corsets, with their layers of canvas and buckram, was hard work, much harder than making dresses or underwear or shirts.

This brings us to another part of the Symington legend. In 1856 Robert Symington, the eldest son of James and Sarah and then aged eighteen, is said to have visited America and met Isaac Singer, 'inventor of the sewing machine'. Young Robert allegedly realised that these machines would be ideal for the hard labour of stitching corsets and shipped one home to his delighted mother, with the result that, within a few years, Symingtons would be producing machine-made corsets on an industrial scale – but this, too, seems to be a myth.

James Symington seems to have tired of drapery and, in the late 1850s, he set himself up as an auctioneer and appraiser (valuer),[4] handing the drapery business over to his two eldest sons, Robert and William Henry; the firm became R. & W. H. Symington. Robert was twenty-three in 1861, William Henry just twenty (see plates 29 and 31). Around that time the brothers took over a disused carpet factory for the corset-making side of their business, which implies that from the outset they were ambitious to expand and confident of their market, and the corsets they made were indeed machine-sewn.

However, though it is possible that Robert Symington visited America in 1856, the meeting with Singer is almost certainly apocryphal. What we do know is that Robert went to America in <u>1886</u> with his wife, his baby son, and the child's nurse.[5] They travelled back on the SS *Umbria* in July 1887 – Robert pasted the passenger list and a brochure about the ship into one of his scrapbooks.[6] We also know that, in December 1886, probably as a result of that visit, Symingtons ordered eighty 'flossing' (embroidery) machines from the House Corset Machinery Co. in Connecticut[7] – could this be the origin of the story about the sewing machine sent from America?

While Robert Symington *might* have purchased a sewing machine in America in 1856, doing so would have been unnecessary and even unwise. To understand why, we need to know a little about the incredibly convoluted history of the sewing machine.

There are numerous claimants to the title of 'inventor of the sewing machine' – various machines were invented by various people in various places between 1790[8] and 1830[9] but none of them worked very well. However, in 1845 an American mechanical engineer, Elias Howe, was awarded an American patent for improvements that created a viable sewing machine.[10]

Elias struggled to get investment in America and eventually his brother came to London on his behalf and sold the English patent for Howe's machine to William F. Thomas for £250. William Thomas owned a firm that manufactured corsets, umbrellas and luggage at 73 Cheapside, London, and was keen to see the sewing machine adapted for use with heavy-duty fabrics and leather. What is interesting about this, and runs contrary to Symington's mythology, is that it was not *their* stay-making firm that first spotted the potential of the sewing machine for use in manufacturing corsets. Elias and his family came over to London, and he worked for Mr Thomas, trying to adapt the machine to stitch the heavy fabrics Thomas's firm used. It appears that he failed and the two men quarrelled – and in 1849 Elias found himself in dire financial straits, with a sick wife, so he decided to go home. He then became embroiled in a series of disputes with other American manufacturers, the chief of whom was Isaac Singer, who was selling a replica of Howe's machine as his own. Eventually, Singer, Howe and a number of other manufacturers settled their differences, pooled their patents and established what we now call the 'sewing machine cartel'.[11]

Meanwhile, in the UK, William Thomas finally found someone to adapt the machines, and allegedly paid them £2,000 to do so.[12] He guarded his patent jealously and set up a factory to make sewing machines under his own name; from 1854 onwards, advertisements for W. F. Thomas and Co's 'Patent sewing machines' appeared in local and national newspapers.

Thomas made the grand claim that the machine could do in one hour the work it would take six or eight men to do by hand,

W. F. THOMAS AND Co.'s
PATENT SEWING MACHINES.
PRICE FROM £15.

THE attention of Tailors, Shoe, Stay, Cap, Dress, and Bag Makers, Upholsterers, and others engaged in various descriptions of Sewing or Stitching, is directed to these Machines, which are rapidly coming into general and profitable use.

No. 1. A Machine producing work, *both sides alike*, which *will neither rip nor ravel*. It will do as much work, in a superior manner, as can be done by 6 or 8 persons, in the same time, by hard labor, and it is not liable to break or get out of order. This Machine, in its construction, differs from all others, the foot or stand being the shape of a *Tailor's Sleeve Board*, which enables persons to put in Sleeves, and stitch round the Cuffs, bottoms of Trowsers, &c., after seams are closed. For the edges of Waistcoats, for Binding, for the raised seams down the sides of Trowsers, and for the *Blind Stitching* of the edges of Coats, it cannot be surpassed. Price £30.

No. 2. A Machine working with immense speed, forming a neat stitch of any size required, *exactly alike on both sides*, *without loop or ridge*. It is continuous in its operations, will work up any length of thread without stopping, either straight lines or curves. It is thus adapted for every description of goods, as Moleskins, Beverteens, Cords, as well as the finer kinds of materials. Price £15.

The clear profit from the use of one of these Machines is from £4 to £8 per Week, depending upon the work done.

They may be seen in operation at

22, Skinner-street, Snow-hill, London.
AGENTS WANTED. [7576]

Advertisement for William Thomas's sewing machine. This advertisement appeared in many local and national papers in 1854 and 1855.

thus – somewhat optimistically, considering the rates garment workers were paid – saving the employer between £4 and £8 a week.

The Symingtons must have seen these advertisements, as they frequently appeared in the Leicester press, and the machines could be viewed in action at Thomas's London showrooms, a short rail journey away from Market Harborough. Furthermore, the adverts specifically mentioned that the machines were suitable for stay-making – and, given that William Thomas was himself a major manufacturer of stays, the family probably knew all about him and his machines well before 1856. At that date Singer's machines did not have the adaptations Thomas had introduced to make them suitable for stitching layers of thick fabrics – so why would Robert have thought that the American machines were superior to the ones that had been available for the previous couple of years back home?

Furthermore, by the late 1850s Thomas's advertisements had taken on a threatening tone. All other manufacturers of sewing machines, they claimed, were infringing Thomas's patent, and firms using them would be taken to court. Such advertisements appeared almost weekly in the Leicester papers and Thomas made good his threat. The Symingtons would almost certainly have been aware of his long-running case against Foxwells of Hinckley, for example.[13] Under the circumstances – is it likely that Robert Symington would have risked sending home a Singer machine, even if he did indeed visit America in 1856? Nevertheless, the story died hard and on the basis of it, the firm celebrated its centenary in 1956.

However, an article in the *Midland Times* on 28 August 1880 dates the establishment of the firm to 1861: 'They commenced business in 1861 employing one machine and three employees, or – as they are usually termed – hands.' The journalist had visited the firm and met the proprietors. It seems unlikely that, just nineteen years after the event, when they were both still comparatively young men, they would have given him the wrong date for their firm's foundation.[14] We do not know where the 'one machine' came from, though the Leicestershire press did report that in April/May 1861 Robert purchased a sewing machine on approval from a firm in Manchester and was dissatisfied with it; however, he failed to secure it in its box when he sent it back. It arrived smashed to pieces – and the dealer sued. The case came to court that June. The supplier was a Mr Laughton and the courts found in his favour.[15]

Despite Thomas's threats, within a very short period of time many corsetry firms were using sewing machines. There were other changes, too. By the 1860s

> ... the cloth is [now] woven double, and, by means of thread binders and reels fixed in the harness of the loom, the stitching for the bones and cords is dispensed with: indeed, it is only required for seaming, goring and binding, and that is done by machine; the only part done by hand now is the sewing around the busks and the putting on the quilling ... [and] stays are made so much lighter than they were, when women fancied they wanted support in the stays ...[16]

The 1880 article is extremely informative and it is clear that Symingtons had grown rapidly in the two decades since 1861. By 1880 the firm employed 1,600 staff, had around 500 machines and had set up a branch factory in Leicester, another in Desborough and two in Rothwell – two small towns near Kettering in Northamptonshire. However, it was the Market Harborough factory that the reporter visited and he described a three-storey building – actually two buildings connected by bridges – between Adam and Eve Street and Factory Lane at the rear of the shops on the Sheep Market. The store rooms were on the top floors and the journalist tells us they contained 'bales of different kinds and colours of cloth from mills in Yorkshire and Lancashire'. Like many nineteenth-century writers, he was fascinated by statistics and he reported that the factory used at least 4,500 yards of fabric a day and made 300 different patterns of corsets 'from some of the plainest to the more elaborately embroidered and trimmed'. They got through 7,500 yards of lacing cord a day, 3,750 yards of edging lace, 3 cwt of steel clasps, 2 cwt of bone and cane – and the amount of sewing thread they used in a year would be enough to wrap three times round the globe!

He visited the sample and designing room, and saw dozens of patterns laid out on counters and cardboard templates hanging on the walls, and then went on to the cutting room, which he obviously found fascinating.

We first noticed three cutting machines at work on some stout material; they have a steel blade with a 'sicklelike' edge, which is made to move vertically, and is of sufficient strength to cut 60 thicknesses of cloth at once. Each machine requires the attention of two men, and occasionally three. The pattern to which the material has to be cut is marked on the topmost piece of the 60 thicknesses, and the whole is guided by hand against the constantly moving guillotine. In addition to these there is an endless saw-band which does its work even more rapidly and correctly ... So rapidly is this cutting done that the material for as many as 250 dozen of corsets is cut daily ...

Not all firms had such sophisticated machinery. Miss Wall, employed at Gargett's in Manchester in the 1860s, found cutting out hard work: 'This cutting out heavy stuff tires me more than working the treddle [sic]; it makes my fingers ache so,'[17] she complained to the Children's Employment Commission.

Most of Symington's corset stitching was farmed out to the other factories or to outworkers, so the next process the reporter described was finishing. Firstly the corsets were shaped by men with large pairs of shears, 'vigorously trimming up the bottoms and tops of corsets that have been stitched'; next, the corsets were brushed with starch and handed over to twenty or thirty men with gas irons for pressing.

The irons are a great improvement on the old fashioned 'goose' which were formerly used, and also on the box-iron that superseded it. They are hollow and contain a mixture of burning gas and air on a similar principle to a gas stove, the gas being supplied by means of a flexible tube from a gas pipe above. By this contrivance the iron is always ready, and no time is wasted in making up fires or charging heaters ...

On the floor below, the corsets were 'bound, trimmed, eyeletted, embroidered and overlooked, all the work being done by females.'

A mechanical punch made the holes and the metal eyelets were inserted by hand:

> We watch one girl seated at an eyeletting machine, and are surprised at the rapid way in which her nimble fingers fix the little circular pieces of metal in their holes, for she was not above ten or twelve seconds fixing those on one side, so that two or three corsets would pass through her hands every minute ...

No doubt she was paid piecework rates, so it was in her interests to work fast. Another girl fixed tags on laces, also at great speed. Eighty sewing machines were used to bind and embroider the corsets, and these too were powered by state-of-the-art systems:

> All the machines were worked from a shaft below the table, and were so arranged that each worker had only to press a pedal down with her foot to set it going. To show how beautifully and thoroughly this power employed was brought under command, we were shown that from half a stitch to 1,500 a minute could be made. This was pointed out to be another improvement on the original system, when each worker had to stand upon one leg while she treadled with the other. Here all were seated, and the actual manual labour was reduced to a minimum. The Singer machines seem best adapted for this work, and are gradually superseding other makes throughout the factory.

This would also suggest that Singer machines were not used from the start – another snippet of evidence that gives the lie to the Robert-Symington-meets-Isaac-Singer story.

After being embroidered and trimmed with lace, the corsets were boned with cane or 'whalebone', which was actually American buffalo horn. The busks were made of steel. Finally, the completed corsets were moulded by being laced on to hollow copper moulds that were shaped like female torsos. The corsets were brushed with more starch; superheated steam was then pumped into the moulds and they were left to dry. Finally, laces were inserted and the corsets were then packed and boxed. Across their five factories, Symingtons were producing around 3,000 corsets a day in 1880.

It may well be that the reporter from the *Midland Times* visited the factory at the brothers' invitation, for his account is overwhelmingly positive. In fact, there were hazards in the stay-making business, as there were in many other manufactures. William Thomas was disarmingly frank:

> All persons who work on articles that have been 'stiffened' in Manchester suffer frequently from the bad size used in the process; it is worse with fustians, moleskins, etc. than with nankeens, sateens and such materials that stay-makers use, but even the latter, particularly in moist warm weather, give out a vapour very offensive and injurious; the girls say they feel unwell and think it is the dye that makes them so but it is nothing less than actual decomposition.[18]

Symingtons certainly used nankeens and sateens (heavy cotton fabrics) from Manchester – but, if their workers complained of ill effects, the journalist obviously thought it wisest not to record the fact.

There was more. Symingtons employed outworkers to stitch corsets and supplied them with sewing machines 'on easy terms of hire or purchase'. Instead of acknowledging this as the cost-saving exercise that it in fact was, the reporter argued that, 'By giving out work they enable many who could not come into the factory an opportunity of assisting the bread winners ...' A brief article appeared in the *Rugby Times* on 31 December 1881; Symingtons had opened a factory in Rugby earlier that year. Sewing machine dealers were targeting people in the locality, offering them machines 'of the kind used at Symingtons', and convincing them that possession of such a machine would enable them to get out-work from the factory. Symingtons refuted this, saying that, 'The sewing machine really used is a Jones.'[19] Again – not a Singer.

Symingtons kept close tabs on their factory workers with a draconian 'clocking on' system, which penalised workers for arriving more than five minutes late, and a system of quality control that enabled any hand doing shoddy work to be easily traced.

> Every worker in the factory is known by a number, and every article manufactured has a label attached, on which is written the numbers of the 'stitcher', 'cottoner', 'binder', 'finisher', etc., etc., so that any defect can at once be traced to the careless worker.

There was an elaborate system of fines 'for being late, and other violations of rule, and these are placed to a sick fund, which has hitherto been sufficient to relieve all hands during sickness' the journalist reported in 1880. It sounds remarkably benign, though a letter in the *Rugby Times* in the mid-1880s hinted at a different interpretation. The writers complained that reports of the earnings of hands at Symingtons' factory in Rugby had been greatly exaggerated, and that most of them earned just 10s or 11s a week, which was often reduced because they were regularly 'fined heavily for mere nothing'[20]. All these rules and regulations were the brainchildren of Robert and William Henry's formidable younger sister, Perry Gold Symington (see plate 30). Perry Gold never married; she worked with her brothers, taking responsibility for the welfare of the firm's young female employees, though as a woman herself she was not invited to join the board until 1911 – after both her elder brothers were dead.

While trumpeting their commitment to the welfare of their work force, Symingtons were quite willing to take their workpeople to court for relatively minor misdemeanours. Staff who left without giving proper notice often appeared before the magistrates. In November 1871, for example, Elizabeth Gilbert was fined 12s for leaving without working her two weeks' notice. Elizabeth clearly hated her job and refused to return, despite being told she could be fined even more heavily. The upshot was that she got a £5 fine on top of the 12s and was also ordered to pay 14s costs. Such sums were far more than a young working woman could find, so instead she was sentenced to two months' hard labour – to modern eyes this seems a totally disproportionate punishment for depriving her wealthy employer of two weeks of her time. She was not alone. Just a few weeks earlier, two other employees had been in court for the same offence – one of them a twelve-year-old errand girl, Charlotte Holmes.[21]

Earlier the same year, in April, Robert Symington prosecuted four girls who had made corsets for themselves using offcuts of material from the factory. He acknowledged that the cloth was of no use to the firm but argued that the girls had stolen the bones, eyelets, laces, etc. that they had used to complete the garments. The newspaper account makes it clear that the girls did not feel they had done anything wrong and were devastated to be in court, and the value of each of the corsets, by Symington's own admission, was only a shilling or two at best and one of them he valued at just one penny.[22] One feels that the appropriate response might have been a severe telling-off and a warning – but instead he stood by while each of the girls was sentenced to seven days' hard labour.

The earliest surviving wages books show that the average wage for workers in most departments at Symingtons in the 1890s was around 9s to 11s a week, though the highest weekly payment recorded was £1 10s and the lowest 4s. Many people seem to have been paid piecework rates; their income fluctuated week by week. These wages are linked to names, not to the jobs the recipients did, so we cannot be sure what the best-paid jobs in the firm were at that date.[23] These wages seem to have been on the low side of the average for workers in the corsetry trade. For example, in the 1860s Guthrie's in Manchester were paying 10s to 16s a week to their machinists, 4s 6d to 5s a week to their eyeletters and 7s 6d to 8s a week to their seamers and casers, who were doing 'coarser and harder work' than the other female workers. Thomas's in Ipswich paid their experienced machinists up to 15s a week.[24]

However, despite the pay, and the rules and the fines, Symingtons was not a bad place to work. The factory – according to the *Midland Times* in 1880 – was scrupulously clean. Later reports would describe drinking fountains on every floor and good 'sanitary arrangements'. However, Symingtons were best known for the facilities they provided for their employees in the form of clubs, sports facilities and so on.

There were also outings. As early as Friday 15 January 1858, the *Leicester Journal* reported that the practice of employers giving 'treats' to their workpeople was becoming increasingly common and commented that 'Mr James Symington and Mr Walpole have each given those employed by them a supper and other entertainments.' William Symington also arranged annual 'treats' for the workers in his pea-flour mills throughout the 1850s and '60s and, as their business grew, R. & W. H. Symington followed the trend set by their father and uncle. In 1870 we find the first reference to such an event: a tea at the Corn Exchange on 5 August to celebrate the marriage of Robert Symington and Mary Louisa Cox. Within a few years the firm was organising annual Christmas parties for their workpeople, and later there would also be summer charabanc outings. In the famously cold January of 1881 there was a much-reported trip[25] wherein staff were taken by a specially chartered train to skate at Welham, about three miles from Harborough.

The firm had its own brass band, set up in 1870, and a social club; in 1901 a special clubhouse was built. But Perry Gold Symington stood no nonsense. Cissy Abbott worked at Symingtons from 1918 and remembered 'Miss Symington ... coming round like a ship in full sail. If you did anything outside the factory that wasn't just right and [she] got to know, the next day she'd have you ... on the carpet.' She even monitored employees' behaviour on the dance floor at club dance nights. 'When they were doing the Lancers, if they lifted them off their feet she'd send one of the forewomen down the room to tell them about it ...'[26] By the time Cissy knew her, Perry Gold was in her seventies – a Victorian martinet unable to cope with changing social attitudes.

The Symington family became firmly enmeshed in the life of their adopted town. The elder William Symington seems to have concentrated on business affairs, but his brother James became an overseer of the poor and a member of the town Improvement Committee. James's sons, Robert and William Henry, both grew up in Market Harborough and became men of substance and influence through their factory. William Henry seems to have been a raconteur, a reciter of poems and singer of comic songs at local events, but Robert took a serious interest in local matters. Like his father, he was a poor law guardian and, when Market Harborough with Great and Little Bowden became an urban district in 1879, Robert Symington was on the 'Local Board', as the council was then called.[27]

His particular interest – almost amounting to an obsession – was with the water supply in Harborough. His concern was largely altruistic; he and his family lived at Little Bowden and their well was not contaminated. He campaigned vigorously for improvements and in 1882 he read a lengthy paper – twenty-two closely argued pages – ending with the motion:

> That the Board do exercise the authority given it by Section 51 of the Public Health Act, 1875, and take steps to provide a supply of water, proper and sufficient for public and private purposes, throughout the district over which it exercises jurisdiction.[28]

When some of his workpeople fell ill through drinking polluted water, Robert took it upon himself to commission a report on the drinking water supply in Market Harborough from E. G. Mawbey C.E., 'certified member of the Sanitary Institute of Great Britain'. The report was delivered in 1883 and made depressing reading. None of the town's wells produced good water and most were downright dangerous – of the twelve samples tested, all were condemned. From 1884 Robert fought his cause as Chair of the Water Supply Committee, but it would be another six years before the Market Harborough, Great and Little Bowden Waterworks opened on 4 December, 1890. Meanwhile he seems to have kept every document he could lay his hands on relating to new water-supply systems, including brochures from as far away as Brighton and Plynlimmon.[29]

Robert kept scrapbooks of press cuttings about the doings of the 'Local Board' with copies of letters he had written to the press about all sorts of local issues – from the length of time cattle were allowed to stand in the streets on market day to the conduct of the local fire brigade. These scrap books tell us a good deal about Robert Symington.[30] At first sight they appear to be all about local government but on closer examination they do contain other material. Robert was a keen bee-keeper and there are articles about that. He was a member of the Volunteers, the local militia – in 1880 he was appointed to the rank of Lieutenant – and he kept programmes of Volunteer camps and sports days and cuttings about the doings of the local troop. The *Midland Times* supplied more information. When their journalist visited in 1880, the firm's porter or doorkeeper was

> ... engaged in what seems a rather incongruous occupation, this being nothing more nor less than the cleaning of rifles, but it is explained by the knowledge that Mr R. Symington is lieutenant of the volunteer corps recently formed in Market Harborough, and the porter being an old soldier, is just the man to know how these arms should be attended to.

Robert was also an Oddfellow at a time when Freemasonry was still very much a secret society – but he did allow himself to keep a cutting from the *Standard* of 12 January 1880 about the discovery under Cleopatra's Needle of a diagram that 'discloses, beyond any doubt, the ancient organisation of a Masonic Lodge – the emblems, principles and customs of which are identical with those today.' He kept a few rather mawkish poems about the bravery of the poor, odd cuttings about the various Symington factories and a longish article from the 11 September 1886 edition of the *Warehouseman's and Drapers' Trade Journal* about 'The Youngest Corsetry Factory in England' – said to be the one run by Mr L. Reynolds and Co. at Southport. There was also a poster about a free excursion to Olathe, Kansas, which offered the opportunity to buy land. It is dated 18 June but there is no reference to the year. Did Robert and his family take advantage of the offer a few weeks before boarding the SS *Umbria* for the voyage home from New York in 1887? There were letters about the ownership of the *William Symington* – a ship apparently named after an ancestor, a Scottish engineer who in the 1760s built the first steam-powered ship – an article about the riots in Market Harborough on Bonfire Night in 1874, notes about social events, an engraving of the house designed and built for him by the architect, William Wright, and meticulous records that Robert himself had made of rainfall in and around Market Harborough. It was an eclectic mix. Robert Symington was a man of many interests and talents.

Under Robert and his brother the corsetry business thrived. They innovated constantly, introducing new lines with evocative, topical names such as the 'Total Eclipse' and the 'Home Rule'.[31] Both these designs were registered in 1886; there was a total eclipse of the sun on 29 August that year and it was also the year the first Irish Home Rule bill was passed. Symingtons made maternity corsets that let out – a little – as the pregnancy progressed, corsets for nursing mothers and short corsets for sport that were 'cut low under the bust to allow for full circular arm movements and high over the hip for riding side-saddle'. One of their best sellers was the 'Pretty Housemaid', the design for which was registered in 1886 and which claimed to be 'the strongest and cheapest corset ever made', featuring a patent busk that would not break when the wearer had to bend over in the course of her household duties (see plate 32b). It was targeted at young working women with a little disposable income, and the box featured a maidservant in a frilly cap and apron. By contrast, there were racy numbers in black and bright colours, trimmed with lace and embroidery, which can only have been intended to titillate whoever the wearer allowed to see them (see plate 32a).

Symingtons' corset boxes were adorned with coloured pictures of shapely ladies with hourglass figures sipping tea or posing in front of mirrors, often described as 'L.S.' or 'lifelike shape' models, when in fact they were anything but. There were corsets that buckled at the front, soft corsets 'boned' with hemp twine or cotton cord, and ventilated corsets with gaps between the bones 'for coolness of wear in tropical zones'. There were corsets with eyeletted seams 'for strength', corsets with double busks to remove 'the gravest objection to the ordinary corset, namely the usual injurious pressure upon the delicate and vital organs of the chest,' and 'Lemon Cup' bust improvers with coiled springs and horsehair pads to replace what nature had failed to provide. There was the 'Bird's Wing' corset, made from forty-two individually shaped pieces of cotton and boned with the same number of whalebone strips, the 'Morn and Noon Corsets – two pairs in one box for the price of one', and the 'Surprise' corset, which was an old design in a new box! Mindful of the concerns expressed by the Rational Dress Society and the anti-tight-lacing movement, Symingtons also produced a range of corsets with names incorporating the word 'health', though none of them differed significantly from any other type of corset.[32] Their ingenuity was endless.

In 1889 they built a grand new factory, which was just across the street from their old one and linked to it by an enclosed bridge at first-floor level. The nineteenth-century records are patchy and not many survive, so it is difficult to get a complete picture of the business. However, we know that by 1888 the firm had eight factories, which between them were carrying stock worth £20,650 11s 7d; by 1894 they had £30,433 13s 3d worth. Of these totals, in 1888 £6,584 8s 9d consisted of made-up corsets; in 1894 that figure was £13,428.[33] By then the firm had branches in Rugby, Leicester, Rothwell, Desborough, Welford (Northants), Manchester and Farnham, while the early years of the new century would see the opening of a factory in Peterborough.

Sarah Symington died in 1890. She had long been a lady of leisure but she must have been proud of what her sons had achieved on the back of her little stay-making workshop. Robert only survived her by two years. Of the two brothers he seems to have been the most colourful – and he died as he lived. One October morning he went out to Sharnford, near Hinckley, for a morning's shooting and then caught the train back to Harborough. He was due to arrive just after one but he never got off the train – the guard found him dead in a first-class carriage. Apparently he had suffered from epilepsy for the previous few years and the inquest concluded that he had had an episode that killed him. His funeral was a grand affair: he was buried with full military honours, a man-servant led his 'charger' behind the hearse and his funeral cavalcade was accompanied by a military band playing the 'Dead March'. Volleys of shots were fired over his coffin as it approached the church and the pallbearers were all fellow captains in the Volunteers. His brother Oddfellows sent a huge wreath of white flowers from St Peter's Lodge, with an intricate arrangement in the centre depicting the square and compasses, and over 100 of his workpeople walked in the procession.[34]

Neither he nor William Henry had children to succeed them and in 1898 William stepped down from the business and retired to the Park, a grand new house that he had built for himself. That year the firm became a limited company, trading as R. & W. H. Symington & Co., which was managed by the two younger Symington brothers, Edward and James, Edward's brother-in-law Robert Howett, and George Wilson, who was one of the firm's agents; William Henry was a sleeping partner. He died in 1908. The capital raised from the sale of shares totalled £130,000 and the factory expanded once more.[35] By 1914 Symingtons was an international company and a market leader; its future looked secure.

Then fashions began to change. In 1956 Symingtons celebrated their 'centenary' – but by then corsetry was becoming a thing of the past. Older women still wore 'foundation garments' but fewer and fewer younger women saw them as necessary. The firm diversified into making swimwear; branches closed; and the operation shrank. In 1967 Symingtons was taken over by Courtaulds and the family relinquished control. Production ceased altogether in 1990 and 150 people in Market Harborough lost their jobs[36] – less than a tenth of the number who had worked for the firm in 1880. The wheel had turned full circle and only the stories – and a large collection of period corsets in Leicestershire Museums – remain.

'Primrose' of Branscombe: Ida Allen (1877–1959), Lace-maker, Beer, Devon

'All these statements I declare to be perfectly true ...' Ida paused. What should she call herself? She was the only Ida in Branscombe; she knew for a fact that some other girls in the village read *The Girl's Own Paper* and she certainly didn't want any of them to know she was the author of the essay she was hoping the magazine would publish. Girls who had entered their competitions in the past had often used made-up names. So would she. What about 'Primrose'? It sounded sweet and modest, and everyone liked the flowers ... you knew summer was on the way when the banks were covered in primroses and violets ... yes, 'Primrose' would do nicely.

It was a wise decision. In August 1897 Ida's essay won fourth prize – a whole two guineas – in *The Girl's Own Paper's* second essay competition for 'Girls who work with their hands'. No doubt there was speculation in the village about the identity of the essayist, but Ida kept quiet. It would be more than fifty years before she finally admitted that, yes, actually, she did know who 'Primrose of Branscombe' was. Fancy Mrs Spencer's[1] sister finding her essay in the magazine after all those years! Of course, she helped out at the museum in Exeter, and there were lots of old books there. Ida was rather in awe of the sisters and she was glad she had had the presence of mind to swear them to secrecy.[2] Even her own husband and children didn't know about the competition win – to tell the truth she was rather embarrassed about it ... This is what she had written:

My Daily Round
Dear Mr Editor,
I have been thinking since I read your last Daily Round Competition letters that I should like to let you see a lace worker's daily round, which work I have to earn my living by.

The summer is my busy time and I rise very early and get my little oil stove ready and make a cup of tea and ready to sit down to work by 5 o'clock sometimes earlier than that. I live quite alone in a little cottage facing the sea and cliffs, and as the days are so hot I like to have the early morning as I have to keep my work very clean so that it does not have to be washed before I sell it. I am today doing point lace cuffs, and I work for the village shop people who give out the work ready tacked to the pattern they require, which first I draw around with needle and fine cotton in every pinhole of the braid; the pattern is covered with; then if we require a new pattern to work on again I place a sheet of paper over the work drawn and with a piece of heel-bore, it is called, rub and the black marks come on the clean paper, and then we have a new pattern to begin another time, then I do a lot of buttonhole bars and pretty stitches which we have learnt, then the last stitch is called pearling; which is done with a coarser cotton, on the outside edge, then we rip it off the paper; and take it to the shop, where I get things to make use of as we are not paid money there.

I sit to work till 8 o'clock then I get my breakfast and put my house tidy and if I have any dinner to cook I get it all ready. I sit to work again by half past nine or ten then work until 12 o'clock, and if very busy for post as we call it, that is the work we are asked to do by a certain time; I do not stop only for a bread and cheese dinner and a cup of tea or an egg for we cannot afford meat dinners every day. I get fish and things very cheap in our village so it helps one a lot where we have not much money to spare so after having my bit of dinner if not busy I take my book and sit down in the fields or indoors in my hour we have for dinner. Sometimes there are two of us have a piece of work between us so then I take my piece to a friend's house to work alike or they come to mine and it is nice to have company at times so I get to work again and work until 4 o'clock and then put on my little kettle on my oil stove which saves coal in Summer; and get my tea, then sit to work until 8 o'clock then I leave off and if I have not finished my piece; I then take my can to fetch my water and do any odd jobs I find to do; I take my little can to a neighbours for her little girl to fetch my milk at the farm in the morning then I fetch other things I may want for my use and if I have time to go and see a dear old woman, who I call granny and who loves to talk to me, and then I go to see how much work my girlfriend has done and then go home to my supper and book for living alone I love books they are my friends now I have lost my mother. Then go to bed and before retiring I thank my Heavenly Father for his mercies which I enjoy which are many I am glad to say then if I am spared I begin my daily round each day but often get weary but glad to get work to do. The lace work is very trying to the sight and I am often very glad of an order from Ladies who pay money and a better price than what the shop people do for after working all day as I have said I earn but bare 7d and then only taken out in the shop.

Ladies often send their Honiton lace to be cleaned and put on new net: which is called transferring and then it will look like new lace; and that is real pillow lace which I have learnt; but it went down in price years ago and now if wanted they don't pay the full price for so the Point lace is done quicker and then we get really more for it. We used in the village to have schools for teaching children the work but it does not do now they have to keep to the daily school and then they go to service. I have learnt all the different sorts and find it most useful now as I cannot live in service my knee gives out so glad to come home to the lace work.

A pair of cuffs takes two days and we get a ½d for them or the worth of it in goods, so I hope if ever my daily round should be in print it will help to show the readers how hard some have to work to earn a shilling before they can spend it if we want clothes we have a book at the shop and they buy us what we want and we work on until we have paid for it.

All these statements I declare to be perfectly true –

'Primrose'
Branscombe
near Axminster
Devon
August 11ᵗʰ

No doubt the editor of *The Girl's Own Paper* was charmed by Ida's story. The lack of structure and punctuation pointed to a limited education, creating a picture of the plucky, motherless young girl living alone by the sea, struggling to make ends meet, a book lover, selflessly spending her precious free time visiting 'granny', too unwell to work in service but still thanking God for His mercies – this was exactly the sort of story subscribers wanted to read.

What the editor probably did not realise was that Ida knew that too. So she had carefully constructed a tragic history for herself – but it was almost entirely fictitious. Both 'Primrose' and Ida lived in homes 'facing the sea and cliffs' but there the resemblance ended. Indeed, Ida was partway through, or had just completed, a five-year dressmaking apprenticeship – she was not working as a lace-maker at all![3] And far from being the brave, lonely, crippled orphan she described, Ida was the youngest child of a prosperous farming family and she lived on a busy farm with her parents and her siblings, George, Minnie and Mary. Ida's father, Emanuel Pike, employed three men and a boy, and the family had a live-in servant to help in the house. They had moved to Great Seaside Farm when Ida was still a child from a slightly smaller farm near Branscombe Mill, where her mother had been brought up. Great Seaside was a picturesque, sixteenth-century, stone-built, thatched house with a 106 acres of land, just 200 yards from the beach.

Should we be shocked by Ida's deception? Probably not, for it did little harm – except in that it may have deprived a less calculating entrant of the two guinea prize. *The Girl's Own Paper* had a wide readership across many strata of society – part of the aim of the competition may well have been to make the wealthier readers aware of their poorer neighbours and to prick their consciences. Ida's essay did that in spades. And it was not entirely inaccurate. There were women in Devon in the 1890s who, like 'Primrose,' did have to live off the proceeds of their lace-making, and earlier in the century there had been many more. The fact that Ida was not one of them is almost immaterial.

Unfortunately, various students of the lace industry – the present writer among them[4] – have taken 'Primrose's' account at face value. Not until the 1891 and 1901 censuses became publicly available was it possible to be reasonably certain where Ida was actually living in 1897, but there are other clues in the essay that we missed.

Ida had little personal experience of the poverty 'Primrose' wrote about, even though she described the practice of paying for work in goods rather than money. This was known as the 'truck' system and had actually been banned in 1831 by Act of Parliament. The Act was reinforced by further Acts in 1887 and 1896 but, if Ida's essay is to be believed, the system was alive and well in Branscombe in 1897. It was certainly in force throughout the lace-making districts a generation earlier. In 1863 Mrs Harriet Wheeker of Sidbury, a lace-school mistress, gave a very full account of the problems it caused.[5] Her girls were expected to take two loaves and half-a-pound of butter each week as part of their wages. Sometimes they were desperate for cash.

The other day a girl who had been working long hours to earn more came to me and asked me if I would buy a pound of white sugar for 6½d if she could get it, 6½d being the proper market price, though the price of this sugar would be put down to the girl herself at 8d.

She gave other examples: five-shilling boots were sold to the girls at 10*s* 6*d*; calico that cost 7*d* a yard would be 9*d* or 10*d*; candles would be 8*d* not 6½*d*; and an extra penny or two would be added to the price of a pound of bacon. Furthermore, if a girl took a private commission and was paid in cash, the shop would boycott her work and, worse still, all the members of the lace-maker's family were expected to shop with the dealer, even when they had actual money. 'I wish the Government could do something to stop this: it is so cruel,' Mrs Wheeker went on. 'I could myself if I had capital to spare. Any shop that would pay ready money and sell on fair terms would make a fortune ...'

John Tucker, who took over the lace shop in Branscombe in 1845, was a notorious exponent of the truck system and his workers disliked him heartily for it. He died in 1877, when Ida was just a baby, but the business remained in the hands of his daughters and son-in-law into the 1890s; however, it had closed by 1897. But it sounds as if other local shopkeepers followed the same practice; Ida's son claimed the system was still in operation in 1905. Certainly Ida's account does not betray the hatred and resentment of 'the shop' that most workers felt, and her interpretation of frugal living is not one that most impoverished workers would have recognised. The truly poor lived on tea and bread, with a scrape of butter or treacle if they had any – cheese and eggs were luxuries. Women who were never paid in cash could not buy 'fish and other things' in the village as 'Primrose' claimed to do, however cheap they were. Not only could they not 'afford meat dinners every day', women solely dependent on their lace-work would have counted themselves lucky to afford a bit of bacon once every few weeks. Women who worked on their own account were not 'allowed' an hour for their mid-day meal; they took what time they could spare. However, Ida was familiar with the workmen on her father's farm and their maid, who would have had set meal breaks, and she seems to have seen this as the normal pattern for working people.

But we should not discount everything Ida wrote. She had certainly learnt to make lace and was good at it. It may be that as a girl she made and sold lace from time to time for pocket money, but in 1891 Ida and her sisters are not recorded in the census as having any occupation. This does not mean that they were ladies of leisure – there would have been plenty for them to do in the house and around the farm – but it does mean that they did not have regular paid work. In 1901, by which time her father had retired, George had a farm of his own and Minnie and Mary were married, Ida was living with her parents at Hole House, a fine medieval manor house a little way inland, and was listed in the census as 'dressmaker on her own account'. Ida had been apprenticed to Aglands of Seaton for five years, working from 8.30 a.m. to 5.30 p.m. and walking the 4 miles there and back each day.[6]

Her mother, Ann Pike, probably encouraged her. Ann was a talented dressmaker and, before her own marriage in 1867, when she was still Ann Bromfield, had made the plain cream silk wedding dress for John Tucker's daughter, Mary, which is now in Exeter museum.[7] It was completely plain to show off a Honiton lace veil and trimmings – Mary was to be a walking advertisement for her father's firm. She married in December 1864. This may also give us some idea of why 'Primrose' is so uncritical of the truck system. The Pikes seem to have been quite friendly with the Tuckers and at some point Ida acquired a huge bundle of lace from their leftover stock, which she later sold, piecemeal, to customers who wanted 'something special'.[8]

Women in Branscombe made Honiton lace and had done so for generations. It was poorly paid and, though the commission for lace for Queen Victoria's wedding in 1841 gave the trade a temporary boost, lace-making was in decline throughout the second half of the nineteenth century. However, the lace Ida describes is not Honiton, which is lace made with bobbins on a lace-pillow (see plates 34 and 35), but Branscombe point, a needle-made lace developed by John Tucker in the middle years of the nineteenth century (see plate 36).

Ida's description is somewhat garbled but she did know what she was talking about. Branscombe point starts with a length of machine-made cotton tape, which is tacked to a printed pattern on coloured paper or cloth to form the outline of a design. The worker then uses a series of fancy embroidery stitches to fill in the spaces in the pattern, and perhaps adds a pearl edging to the tape to prettify it. The backing holds the work in position until it is complete, when it is removed and discarded; it is fiddly work, but much quicker to make than pillow-made Honiton lace. We know that Ida learnt to make both types of lace but we do not know who taught her. By the time she was five, schooling was compulsory for all children up to the age of thirteen. There were no longer lace 'schools', where little girls as young as six or seven sat hunched over their pillows for hours on end, day after day, learning to make the Honiton lace 'sprigs' (motifs), which would be joined together to make collars and cuffs, wedding veils and handkerchief corners. However, in some of the Devon schools lace teachers came in to teach the craft for a few hours a week. Maybe that happened at Salcombe Regis, the school that we know Ida attended[9] – or maybe one of the older villagers taught her outside of school hours. It was a rather strange choice of occupation for a relatively well-to-do young girl of her generation – as she said in her essay, most of her contemporaries preferred to go into service rather than take up a poorly paid, old-fashioned trade like lace-making. In 1891 there were fifty lace-makers in Branscombe, but only thirteen of them were under the age of thirty.

Ida knew enough about the trade and its workers for most of her descriptions to be credible. The details she gives all tally with what we know from other accounts: working early in the morning when the light was good and it was not too hot, keeping the lace clean so it did not have to be washed before being sold, remounting old lace on new net, the gratitude workers felt when ladies paid ready money, the 7d-a-day average earnings and the length of time it took to make a pair of cuffs – though the ½*d* Ida claimed to have been paid for the cuffs is unrealistically little.

In 1902, five years after the essay was published, Ida married. She was then twenty-six, an ambitious young woman, and she married well. Her husband was George Edwin Farrant Allen – though by the time of the marriage he seems to have dropped the 'George' – and he was an engineering draftsman. He was a couple of years younger than Ida and had been brought up in Cardiff, where his father was an engineer; but his mother, Evaline Good, came from Beer, a small town about two miles up the coast from Branscombe. By 1891 Evaline seems to have been living apart from her husband, and she and her two children – George Edwin and Olive – were back home with her parents. After the wedding Edwin and Ida moved to Wales, and then to Dorset, and had three children. The names Ida gave them give us some insight into her character. Her second son was called Edwin after his father and Pike after her family – nothing surprising there – but her eldest son was called Roydon Farrant. Farrant was a family name, but Roydon was modern and rather pretentious. It was a surname, but as far as we know there were no Roydons on either side of the family. Her daughter fared even worse. She was christened Inez Bidney, though she was always known as 'Biddy'. Inez was an unusual name for the period but it is the 'Bidney' that is striking. Ida had discovered that her husband was distantly related to Jane Bidney.[10]

Jane Bidney was born in Beer in 1802; she was an astute businesswoman and moved to London to set up a lace dealership. It was Miss Bidney who was entrusted with the commission for Queen Victoria's wedding lace and who came back to Devon in 1839 to scour Beer, Branscombe and the surrounding area for women sufficiently talented to make up the designs William Dyce had created.[11] As we have seen, Ida was not one to allow the truth to get in the way of a good story and she exploited the relationship shamelessly, claiming to be Jane's 'descendant'. There was no blood relationship between the two women but that did not deter Ida – she repeated the story endlessly and used her daughter's name to reinforce it.

In August 1910, Edwin and Ida moved back to Beer. They had purchased the remaining twenty-five years of a lease on a property on Fore Street in 1904 for £80 from the Clinton Estate, on the understanding that the Estate would make various minor improvements, notably moving the privy from the end of the garden to outside the back door. Nevertheless, once the improvements were made, the sitting tenants were unwilling to leave and it was six years before the Allens were able to move in.

It was not a particularly comfortable residence. There were only two downstairs living rooms and Ida commandeered the best one as a lace shop, while the family living room doubled as her workroom. In later years Ida's son Ted recalled how cold it was when he and his wife visited for Christmas. Ida insisted on having the bedroom windows wide open even in the coldest weather, and the sheets over the hard horsehair mattress were linen – like sleeping between sheets of plate glass, Ted said. By the time you got warm it was time to get up. It had been the same when he was a child, but in those days he accepted the discomfort as normal. The house had dry rot; the ceilings were bowed; and the lath and plaster walls were flimsy. A huge flint was incorporated in the living room wall, making an unsightly bulge – but a gypsy woman assured the family this was a good luck sign. The bedrooms were poky with sagging ceilings and there were only two of them, though one was later divided in two to make a separate room for Biddy. They were reached by a narrow spiral staircase. Ida's husband died in 1936; he was a big man and the undertakers had to dismantle the staircase to get his coffin down. There was no running water, and so the family used rainwater from a butt out at the back or water from a tap over a conduit on the other side of the road. The kitchen was a lean-to at the back of the property. The toilet was in the back yard and Ida would never allow it to be roofed in, while the idea of an indoor water-closet was anathema to her – she 'didn't believe in them'. She even threw out the mat her daughter-in-law placed in the privy because she thought it unhygienic.

Ida's son remembered that the house was always infested with rats – they set traps and some nights would catch as many as thirty.

Years later they discovered there was a hole that led directly into the sewers through which the rats came. They also bred in the roof and the noise they made kept the children awake at night. However, there was another reason why there were so many of them. The man over the road was a butcher and used to slaughter beasts in his back garden – a garden that could only be reached by driving the beasts through his house! His pony and trap were kept in the same garden. Any meat he could not sell, offal, or things that had gone bad were handed over to the Allens' neighbour who bred maggots for fisherman. He used to hang the rotting meat on the trees in his orchard until it was crawling with maggots and no doubt smelling disgusting – and attracting rats and other vermin.[12]

Once installed in Beer, Ida set about making herself the face of lace-making in Devon (see plate 33). She was a canny businesswoman. While fewer women were becoming lace-makers, there were still married women who had learnt the craft and wanted to earn a little extra money, and a diminishing band of older ladies who had never done anything else. In Beer and Branscombe alone, 145 women identified themselves as lace-makers in the 1911 census. Ida gave these women an outlet. What is more, she paid cash and offered a fair price for high-quality work. Beer was a small town and the Devon coast was beginning to attract tourists and day-trippers – there was a new market to exploit. What better souvenir of a visit to Beer than a little piece of Devon lace? Ida knew how to sell.

She set high standards. 'The work that one woman starts cannot be completed by another', the *Western Morning News* reported her as saying.[13] This was not strictly true, but what she meant was that each lace-maker worked in a subtly different way which would – to the trained eye – affect the quality of the finished product. 'Old Mrs Allen was a very good lace-maker herself. She had a keen eye like a hawk and she could pick out the little mistake', Lesley Collier told Barbara Farquharson and Joan Doern. Lesley's mother had been a lace-maker; she used to work for Ida and would take Lesley with her to Beer to deliver the lace. Ida herself did much of the 'making up' – mounting Honiton sprigs in a tasteful design on net – and kept a sharp eye on which designs would sell. 'Oh – I want four of those and a big one', was the sort of thing Lesley remembered her saying.[14]

Like Lesley's mother, many of Ida's lace-makers came from her home village of Branscombe. There were various collecting points for lace in the village – Miss Farant's in Street, Ida's sister in 'the council houses' – and every few weeks Ida herself would visit Branscombe. No doubt there were similar arrangements in other villages where her workers lived and, of course, some chose to walk into Beer to deliver their lace in person. Betty Rowson explained:

My mum, every Saturday morning, when we were kids, we used to walk to Beer with little parcels of my mum's and my granny's lace and take it to Mrs Allen in the Lace Shop. She used to buy it from my mother, give us the money, and we had to walk home again to Sellars Wood ... Mrs Allen provided the cottons. Like when you took your lace work, they was done up in blue paper, and you used to hand it over to Mrs Allen and she'd look at it, price it off, give you the money, and then she'd give you how much thread she thought you had used. But you could buy – if mother needed any extra she'd ask Mrs Allen and buy a 'skip', they called it, which was a lot of little tiny skeins fixed together. Very, very fine thread.[15]

At least Ida did not copy the Tuckers and weigh the thread she doled out against the finished lace – hatred of this and other manifestations of the Tuckers' meanness still simmered in Branscombe well into the 1960s. 'Mother used to tell us ... they'd only give them so much money, make it up with groceries,' said Lillie Gush. 'Tucker sisters – Abbie, Louisa, Sophie. Two died one night. They didn't live very long. No, because they cheated, the Lord paid them.'[16]

Not only did Ida cater to the tourists, but she attracted royal commissions as well. It is not entirely clear how she first became known to the Royal Family – but she had boundless self-confidence and probably made the first approach herself. There was a long tradition of royalty patronising the Honiton lace-makers in increasingly futile attempts to keep the failing industry alive – the most publicised order being the one for Queen Victoria's wedding lace – and this continued well into the twentieth century. Queen Mary, consort of George V and grandmother of the present queen, patronised Ida's shop, sending 'much of her valuable old lace for reconditioning'[17], but there is no evidence that she ever actually visited in person. However, Princess Marie-Louise of Schleswig Holstein,[18] Queen Victoria's granddaughter, visited Mrs Allen several times and made a number of purchases. She seems to have visited incognito or, at least, without attracting the attention of the newspapers; but, when her uncle, the Duke of Connaught[19], visited Beer in November 1932, his meeting with Mrs Allen was widely reported. He expressed a courteous interest in what she did and spoke of his niece's interest in lace, while the newspaper reports of his visit presented an optimistic view of the industry. 'There are still about fifteen of the older women of Beer making lace, and successful efforts are being made to train the rising generation in this beautiful art', announced the *Exeter and Plymouth Gazette* on 2 December 1932. The 1930s were the highpoint of Ida's career. She was then employing upwards of 100 workers, including, she said, two men. If only fifteen of them came from Beer, Ida must have had workers in villages over quite a wide area.

The royal commissions continued but they were not enough to keep the industry afloat. In May 1939 Queen Elizabeth asked Mrs Allen to send her a selection of handkerchiefs edged with Honiton lace; she kept two and ordered a special one to be decorated with roses and thistles.[20] These commissions were good publicity but the royals did not always pay; they expected the honour of the commission to be sufficient reward. And Mrs Allen played along. As late as 1946 she had her workers make a lace-edged handkerchief as a gift for Queen Elizabeth to take as part of her wardrobe on her tour of Canada and the USA.[21] Apparently the Lord Chamberlain suggested that she should apply for a Royal Warrant – but Ida rejected that idea when she discovered it would cost her 100 guineas a year. Instead she had her stationery printed with the words 'Patronised by Royalty' – a perfectly legitimate claim that cost her nothing.[22]

It was not only royalty who received gifts in return for publicising Mrs Allen's wares. Society brides from influential local families – like Brenda Physick of Alphington who married in May 1932[23] – were equally likely to be presented with a lacy handkerchief to use on their wedding day on the understanding that an acknowledgment of the gift appeared in the press.

As Ida's reputation grew, there were other notable visitors – from Daisy Countess of Warwick (one of the Prince of Wales's mistresses), Lord Hailsham, Winston Churchill, Dwight D. Eisenhower and Field Marshall Montgomery of Alamein, to the world light-heavyweight champion (1948–50) Freddie Mills.[24] Presumably these men made purchases for their wives and girlfriends.

Ida was quite pushy with customers she judged to be susceptible. One such was a Mrs Ratcliffe. 'If I get anything rare I always

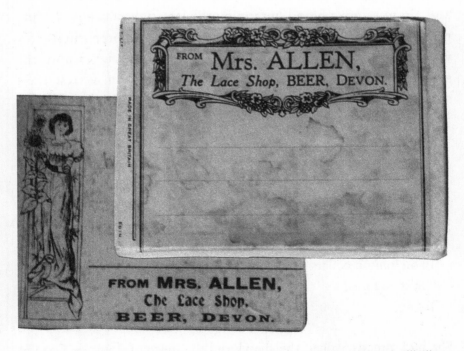

The designs on some of Ida Allen's packaging materials. (Courtesy of Allhallows Museum, Honiton)

think of you', she wrote in March 1948, trying to persuade her to buy a lace veil of 1864, 'just like one in the Victoria and Albert Museum'. She told a – probably apocryphal – story about how a local lace-maker had gathered ferns on Beer common from which she had created the design. The veil cost the hapless Mrs Ratcliffe £35, though Ida cannily claimed the owner had wanted £50 for it. She also persuaded her to buy some letters worked in lace, and two large sprays to decorate a dress to celebrate the Coronation. These cost £12 each but Ida assured her nothing comparable was available – 'if you offered me £100 I could not get them copied'[25].

Ida did not just sell lace, but she also identified and valued lace items – no doubt at rates that made her own prices look reasonable – and offered a cleaning and repair service, though Ted Allen said that if customers had known the methods she used they would never have entrusted precious items to her. Apart from the rats and the lack of a clean water source, Ida's methods were cavalier. She used chlorine bleach and salt to remove stains, and gin to remove blood, wrapping the lace tightly round a white pottery jam jar (the tried and tested method of preparing it for washing) and dabbing the chemicals on with her finger until the stains disappeared. Her prices were quite high. In March 1934 she charged a Miss Lockwood the following prices for cleaning lace items:

Swiss appliqué shawl	5s-6d
Limerick bertha [a wide collar]	2s-6d
Wide Brussels flounce	7s-6d
Point de Gaze	4s-6d
Narrow Brussels lace	5s-0d
Two Honiton collars	2s-6d
Registered post	9d
Total:	£1-8s-3d

She had already valued the shawl and the piece of Point de Gaze at £10 each and the flounce at £5, and she offered to remount some of the lace on to new muslin for a further 15s – but that seems to have been an expense too far for Miss Lockwood.[26]

Mrs Allen also exhibited her wares at county shows and local exhibitions – but no amount of publicity could keep lace-making alive as a viable industry. Ida acknowledged as much in 1940. While lace-making was taught in Devon schools in the 1930s, few girls continued to make lace after they left school and virtually none of them saw it as a way of making money. She had no new recruits and by 1940 many of her workers were in their seventies and eighties. 'Lace-making is too slow for modern times', Ida told the reporter 'wistfully'[27]. But in all probability it was the low rate of pay that was the real problem. Employment opportunities for women were opening up and men's wages had improved; few married women needed a few extra shillings so desperately that they were willing to work at the tedious business of making lace to earn them.

Ida was loath to shut up the shop she had worked so hard to establish. In 1956, then aged almost eighty, she was interviewed by the Exeter *Express and Echo* and at that time she still had five people working for her. One of them was Mrs Elizabeth Dart, who was over ninety. She was interviewed along with Ida and said proudly, 'I've been working for Mrs Allen for over thirty years and I'll continue if she's carrying on!' Elizabeth Dart died in 1960, outliving Ida by almost a year. The other thing that stands out from that interview was that, even in 1956, Ida still had a rose-coloured view of the truck system.

> A piece of lace 50 years ago was regarded as currency. A fisherman's wife could put the children to bed and make a sprig. She would take it to the grocer and get half a pound of butter, a pound of sugar and ½d change – all the result of her evening's work.[28]

Sugar cost 5d to 7d a pound and butter cost 5d to 6d a half pound in 1906.[29] The dealer would therefore have paid the equivalent of 1s 6d for an 'evening's work' – at a time when by Ida's own admission the amount of lace a worker could make in a full day would only bring in 7*d*! As we have noted before – Ida was not one to let facts spoil a good story.

Mrs Ida Allen died of cancer in the summer of 1959, by which time she had moved to Seaton to live with her daughter. But she need not have worried. The craft of lace-making would not die out with her as she had feared – it still flourishes as a hobby and some beautiful, delicate work is produced to this day.

Epilogue

I never wanted to return to this work. But I don't know anything else. The first day I returned to work, the deafening noise of the sewing machines made me so scared that I wanted to leave right away … The other night I dreamt that this factory also collapsed … God saved me once. How many times do you think God would save me? (Sharmin Akter)

Sharmin Akter survived the collapse of Rana Plaza on 24 April 2013, in which over 1,130 people were killed and more than 2,500 were injured.[1]

Rana Plaza was an eight-storey building in Savar, a district some fifteen miles north-west of Dhaka in Bangladesh, where garment workers from a number of different firms were employed. Westerners were shocked to learn that the firms renting space in the building made garments for Primark, Mango, Monsoon, Bon Marché, Benetton, Matalan and other well-known high street brands. For several days our television news programmes broadcast interviews with the grieving relatives of the dead and missing, and showed images of survivors dragged from the rubble, their brilliantly coloured *salwar kameez* coated in white dust. For a brief time these garment workers became real people with names and faces, homes and families, hopes and dreams. Big companies promised to act more ethically in future and to check on the conditions of the workers in the firms to which they subcontracted. Then the dust settled, the media caravan moved on – and most customers no longer question whether or not Matalan, Primark and the others have kept their promises.

If, in this age of instant mass communication, we are so wilfully ignorant of the conditions in which our clothes are produced, we can scarcely blame our nineteenth-century forbears for ignoring the plight of the garment workers of their day. Admittedly nineteenth-century clothing workers lived closer to their clients; but, for the most part, they were hidden away in closed workrooms and factories, and they arrived early to work and left late, seldom sharing the streets with the people who wore the clothes they made. Yet these people were not members of an underclass; like the Bangladeshi machinists in Savar, they were skilled workers.

There are many parallels between workers in the nineteenth-century garment trades in the UK and workers in the twenty-first-century garment trade in Asia. In places like Bangladesh there is a cheap and plentiful supply of labour; workers are afraid to complain for fear of losing their jobs; and employers often show a callous disregard for health and safety and the worker's well-being. The customer is king, while orders have to be filled at breakneck speed whatever the cost to the people on the shop floor. Owners of businesses make a comfortable profit while the workers barely make a living. It is a picture that would be familiar to most of our subjects. *Plus ça change, plus c'est la même chose …*

Endnotes

Biographical information that comes from normal family history sources – censuses, the 1939 household register, parish registers, civil registration records, individual birth, marriage and death certificates and probate records – and other information that comes from trade directories is **not** referenced. Each of the biographical chapters is based on an individual source or collection of sources, which is referenced **once**.

CEC = Report of the Commissioners into the Employment of Children and Young Persons (Children's Employment Commission) CRO = County Record Office

Introduction

1 The office has now moved to Museum Street, YO1 7DS.

Chapter 1

1 Quennell, Peter (ed.), *Mayhew's London* (Bracken Books, 1984, p. 574 and p. 341).

2 For further information see, for example, http://www.zum.de/whkmla/sp/1011/pope/sje1.html3.

3 Diary of Emma Jane Longsdon in Derby CRO, D3580/FP/5.

4 For further information see Inder, P. M., *British Provincial Dressmakers in the 19th century* (PhD thesis, De Montfort University, Leicester, 2000).

5 Information from *Dressmakers' Chart and Cutting Guide,* 1888–9.

6 Inder, op cit.

7 For more information about Charles Booth see: booth.lse.ac.uk.

8 Jackson, R. V., 'Pay in Nineteenth-Century Britain' in *Economic History Review* (2nd series, Vol XL, no 4, Nov 1987).

9 Perkin, Joan, *Victorian Women,* 1994, Chapter 9.

10 Inder, op cit.

11 National Archives of Scotland, CS96/3562.

12 CEC Vol X.

13 CEC Vol XIV.

14 A coarse braid sewn round the underside of the hem of a dress and protruding slightly below it, thus protecting the hem from wear as it brushed the ground (see plate 14d).

15 Crossick and Joumain, 'The World of the Department Store: distribution, culture and social change' in *Cathedrals of Consumption,* 1999.

16 For example, Mrs Woodgate Low (*Technical and Practical Lessons in Dressmaking,* 1893), Jeanette Davis (*The Elements of Modern Dressmaking,* 1894), Mrs Dobson (*Dressmakers' Chart and Cutting Guide,* 1888–9) and Mrs Grenfell of Liverpool, who produced a series of manuals for pupils and teachers between 1892 and 1894.

17 Deduced in part from a study of dresses in the Leicester Museum collection. Of twenty-seven 1850s dresses, eight were partly or wholly machine sewn; of thirty-three 1860s dresses, twenty-five were machine-made; of twenty-nine 1870s dresses, twenty-four were machine-made.

18 For more information about the 'watershed of the 1870s', see Inder, op cit.

Chapter 2

1 This letter and most of the information in this chapter comes from a scrapbook of family letters and papers in the National Library of Scotland, MS9685.

2 For more detail, see Inder, P. M. *English Provincial Dressmakers in the 19th Century* (PhD thesis, De Montfort University, Leicester, 2000).

3 10 April 1867.

Chapter 3

1 Unless otherwise stated, all the information in this chapter comes from documents in Gloucestershire CRO, CBR B1/4/8.

2 I am grateful to the staff at Cheltenham Local History Library for their detective work in discovering the original location of no. 13.

3 CEC Vol XIV, interviewee no. 91.

4 ibid. interviewee no. 88.

5 The *Cheltenham Directory* was published annually and the last entry for Rebecca Thomas appears in 1888.

Chapter 4

This chapter is an expanded version of an article published by the author in *Costume and the Textile Trade,* the proceedings of the 2009 Annual Conference of the ICOM Costume Committee.

1 It is on that collection of documents that this chapter is based. They are in the Barrow branch of Cumbria CRO, BDB/38.

2 For more detail, see Inder, P. M. *English Provincial Dressmakers in the 19th Century* (PhD thesis, De Montfort University, Leicester, 2000).

Chapter 5

1 It is on that diary that most of this chapter is based. It is in Hampshire CRO, 8M62/27.

2 Hampshire CRO, 8M62/8.

3 Hampshire CRO, 10/757/238.

4 Hampshire CRO, 5M62/11, page 155.

5 National Probate Calendar, 1883.

Chapter 6

1 The information in the first five paragraphs comes from an *Account of a Voyage to France.* Plymouth and West Devon CRO, 1217.

2 Most of the information in this chapter comes from that diary. Plymouth and West Devon CRO, 810.

3 Holbeton Parish Churchwarden's Rates and Accounts, Plymouth and West Devon CRO, 633/18.

4 Undated but *c*. 1836.

5 For example, Mansbridge in Basingstoke (see previous chapter, Hampshire CRO, 8M62/8) and Edward Stedman, James Edwards's father-in-law in Shropshire (see chapter 10, Herefordshire CRO, E61/2/1), were charging very similar sums, as were David Allison in Northampton (Northamptonshire CRO, D10388-90) and William Waslin in Skidby, East Yorkshire (E. Riding Archive and Local History Service, DDX476), while over in Garstang in Lancashire in June 1848 the master tailors came to a detailed agreement about their charges for making a huge range of items (DDX109 6/8 Lancashire CRO). Their rates were slightly lower than those of the other tailors listed above. Men's coats were to cost 6*s* to 6*s* 6*d*, jackets 4*s* 3*d* to 5*s* 6*d*, trousers 2*s* 7*d* to 3*s* 6*d* and waistcoats 2*s*. Boys' clothes were proportionately less; other jobs were costed at 3½*d* an hour.

6 The text of the report can be found at www.historyhome.co.uk/peel/economic/ duties.htm.

7 For more detail, see Spence, Jack, *The Smugglers of Cawsand Bay*, 2007; www.hansonclan.co.uk/coastguards_1.htm; and www.genuki.org.uk/Coastguards.

8 Spence, op cit.

9 www.historyhome.co.uk/peel/economic/duties.htm.

10 Holbeton Parish Churchwarden's Rates and Accounts, Plymouth and West Devon CRO, 633/18-19 and Holbeton tithe map – www.devon.gov.uk/ tithemaps.uk.

11 Plymouth and West Devon CRO, 633/18-19.

Chapter 7

1 'Thank you' in Yiddish and Russian – it is reasonable to suppose Adolph spoke a little Russian.

2 The name appears with a whole variety of spellings at different times and in different sources – Kutcheneer, Cushner, Cushneer, Kushner, etc. – but by 1911 he seems to have settled on 'Kashner'. His first name appears as both 'Adolph' and 'Adolf'.

3 The story and all the details in this account appear in the *Huddersfield Gazette*, 7 Jan. 1892, *Lloyd's Weekly London Newspaper* and *Reynolds Newspaper*, 10 Jan. 1892. The case was also widely reported in other newspapers.

4 Asaf, David, *Journey to a Nineteenth-Century Shtetl, the Memoirs of Yekhezkel Kotik 1847–1921*, 2002.

5 See, for example, www.simpletoremember.co./articles/a/pale_of_settlement.

6 Jewish Museum, London, oral history interview, tape no. 05.

7 Asaf, op cit.

8 Or 13 March according to the Gregorian calendar.

9 Asaf, op cit.

10 http://www2.le.ac.uk/centres/stanley-burton-centre/documents/research/lectures/union%20castle%20line%20and%20emigration.pdf/view.

11 Beatrice Potter quoted in Green J., *A Social History of the Jewish East End of London 1914–1939*, 1991.

12 Jewish Museum, London, E1991.259.

13 Eva Cushneer's death certificate, July 1893.

14 Mendelsohn, Adam D., *The Rag Race*, 2015.

15 This seems to be the only record of Barnet Kushner. It may that he emigrated or simply changed his name.

16 Jewish Museum, London, oral history interview, tape no. 123.

17 Zangwill, Israel, *Children of the Ghetto*, 1892 (a novel).

18 ibid.

19 ibid.

20 Green, op cit.

21 Jewish Museum, oral history interview with Israel Scheef, tape no. 490.

22 www.hackneybuildings.org/items/show/19306.

23 British Army First World War pension records no. 4995.

24 Mendelsohn, op cit.

25 However, his daughters were Barbara and Judith *Kashner*.

26 www.hackneybuildings/items/show/19306.

27 *Daily Herald*, 4 July 1939.

Chapter 8

1 The first part of this chapter is based on Joseph Burdett's *Reminiscences*, Nottinghamshire CRO, DD1177/1.

2 *Nottingham Gazette*, 5 Nov. 1813.

3 Felkin, William, *History of the Machine-Wrought Hosiery and Lace Manufactures*, 1867.

4 *Memories of Lambley 1890–1900*, an entry in an essay competition in the 1960s. Nottinghamshire CRO, DD121/1/42.

5 www.frameworkknittersmuseum.org.uk/about-framework-knitters/.

6 This part of the chapter is based on Joseph Moss's *Memoir*, Nottinghamshire CRO, DD/1487/1.

7 The master tailors of Garstang set the rate for making a smock as follows 'Frock Smock plain 2s/- if buttoned down frunt & taped seams 3s/-' in June 1848. However, their rates do seem to have been rather lower than average.

8 Felkin, op cit.

9 ibid.

10 *Report of the Commissioner Appointed to Inquire into the Condition of the Frame-Work Knitters,* 1845, Volume 2.

11 ibid.

Chapter 9

1 Unlike most of the scenarios in other chapters, this is artistic licence – but based on probability and the fact that on most roads the toll for a man on horseback was 2*d* or 3*d*.

2 See entry for Robert Harley in the *Dictionary of National Biography*.

3 In *The Guide to Trade,* 1842, published by Charles Knight.

4 CEC Vol XIV, interviewee no 321.

5 It is on the various sets of records from the Old Post Office, Brampton Bryan, that this chapter is based. Herefordshire CRO, E61, notably the records of the grocery business E61/1/1-7 and the shoemaking business E61/3/1-7.

6 Or the first Lord Ruthven if you follow *The Complete Peerage,* or the eighth if, like some other authorities, you refuse to recognise his grandmother as a Lord!

7 *The Guide to Trade,* op cit.

8 E61/32/1-4.

9 E61/5/8.

10 E61/18-31.

11 E61/9/1.

Chapter 10

Much of the information in this chapter comes from Moberg, Donald Reed, *George Odger and the English Working Class 1860–1877,* (unpublished PhD thesis, London School of Economics and Political Science, 1953).

1 Helen Taylor, the stepdaughter of J. S. Mill, described him thus in a talk given the day after his funeral, quoted in the *Standard* 12 March, 1877.
2 Quoted in the *Wikipedia* entry for George Odger but unsourced.
3 The Howell Collection in Bishopsgate Institute.
4 *George Odger's Biography,* reprinted from *St Crispin, the Boot and Shoemaker's Journal*, 1877.
5 ibid.
6 ibid.
7 Marx writing in *Das Volk,* August, 1859.
8 *George Odger's Biography,* op cit.
9 In *Rhymes for the People,* London, 1871.
10 Chapter III.
11 19 March, 1864.
12 *Sources for the Study of the Sheffield Outrages,* Libraries, Archives and Information, Sheffield City Council, 2011.
13 It folded in 1867.
14 *Punch*, 1 June, 1867. Edmond Beales, Charles Bradlaugh and John Bright were prominent members of the movement for parliamentary reform.
15 21 Nov. 1868.
16 Information from George's great-great-great-great-granddaughter.

Chapter 11

1 www.symingtons.com/about-us/.
2 *Leicester Journal,* 11 February 1848.
3 *Leicester Chronicle,* 8 January 1842.
4 His advertisements begin to appear in the local press in 1859.

5 'Master W. C. Symington and his nurse' (unnamed) appear in the passenger lists, though there is no record anywhere else of Robert and Mary Symington having a child.

6 Leicestershire CRO, 7D73/2.

7 Leicestershire CRO, DE3730/71.

8 Thomas Saint is credited with the invention in 1790.

9 Barthélemy Thimonnier patented a sewing machine in France in 1830 and his machines were in use in a Parisian factory manufacturing military uniforms in the 1830s. However, the factory burnt down and all the machines were destroyed, though the Science Museum in London has a replica.

10 These were: a needle with the eye at the point; a shuttle operating beneath the cloth to form the lock stitch (previous machines had created a chain stitch with a single thread, which unravelled unless the final stitch was secured by hand); and an automatic feed.

11 See, for example, *Wikipedia.*

12 *Leicester Journal,* 17 March 1865. The mysterious inventor who modified the machine has never been named, and one wonders whether he existed or whether in fact Elias Howe did modify the machines as Thomas requested but was never given credit for doing so.

13 See, for example, *Leicester Mercury,* 12 February 1859.

14 Robert Symington's obituary in the *Leicester Chronicle,* 8 October 1892, also states that the firm was established 'in the early 1860s'.

15 *Leicester Chronicle,* 29 June 1861. The case rumbled on for some months and was widely reported in the local press. It seems that Mr Laughton overcharged for his expenses in attending court and this prolonged proceedings. Eventually the matter was settled by arbitration and the final figure he received was not reported.

16 CEC Vol XIV, Interviewee 252. This was in fact Mr W. F. Thomas, the stay-maker who bought Elias Howe's patent.

17 CEC Vol XIV, interviewee 258a.

18 ibid.

19 Leicestershire CRO, 7D73/1.

20 ibid.

21 *Leicester Journal,* 10 November and 27 October 1871.

22 *Leicester Chronicle,* 15 May 1871.

23 Leicestershire CRO, DE2262/115.

24 CEC Vol XIV, interviewees 252 and 257.

25 *Midland Times,* 22 January 1881.

26 Warren, Philip and Nicol, Sarah, *Foundations of Fashion,* 2013.

27 Leicestershire CRO, 7D73/1 & 2.

28 ibid. 7D73/14.

29 ibid. 7D73/1 & 2.

30 ibid.

31 Leicestershire CRO, DE3730/105 – a scruffy little notebook labelled 'Trade marks'.

32 *Foundations of Fashion,* op cit. and the Symington collection at imageleicestershire.org.uk.

33 Leicestershire CRO, DE3730/14.

34 *Leicester Chronicle,* 8 October 1892.

35 *Foundations of Fashion,* op cit.

36 ibid.

Chapter 12

1 She was 'Lady Spencer' after 1959 – but that was the year Ida died. She would have known her as 'Mrs Spencer', or 'Phoebe'.

2 They kept their promise. Not until some years after Ida's death did Freda Wills, Lady Spencer's sister, make a note in the museum records to the effect that 'Primrose of Branscombe', who wrote the essay in the August 1897 edition of *The Girl's Own Paper,* was Mrs Ida Allen, née Pike.

3 Recording of an interview with Ida's son, Ted Allen, 1970s. He knew she served a five-year term with Aglands, but didn't know exactly when in the decade this was. Courtesy of Norman Lambert.

4 Inder, Pamela, *Honiton Lace,* Exeter Museums, 1971; Farquharson, Barbara and Doern, Joan, *The Branscombe Lace Makers,* Branscombe Project, 2002.

5 CEC, Volume XIII.

6 Ted Allen, interview.

7 Royal Albert Memorial Museum records and Farquharson and Doern, op cit.

8 Farquharson and Doern, op cit.

9 Ted Allen, interview.

10 Edwin Allen was Jane Bidney's first cousin three times removed, on his mother's side of the family!

11 Staniland, K., *In Royal Fashion,* 1997.

12 Ted Allen, interview.

13 29 Nov, 1932.

14 Farquharson and Doern, op cit.

15 ibid.

16 ibid.

17 *Western Morning News,* 13 Dec. 1946.

18 1872–1956. She was the daughter of Princess Helena and Prince Christian of Schleswig Holstein, and was married to Prince Aribert of Anhalt.

19 1850–1942. He was Queen Victoria's third son and seventh child, Prince Arthur.

20 *Sheffield Daily Telegraph,* 12 May 1939.

21 *Western Morning News,* 10 May 1932. 'Queen Elizabeth' in this context was the 'Queen Mother' – mother of Elizabeth II.

22 Ted Allen, interview.

23 *Western Morning News,* 20 May, 1932.

24 Ted Allen, interview.

25 Correspondence in Allhallows Museum, Honiton.

26 ibid.

27 *Western Morning News,* 10 Feb. 1940.

28 Undated press cutting in the *Express and Echo* archive, seen in the 1970s but now untraceable.

29 Burnett, John, *A History of the Cost of Living,* 1969 and www.1900s.org.uk/1900s-shopping.htm.

Epilogue

1 Reported by Shahnaz Parveen for BBC Bengal, Dhakar, on the anniversary of the disaster. Sharmin's mother was among the dead and it took the family ten months to find where she was buried. www.bbc.co.uk/news/world-asia-27107860.